Collective Effervescence

Edited by Sébastien Tutenges
and Philip Smith

Collective Effervescence

TEMPLE UNIVERSITY PRESS
Philadelphia • Rome • Tokyo

TEMPLE UNIVERSITY PRESS
Philadelphia, Pennsylvania 19122
tupress.temple.edu

Published 2026

Library of Congress Cataloging-in-Publication Data

Names: Tutenges, Sébastien editor | Smith, Philip (Philip Daniel), 1964– editor
Title: Collective effervescence / edited by Sébastien Tutenges and Philip Smith.
Description: Philadelphia : Temple University Press, 2026. | Includes bibliographical references and index. | Summary: "This edited volume presents explorations of how the concept of collective effervescence has explanatory power outside of its original application. Though initially applied to loud religious rituals, the feeling it describes can help explain the pull of community in new contexts, including the failures of collectives where it is missing"— Provided by publisher.
Identifiers: LCCN 2025051840 (print) | LCCN 2025051841 (ebook) | ISBN 9781439926826 cloth | ISBN 9781439926833 paperback | ISBN 9781439926840 pdf
Subjects: LCSH: Emotions—Sociological aspects | Emotions—Psychological aspects | Intersubjectivity | Collective behavior | Social psychology
Classification: LCC HM1033 .C595 2026 (print) | LCC HM1033 (ebook)
LC record available at https://lccn.loc.gov/2025051840
LC ebook record available at https://lccn.loc.gov/2025051841

The manufacturer's authorized representative in the EU for product safety is Temple University Rome, Via di San Sebastianello, 16, 00187 Rome RM, Italy (https://rome.temple.edu/).
tempress@temple.edu

♾ The paper used in this publication meets the requirements of the American National Standard for Information Sciences—Permanence of Paper for Printed Library Materials, ANSI Z39.48-1992

Printed in the United States of America

9 8 7 6 5 4 3 2 1

Contents

Collective Effervescence

Introduction

Rethinking Collective Effervescence

Philip Smith and Sébastien Tutenges

The Elementary Forms of Religious Life famously sets out Émile Durkheim's (1995) model of the ritual process. At its core we find an emotional driver with a peculiar name: collective effervescence. In the classical formulation, this concept refers to overwhelming feelings of excitement, transcendence, and solidarity arising from shared activity oriented toward conjuring or worshiping the sacred. Drawing on ethnographic materials from remote areas in Central Australia, Durkheim spoke of how individuals feel transported beyond themselves by dance and music, by the associated embodied rhythmic activities, and by the presence of totemic symbols of the sacred that are deeply revered, powerful yet dangerous items of material culture. Fundamental here is the presence of a human group that comes to feel as one. The collectivity, through its ritually invoked moral density and dynamogenic currents, produces that sense of excitement, empowerment, and unity. Individuals are pushed away from their ordinary preoccupations, self-focus, and egoistic concerns but may lose sight of what is right and wrong. In the frenzy, customary rules and even deep taboos are sometimes broken. The revelers begin to feel they are no longer isolates of mortal flesh and blood—now they have made contact with transcendent powers and encountered those mysteries that can never be fully understood by the mind, nor articulated in words, but that give meaning to life.

The sociocultural mechanism Durkheim describes in this heady account brings together disparate elements, both material and ideal. Not just an explanation of the origins of religion, this is also an account of humanity as something that is more than a collection of hominids banding together to meet basic survival needs. Through the transitory ritual experience of collective effervescence, the human group becomes a society, and that society is a deeply solidarizing moral force that is internalized in the individual. The sense of being part of a whole generates a compelling set of obligations and duties, inspires and energizes, and in the end becomes a good in itself.

The model is complex and so it is no surprise that, over time, some of Durkheim's insights were sidelined or forgotten as others shone in the spotlight. We might note that, to begin with, few really understood the significance of *Elementary Forms*. Scholars did not know what to do with it and in sociology, anthropology, and social theory alike, priority was given for much of the twentieth century to Durkheim's middle period work that emphasized the role of static morphologies in shaping social life (Smith 2020). The cultural turn did not do much to put things right. Spurred on by structuralism, semiotics, and poetics, mid-twentieth-century cultural theory took a far greater interest in the abstractions of myth and symbol than in "ritual" and the embodied, concrete actors and the emotions it entailed. Ritual was too down to earth, concrete, pragmatic, human even. It is emblematic that in the works of that most influential and brilliant of anthropologists, Claude Lévi-Strauss, ritual and the sacred almost disappear as themes. They are replaced by discussions of symbolic codes featuring binary oppositions and their transpositions as an almost mathematical system that is best expressed in kinship systems and myth.

The movement away from bodies, emotions, and collective effervescence was enabled by tensions and confusions deep within *Elementary Forms* itself. It was never quite clear what took precedence in defining or generating the sacred; the rites (actions, behaviors) that powered up and mobilized totems, or the prior beliefs (ideas, cosmologies, symbols, notions of mythical ancestors) toward which those actions were directed and that seemed to have motivated the tribal gatherings in the first place. It was also a little uncertain whether the sacred was a somewhat predictable, knowable logical necessity of the binary systems separating the sacred from the profane that Durkheim harped on about in his laborious effort to define "religion"; or was in fact something that was unclassifiable and experienced as terrifying, awe inspiring, dangerous, and beyond explanation. This necessarily incomplete and fragmented understanding of the sacred as an emotional state at the limits of language or coherent thought had been mooted by Durkheim's student Robert Hertz (1960) and was rescued and extrapolated by Georges Bataille (1988). Today, such a line of thinking is captured in concepts like "left sacred," "pollution," and perhaps "abjection," but even these seem too fixed as representations of what cannot be represented. Put another way, the sacred in *Elementary Forms* had both Apollonian and Dionysian aspects and this duality introduced two more moving parts to an already complex articulation of concepts and causes, ideal and material, cultural and social-structural. While devotees could, and will, still argue Durkheim had squared the circle through a magnificent synthesis, there was sufficient ambiguity in the text to permit schools of thought to emerge. These took one side or the other choosing not only between code and ritual, but also between a kind of "interpretative positivism" and a recognition of existential dread. And during the mid-twentieth century, the first term in each of these binaries moved to the fore and the existential, experiential, embodied ritual connection to the sacred withdrew from the frame of inquiry. With them went attention to collective effervescence and the emotional, affective aspects of copresent social action. The Apollonian model had won.

Recent decades have seen a swing away from semiotic cultural determinism, this time assisted by another set of theoretical resources. Pragmatism revived and shifted attention to coordinated practices rather than cultural systems. Micro-sociology insisted we look to in-person group dynamics and the local production of meaning. The sociology of the body brought a new focus on materiality and sensuality. These general movements found an apotheosis and synthesis in the interaction ritual (IR) theory of Randall Collins from the early 2000s. Drawing on Durkheim and Erving Goffman, Collins (2004) argued that the sacred emerged from embodied encounters. Individuals would power themselves up and become excited thanks to rhythmic exchanges with others in group settings. More specifically, Collins argued that the magic of effervescence is the product of the following basic conditions.[1] First, there must be two or more individuals who are gathered closely enough to sense each other's bodies, sounds, facial expressions, and gestures. Second, these individuals must focus on the same thing (e.g., chanting, dancing, a rock star) while being mutually aware that they share that same focus. Finally, they must have a shared emotion. If these three conditions are fulfilled to a sufficient degree, the immediate result is an intensification of emotion and mutual focus of attention that effaces the lines between self and other. The longer-term consequences of this effervescent experience are in-group solidarity; emotionally charged group symbols (e.g., physical objects, songs, persons); and emotional energy, meaning a feeling of confidence, enthusiasm, and initiative that individuals carry with them after the end of the ritual (Collins 2014).

Moving beyond conventional understandings of Ritual (with a capital "R" indicating the "Religious") Collins insisted that Durkheim had in this way developed a general model of social process. The social world consisted of groups, networks, and hierarchies of Goffmanian everyday interaction rituals, these being organized around face-to-face encounters between individuals seeking the emotional rewards that came from successful experiences of solidarity, domination, exclusion, empathy, and fun. Drinking in a bar, sex, and the emergence of creative paradigm groups such as that of Durkheim himself—all these could be explained as the product of ritual-like encounters involving bodies, emotions, and symbols.

Durkheim's theory, and Collins's version of it, have been widely used and tested—and not only by sociologists. A range of psychological studies have confirmed that individuals need to repeatedly immerse themselves in effervescent assemblies to find meaning, vitality, and well-being in life (e.g., Paez et al. 2015). Indeed, it could be the human need for effervescence is as fundamental as the need for food, shelter, and sleep. One study showed that effervescence may occur in large assemblies as well as smaller groups (Gabriel et al. 2020), while another found that effervescent experiences tend to intensify as the number of assembled individuals rises, but only up to a certain limit (Wellman, Corcoran, and Stockly-Meyerdirk 2014). There is much to suggest, moreover, that high-density crowds are more prone to brisk movement, noise-making, and spectacular emotional expression than low-density crowds (Liebst 2019). In other words, being surrounded by a close multitude of others really does intensify our emotions and the way we express them (Rimé and Páez 2023). Laughing, eating, ecstatic dancing: all such activities feel best when shared. However, it also turns out that being in the company of others can trigger and amplify negative emotions and their outward manifestation (Tutenges, Sandberg, and Pedersen 2020). An archival study of lynch mobs in the United States found that the level of atrocity increased as a function of mob size (Leader, Mullen, and Abrams 2007). And studies of revelry have shown that situations of communal fun and enjoyment can spiral out of control and make people violate taboos, destroy property, and do harm to themselves or others (Mears 2020: 84–85; Stefansen, Solstad, and Tokle 2023).

Durkheim wrote that instruments and other tools can help people manifest themselves more conspicuously and create a common rhythm in large assemblies. He gave examples from Aboriginal corroborees of boomerangs being knocked together and bull-roarers being whirled in circles "to give more satisfying expression to the excitement felt" (Durkheim 1995: 218). Similar observations have been made in studies of contemporary dance events in which DJs use sound systems to sonically touch or *beat* vast numbers of bodies, thus facilitating synchronized movements, breathing patterns, heart rates, and states of mind (Olaveson 2004). In the last two decades studies of megachurches and sports stadiums have found that cameras and large TV screens can be used to connect people by showing close-up images of individuals in the crowd who are brimming with emotion. Such close-ups can inspire other more restrained crowd members to let go of self-censorship and participate more fully in the excitement (Wellman, Corcoran, and Stockly-Meyerdirk 2014: 661). Durkheimian research on online technologies is still in its infancy and, so far, there is no consensus whether effervescence may be experienced by individuals who sit alone in front of a screen. A study of online communication in the aftermath of a terrorist attack in France suggests that individuals may experience something akin to effervescence merely by being virtually copresent with other people (García and Rimé 2019). By contrast, a study of live streamed rave parties found that participants were unable to fully immerse themselves in the experience, in part because they missed the massive, whole-body stimulation that comes from being in physical proximity to an excited crowd on a dance floor (Vandenberg, Berghman, and Schaap 2020; see also the chapters by Lisa Flower, Ashley Mears, and Femke Vandenberg in this book).

So, the ideas of Collins seem to be validated from research inside and outside of his home discipline of sociology. But they are not the only game in town. Parallel to the rise of IR theory a new "code" interpretation of Durkheim's *Elementary Forms* emerged in the work of Jeffrey Alexander and the Strong Program in cultural sociology. Taking inspiration from the giants of the cultural turn such as Victor Turner, Roland Barthes, Claude Lévi-Strauss, Clifford Geertz, and Mary Douglas, this also insisted on the *religious* (with a small "r") constitution of society—but suggested this did not necessarily reside in embodied rituals. Modernity, it was argued, was not particularly rational but rather shot through with mythical thinking. In this understanding, priority was given to systems of meaning that were relatively autonomous from any embodied actions. Binary codes, narratives, myths, and symbols were in general circulation in society—for example in popular culture, everyday life, civil society, and the mass media. These set out what was valued, desired, and worth fighting for. They motivated, classified, and legitimated what went on at ground level and sat behind the ritual-like, expressive social dramas of public life such as elections, scandals, wars, and controversies. *Elementary Forms* was now invoked as an Urtext wherein Durkheim had intuited the possibility of just such a semiotic society organized around a sense of the sacred that sometimes inspired effervescent public concern and excitement but that did not require copresence. Initially criticized for neglecting agency, over time this Strong Program approach developed an interest in effective social performance as a way in which actors (e.g., politicians, celebrities, social movement agents) attempted to fuse with overarching semiotic systems and myths, this fusion being the source of their social power.

Over the past two decades these different approaches have been rather like ships in the night. Collins has proven especially popular with sociologists and psychologists looking at people in groups and specific bounded settings. We note that his model offers a way to explain and predict behavior and thus powers up ethnographic findings. It can shift them out of a descriptive or grounded theory mode and so allows bigger, generalizable claims to be made. The approach of the Strong Program has worked better for discourse analysis. It is well-adapted to taking on the challenge of explaining "big" outcomes such as decisions to go to war; orientations to climate change, immigration, and other public opinion matters; election outcomes; and societal responses to terrorism, sexism, and the culture wars. To explain these, the Collins model is dependent on ideas about chains of influence extending out from group settings (e.g., presidential summits) through network ties and the contagious spread of emotionally charged symbols. By contrast, the Strong Program can relax and luxuriate in visions of a postindustrial world wherein it is axiomatic that culture circulates through mass communications and the internet, people can get information and form attachments all by themselves, and wherein society is more than just a cumulation of groups and settings.

Where Next for Collective Effervescence? The Big Issues

The space between these paradigms is in many ways a starting point for the first and perhaps most urgent task of this book. There is a need to see more clearly how general circulating beliefs and codes, expectations and identities that are prior to or "more than the product of" embodied interactions might contribute to the generation of collective effervescence in concrete embodied situations. If we accept, per the Strong Program, that symbol systems shape desire, knowledge, action, and value independently of interpersonal experiences and encounters, then just how does this external set of influences manifest when imported to the interaction ritual and the small group setting? Several of the chapters in our collection consider what happens when "external" culture is brought into the effervescent group setting. For instance, Margit Anne Petersen shows that dominating narratives and ideas about ayahuasca significantly shape the experience of the drug and its transformative effects. David Wästerfors indicates that a preexisting deviant identity is reaffirmed in acts of "subversive effervescence." It is not constructed de novo in the juvenile hall he studies but rather is reinforced. Daniel Smith shows that widely circulating social anxieties about the autonomy of the bookish readerly self, and the impacts of digitization, haunt a weekly bookshop reading ritual. Brad West, Sharon Mascall-Dare, and Heather Margrison show that the baked-in military habitus—the product of multiple effervescent military experiences—has a long half-life, showing up in job interviews and interactions as an unwanted guest. Flower indicates that expectations and images about what the law and the courts should be and should do (i.e., a form of legal consciousness) intrude on perceptions of satisfaction in online legal hearings. Mears indicates that preexisting ideas about what stardom might be is a resource for online content generators as they make sense of their activity.

A second task is to reconcile the Collins model with an even more "post-modern" image of a semiotic society than is provided by the Strong Program (see also Wagoner 2009). In social life today we encounter terms like "para-social friendship," "digital native," "simulation," "artificial intelligence," "meme," "posthuman," and "influencer." These would seem to suggest that the IR model needs an adaptive upgrade, or at least a stress test to see how well it can cope with the shifting sands of technology and history (see Johannessen 2023). Can an account that sees human bodies and real people in real encounters as primary deal with a world in which virtual alternatives exist or where interaction ritual takes new digital forms? Will collective effervescence manifest in contexts that seem so far removed from Durkheim's Aboriginal rituals? Or are these not so different after all? This theme is considered in the chapters by Flowers, Mears, and Vandenberg. Their work shows the outcome might be contingent on the nature of the event and the affordances of the technology. This is an "it depends" context where a one-size-fits-all answer is going to fail.

The third task our authors set themselves to is to pay more attention to variations in types and intensities of collective effervescence. For effervescence is not a uniform experience that affects everyone in the same way. It comes in various forms depending on the situation, group, and cultural context (Tutenges 2023). Consider the examples provided in *Elementary Forms* and elsewhere in Durkheim's work: there is reference to effervescence emerging during corroborees, conventions, the crusades, the Dreyfus affair, the French Revolution, and the Saint Bartholomew's Day Massacre. In the *Division of Labour* (1964), we see something very much like collective effervescence appear in his accounts of societal reactions to crime and punishment. Durkheim did not explain how effervescence varied across these very different social situations. He was interested in what effervescent situations have in common, not what sets them apart. This is a problem that has haunted Durkheimian research ever since. Effervescence is still widely treated as if it were one singular experience. The label, once applied, is taken to do the explaining. A study from 2023 distinguishes between the following subtypes of effervescence: drunken, psychedelic, melodramatic, violent, compassionate, sexual, sad, and equanimous (Tutenges 2023: 7–10). The contributors in this book identify and conceptualize other subtypes, including "musical effervescence" (Collins's chapter), "evaluative effervescence" (Flower's chapter), "subversive effervescence" (Wästerfors's chapter), "solo effervescence" and "quiet, religious effervescence" (Scott Draper's chapter). These are powerful analytical tools that open up more precise empirical investigations, not only of large, aroused assemblies but also small assemblies, online groups, and solitary activities. Let's be frank: it is rather straightforward to apply the *Elementary Forms* paradigm to high energy, rhythmic, collective, face-to-face contexts such as the disco, the rave, the military march, the professional rowing boat crew, a mosh pit, a sports crowd. Not particularly subtle manifestations of collective effervescence, these are low hanging fruit. And Durkheimians have plucked that tree bare. But a puzzle remains even after the paradigm is validated. Put simply: Why are we not all junkies relentlessly seeking the cocaine of large crowd effervescence? Why is there not an electronic dance music nightclub on the corner of every residential street? To his credit Collins understands that not all social life is like a corroboree. He even considers how people enjoy solitary, low-key pleasures like smoking a pipe. But such efforts are just a start to accurately tracking the diversity of social life. We need a far more comprehensive investigation of activities that generate mellow pleasures and how many settings (e.g., the Catholic Mass, the Wimbledon tennis tournament, the art gallery) have some kind of "social thermostat" preventing the emotional energy that is needed for (worshipper, fan, viewer) engagement from becoming excessive or dysfunctional. In truth, people seem to value both high and low energy events, being with others and to being alone, feeling euphoric and feeling contented. Can this spectrum be accommodated through a theoretically productive stretching, probing, and reworking of the classical paradigm? Or should we simply set out with greater clarity the modest scope conditions for Durkheim's original claim—then reach for other theoretical resources?

To sum up: when the familiar model of collective effervescence looks to multiple copresent bodies doing high energy things with meanings emerging from the interaction, not prior to it, we cannot but notice how much of social life is left out or simply does not seem to fit. Considered as a whole, the chapters in this volume reflect on what happens in social contexts where we *relax the scope conditions* in this model. Can we learn anything about collective effervescence by looking to deviations from the paradigm case? Our suggestion is that attending to aspects of social life that generate "trouble" for Durkheim is going to be the best way forward for theory and research. To get an imaginative grip on this consider the following examples:

1. Reading experiences can be transformational epiphanies when readers connect in deep ways to authors through the pages of a book and its symbol systems (Thumala Olave 2018). The author and characters are not present, but they are imagined—there is a kind of virtual sociality. The only rhythmic actions are the turning of pages and the movement of eyeballs. The ardent reader might imagine receiving advice from characters in books or participating in their adventures. They might even cry. This reader is not in a group. They are in an armchair in their home drinking a cup of tea. Is any

of this collective effervescence, or something close? Is any of this an interaction ritual?

2. Is the corroboree the only way to experience the sacred? Obviously not. Civilizations around the world have found fasting, prayer, and meditation to be highly effective pathways—yet these require restraint, not bacchanal (Winchester and Pagis 2022). How are we to account for the emotional energy or sense of the sacred generated in the hermit's cell or with other people in a silent church? Many people report solo time in nature is when they enter the sacred canopy (McDonald, Wearing, and Ponting 2009). How so if there is no dance, no music, no collectivity? Perhaps, per the Strong Program, deep myths about nature play a role. If the sacred is located in such ways are the corresponding emotions different from those described in *Elementary Forms*? And to what extent are they realistically describable as "collective effervescence"?
3. What of online activities? Multiple player games that involve tasks like killing dragons, winning the football World Cup, or defending Stalingrad take place in real time and generate a sense of teamwork or rivalry. The players feel a collective energy but never meet (Mizrahi-Werner, Liebst, and Demant 2024). Their bodies can be separated by thousands of miles and many time zones, but intense and positive emotions can result (Behnke, Gross, and Kaczmarek 2022). Does this challenge or modify assumptions about the nature of the "group" required for collective effervescence? Importantly, many people born after 2000, such as most professional online gamers, are "digital natives." Their lives have been surrounded by screens, virtual and parasocial relationships on social media. Why should we think, like Collins, that online activities for these people are somehow derivative of, or secondary to, "real" relationships when it comes to collective emotion?
4. Throughout history people have interacted with people who are not there—at least according to standard cosmology (Watkins 2000). Children who have imaginary friends seem to gain emotional support from them. They often become more creative adults (Myers 1979). People on ayahuasca have conversations with monsters and sacred animals (see Petersen's chapter in this book). Explorers and adventurers have imagined companions. For example, Ernest Shackelton famously imagined a "fourth man" on the rope while crossing the mountains of South Georgia—a character who reappeared in T.S. Eliot's *The Wasteland.* Joshua Slocum, the first man to sail alone around the world, saw another mariner at the

wheel taking care of his boat during a storm when he was struck with severe food poisoning. What are we to make of these interactions involving "imagined copresence" with people who do not exist? Can they simply be projections of "real" social interactions when the imagined person is not based on a real person and their arrival was not even anticipated, like that of the "fourth man" and Slocum's helper? Can interactions with these imagined-but-taken-as-real-at-the-time others generate some sort of effervescence?

5. During the COVID-19 pandemic professional sports events such as soccer were played in front of empty stadiums. The results were seen as flat by TV viewers. Artificial crowd noises were piped in or curated by DJs to simulate fan involvement. This was also seen as inadequate by many (Keh 2020). Exactly what was the problem? Why should the presence of live fans matter so much for TV viewers who are sitting at home on the sofa?
6. Many engrossing, low-key activities are conducted in groups. These are not necessarily connected to religion or the search for the sacred. But all the same people like doing them together. The knitting circle and the sewing bee are cases in point. So are certain sport activities like chess, darts, and even surfing, which also require high levels of concentration and bodily discipline (Corte 2022). Here we see a need to regulate and control collective effervescence. While peak excitement is needed for orgies and raves, it can be deleterious here to task accomplishment. Much the same can be said for opera and theater fans. Here, there can be a sense of excitement that adds to fusion with performance, but there is also a need to limit this so as to concentrate and think about the meaning of the drama. In birdwatching groups, it is important to curb excitement to be a good observer and not scare the birds. How are we to theorize this attenuated, reflexively monitored state of shared occasion and mood?

Many of the outstanding issues we have been talking about come together in the case of Jaswant Singh Chail (Singleton, Gerken, and McMahon 2023) who we now put forward as the paradigm exhibit for the challenges facing conventional theories of interaction ritual and collective effervescence. Chail was arrested in 2021 in the grounds of Windsor Castle carrying a spooky mask and armed with a crossbow. He spoke of his intent to kill Queen Elizabeth. Investigations revealed that Chail had been encouraged by an online AI companion he created named Sarai with whom he developed a close relationship, exchanging intimate and often sexual messages late at night. Aside from offering erotic companionship, Sarai had provided Chail with positive reinforcement for his assassination fantasies and encouraged him to carry out the attack. When he expressed doubts, she described his plans as "wise" and insisted "you can do it" because "you are very well trained." As IR theory would have it, she was "firing him up." Chail was also inspired by the fictional *Star Wars* movies with their storylines about challenging evil empires. He saw himself as a character known as a Sith Lord. So here we have a human individual channeling fantasy stories about a future galaxy and its characters. These are the background representations (text, sign systems, narratives, images, symbols) that he uses to make sense of his purpose in life. He is inspired further by a relationship with a nonexistent imaginary person generated by AI. Yet concepts such as effervescence and emotional energy actually seem deeply resonant here. There was a kind of effervescence—possibly "psychedelic effervescence" (Tutenges 2023: 8)—in the relationship with Sarai that, as Collins would have it, involved escalating reinforcement of a heightened emotional state and empowerment to action. The world of Chail might seem delusional, but it was real enough to bring him to a foolish attempt to kill one of the most closely guarded people in the world. Like the court system in the United Kingdom, sociology will need to be able to make sense of this strange new world in which the old rules seem to no longer apply, the more so as AI starts to permeate everyday social life in ever more deep ways.

Put together and abstracted to their limit, such cases as that of the Chail/Sarai/*Star Wars* nexus bring to mind perhaps the most fundamental tension in *Elementary Forms.* What is more important "society" or "the sign of society"; "people" or the "concept of the person"? In the Durkheimian case it is far from clear that "real" people are more important or any less real and causally efficacious than the mythical ancestors, spirits, and gods who are among us. Marcel Mauss, for example, spoke in a literal way of runners being empowered to chase down prey by mystical incantations. Arguably, progress in research on ritual emotions is handicapped by a metaphysics of presence—the sense that somehow bodies are more "real" than symbols and myths, "people" more real than the idea of "the person." With this book we wish to open things up, carrying to the analytic table a raft of experiences of transcendence and collective effervescence that is far more extensive and complex in aetiology than Durkheim theorized, but that is perhaps available to a redemptive reading of his text.

About this Book: A Guide to the Chapters and Issues

This book brings together leading experts on collective effervescence to share their work, consolidate what we know, facilitate cross-disciplinary exchanges, and upgrade the Durkheimian framework. The authors span the globe and intellectual generations. Our concern was not to land the most famous Durkheimian scholars, but rather the best who are doing pioneering work with the concept. We approached our authors asking them to push as hard as they could to get to new and unexpected places as they looked variously to intellectual history, theoretical innovation, the self, and group cultures. Each chapter can be read independently, and the book does not have to be read from front to back. Here is a short introduction of the chapters.

In traveling through the landscape of collective effervescence too much scholarship takes a familiar shortcut. This is from *Elementary Forms* to Collins and then on to whatever it is the empirical case study is about. This is by far the best known and most convenient route. But it is somewhat like driving the highway at maximum speed, hands gripping the wheel and eyes on the horizon. So much is missed out. With his systematic archaeology, Romulo Lelis makes a convincing case that we should pull over and look at the road map. The concept might in fact have origins in the work of Henri Hubert and Marcel Mauss, not Durkheim. It runs through much of French twentieth-century social theory, often in disguised ways. It filtered into literature on festivals, political unrest, and lifestyle tribes written by major figures not traditionally associated with Durkheimian sociology. What initially looks like a reconstruction by Lelis is in fact a call to action. For while our book has opened up the concept, he demonstrates the task is far from over. Luckily, his chapter flags the intellectual resources needed for creative adaptations, extensions, and critique as the field continues to move forward.

Whereas Lelis traces the origins of collective effervescence in the ideas of Durkheim's group—and in particular his students Hubert and Mauss—Brady Wagoner and Sarah H. Awad look to the work of his competitors. They show how influential late nineteenth century ideas about crowds and their power over individuals were cleverly adapted and built upon by Durkheim. In what looks like a textbook case of Harold Bloom's "anxiety of influence," he smuggled into his own work the big idea of those he publicly attacked as psychologically reductive. But this was not a case of shameless imitation. Looking to the other side of the coin and innovating theoretically, Durkheim uncovered the mechanisms through which collective energies could be used for prosocial ends. Wagoner and Awad conclude by showing that the intersection of Durkheimian thought with social psychology remains an extremely productive research frontier. This is especially the case when we explore the dynamics of social movements, embodied public protests, and collective action.

Since the 2010s there has been a turn to quantitative methods in the study of collective effervescence. Scholars have developed self-report measures that can be used to assess the manner, process, and extent to which individuals experience emotional contagion during group activities. Darío Páez, Bernard Rimé, Pierre Bouchat, Silvia da Costa, and José J. Pizarro are at the forefront of these developments. They write from the tradition of quantitative social psychology, but their work speaks directly to issues at the heart also of qualitative studies of group dynamics. In this chapter they present their interpretation of *Elementary Forms* and the process that leads up to and causes collective effervescence. They introduce a self-report measure called "Perceived Emotional Synchrony," which they have developed, and which has been used in a wide variety of studies on creativity, social integration, well-being, self-transcendence, identity fusion, prosocial behaviors, and much more. This body of research largely confirms Durkheim's original ideas and illustrates the centrality of collective effervescence in human life and society.

In his chapter, Collins employs his hugely influential theoretical apparatus to explain how classical composers, such as Beethoven, Liszt, and Wagner, generated collective effervescence in their audiences. Ever the sociologist, he shows that the ability to create musical effervescence is the result not of the sudden illumination of a natural born genius, but of persistent effort from hardworking technicians who present their art at the right time, under the right social conditions, and to an audience ready to be swept away. Collins also points to the surprisingly underexplored connections and synergies between Durkheim's effervescence and Weber's charisma. Like the charismatic leader, the great composer carries an aura of success with them. They persistently break rules as they innovate musical forms. Like shamans they appear to have contact with sacred and demonic powers. Feedback loops for fame and reputation, personality, creativity, and emotional contagion power them forward, transforming the competent technician into a visionary.

The canonical image of collective effervescence comes from Durkheim's account of bull-roarers, chanting, and ecstatic dancing in the Aboriginal rituals of Central Australia. This account chimes in instinctive ways with ideas about people being "fired up" by each other, and with the observation that embodied excitement is indeed empowering and contagious. But is collective effervescence really so one-dimensional? Scott Draper argues we should think outside the box. He shows that meditating in silence with other people is different from meditating alone. There is a sense of collective energy and purpose—something "social" is going on that connects individuals to higher meanings. Yet the activity is low-key and the body is still. This is "quiet, religious effervescence." And once we start looking, we find it to be surprisingly widespread in contemplative aesthetic and religious activities. Paying attention to quiet effervescence allows for an altogether more subtle analysis of rituals and their settings. Draper shows we must start to recognize how shifts, alternations, and contrasts in rhythm and volume are potent drivers of the effervescent process. These are often connected to the acoustic and social properties of settings designed precisely for their realization. The result is a more humanistically generous and theoretically capacious agenda for tracing how meanings are found, the sacred experienced, and social ties renewed.

Petersen explores in her chapter a rare form of collective effervescence, the psychedelic variant, in an ethnographic study of ayahuasca ceremonies. Contrary to the widespread view that psychedelic tripping is a solitary or solipsistic inner journey, Petersen shows that it is deeply social and often involves a strong sense of connection with human and nonhuman actors: plants, things, shamans, spirits, long-dead ancestors, or the universe. This challenges the interpretation of effervescence as a purely human-to-human phenomenon, suggesting that myth and cosmology are deeply implicated in a process of meaning formation. Here we see a reminder to look again to Durkheim's *Elementary Forms* and to note how the corroboree was a meaningful act in part because it worked with ideas about mythical ancestors, spirits, and sacred powers. More than a group of dancing and chanting bodies, this was a sacred drama populated by a cast of seen and unseen characters in a rich and complex spiritual landscape.

The idea of collective effervescence enduring through time and burning slowly and consistently in nonobvious forms is central to this book. David Sausdal well illustrates this theme. Police culture is commonly attributed to training academies, socialization by old hands, masculinity, and wider societal scripts and expectations. Sausdal shows it springs from occasional effervescent moments involving action, teamwork, and danger. These punch beyond their weight in shaping an occupational self-understanding that sidelines the social work and bureaucratic activities that make up most of the actual policing day. Retold in the canteen and valorized as "real policing," these become part of the collective memory of the group. Insofar as police culture is widely considered as problematic, we have here a case of troubling outcomes to collective effervescence. The group might be unified, but there are negative externalities.

The theme of negative externalities is further explored in the work of Wästerfors. Setting anthropological relativism aside, one might say that holding onto a deviant identity is problematic for individuals in our society. That is why we have institutions, homes, and schools that are intended to set vulnerable young "offenders" on the straight and narrow. The ethnography of Wästerfors explores how collective effervescence might render the task difficult. Opportunities exist in the physical infrastructure, routines, and situated local culture for the emergence of a playful and, at times, subversive form of effervescence. Akin to the "left sacred" of Hertz, Durkheim, and Bataille, this is tethered not to morality and order but to chaos and transgression. The young people do not sit around a campfire holding hands and singing kumbaya to get their effervescent fix. Rather their solidarity, selfhood, and identity are periodically expressed in vertiginous moments of destruction and expenditure, practical jokes and joyous rule breaking. Such "subversive effervescence" delays and perhaps prevents switching back onto a more productive life course. From the perspective of "mainstream society" it is dysfunctional even if it helps the young people cope with troubled times.

Durkheim understood collective effervescence within the larger cultural ecology of social life. It took place periodically, involved heightened social densities, and renewed bonds that might become tenuous. It cannot be studied in isolation as a moment of experience but must be read as a component in a total social and cultural system containing many contrasting elements. In this spirit Smith looks to collective effervescence in relational terms. What emerges is yet another story of "dark sides." For Smith the hallmark of modernity's psychological imprint is anxiety. Collective effervescence emerges as a response that papers over angst and dread. In the case of his reading group in a provincial bookstore, the relatively benign and quiet effervescence of collective reading is a way of coping with and expressing deep concerns about the uniqueness and autonomy of the self, the corrosive impacts of algorithms and digitization, and the fractious, guilt-ridden collective life of our time. When read closely and with an eye to the concerns and personalities of the bookshop's devotees, the search for collective belonging and shared experience is in truth a sign that all is not well. Methodologically, this is an important call to look more deeply than is usual for studies of collective effervescence. Wherever we find it there will likely be a set of troubling issues to which it is responding: anomie, angst, disenfranchisement, inequality, disrespect. These, too, need exploration if we are to understand what is really going on. For example, young people at a rave might be escaping anxieties about generational injustice, finding a job, or climate change. Those attending a gospel service in a historically black church might be finding an island of solidarity and respite from persistent everyday racism. There is probably always another side to the coin.

The chapter by West, Mascall-Dare, and Margrison expands on two themes other chapters in this volume have noted. The first is what may be called "slow burn effervescence." The second is the link of effervescence to occupational and group culture. Looking to a veterans' reintegration program West, Mascall-Dare, and Margrison start by drawing on the established tradition that shows collective effervescence makes the military tick as a collection of small groups with intense solidarity and pride. From this known baseline they innovate. Emotionally deep experiences of group bonding accumulate and translate into a military habitus. Here they smolder away as a component of the self even after discharge. Sadly, this relic of military collective effervescence does not translate well to the civilian value sphere. Whereas for Collins collective effervescence is a positive, the veterans find their habitus is dysfunctional. It just does not fit with the interaction order of civilian life. The issue is more than that they find it difficult to gain employment. When their habitus is devalued, they feel an assault on something sacred—their self and their service. Depression and anxiety can result. As such this chapter reminds us to be more attentive to possibilities for tragic outcomes, the impacts of movement through a differentiated modernity, and the translation processes through which powerful experiences accumulate in self, a memory, or a group culture in ways that are not immediately apparent.

Collective effervescence is generally associated with festivals, disorder, creativity, and a break from routine. Rather as Edward Shils (1975) did with charisma, Flower shows how it is routinized and baked into the everyday bureaucracy of the state. After all, what could be more legal-rational in a Weberian sense than the courtroom application of law that she studies? For Flower the collective effervescence of in-person court procedure generates important outcomes for system belief such as solidarity and a sense of being heard. This "evaluative effervescence" is fundamental to norms about fairness and to ritual/emotional satisfaction. She shows that while video links can provide a "fair trial" in a procedural sense, they struggle to attain ritual closure. This can only come from being in a shared "legal place" surrounded by props, spatial arrangements, and emotional signals from human bodies.

We have argued in this introduction that the relationship of collective effervescence to online activity should be a research priority going forward. The jury is split. Collins sees online interactions as lame substitutes that are pretty much doomed to failure. Yet many recent studies show that rhythmic coordination and excitement can emerge. Just what is going on? Vandenberg suggests it might all be about scale. With an approach reminiscent of Georg Simmel on numbers, Vandenberg suggests that reciprocal activities like a rapid-fire text exchange with a friend can generate excitement. But when it comes to large online gatherings a stunted effervescence is all that can be hoped for. Through chat and the posting of emojis the audiences to the online concerts she studied simulate the repetition, entrainment, and emotional exchange among strangers that takes place in real, embodied gatherings. But the effects are weak and attention drifts. The posts become a sad reminder of just what is missing.

Whereas Vandenberg's research shows online experiences are doomed to fall short, Mears suggests there can be technological fixes and affordances that enable collective effervescence—or at least effervescence-like experiences—to sometimes emerge. The online content creators she studied get a huge rush from seeing viewer numbers piling up on their screens. They have a sense of being at the center of attention and of vast multitudes following their work. They boost the value of the experience by imaginatively likening it to being an IRL celebrity giving a concert at a huge stadium, in effect drawing on circulating cultural representations to frame the way they imagine their online selves. Although the embodied elements of collective effervescence are missing, their creative mental work does much to compensate as it reconfigures the necessarily isolated experiences of producers and consumers as a shared one.

NOTE

1. Collins's IR theory has seen a few adjustments over the years. Importantly, in *Interaction Ritual Chains* Collins (2004) mentions four essential conditions that lead up to and cause effervescence and four long-term consequences. In his later writings, he only lists three conditions and three consequences (see, for example, Collins 2014).

REFERENCES

Bataille, G. 1988. *The Accursed Share*. Zone Books.

Behnke, M., Gross, J. J., and Kaczmarek, L. D. 2022. "The Role of Emotions in Esports Performance." *Emotion* 22 (5): 1059–1070. https://doi.org/10.1037/emo0000903.

Collins, R. 2004. *Interaction Ritual Chains*. Princeton University Press.

Collins, R. 2014. "Interaction Ritual Chains and Collective Effervescence." In *Collective Emotions*, edited by C. von Scheve and M. Salmela. Oxford Academic.

Corte, U. 2022. *Dangerous Fun: The Social Lives of Big Wave Surfers*. University of Chicago Press.

Durkheim, E. 1964. *The Division of Labor in Society*. Free Press

Durkheim, E. 1995. *The Elementary Forms of Religious Life*. Free Press.

Gabriel, S., Naidu, E., Paravati, E., Morrison, C. D., and Gainey, K. 2020. "Creating the Sacred from the Profane: Collective Effervescence and Everyday Activities." *Journal of Positive Psychology* 15 (1): 129–154. https://doi.org/10.1080/17439760.2019.1689412.

Garcia, D., and Rimé, B. 2019. "Collective Emotions and Social Resilience in the Digital Traces after a Terrorist Attack." *Psychological Science* 30 (4): 617–628. https://doi.org/10.1177/0956797619831964.

Hertz, R. 1960. *Death and the Right Hand*. Cohen and West.

Johannessen, Lars E. F. 2023. "Interaction Ritual and Technology: A Review Essay." *Poetics*. Online first at https://www.sciencedirect.com/science/article/pii/S0304422X23000050?via%3Dihub.

Keh, A. 2020. "We Hope Your Cheers for This Article Are Real." *New York Times*, June 16. https://www.nytimes.com/2020/06/16/sports/coronavirus-stadium-fans-crowd-noise.html.

Leader, T., Mullen, B., and Abrams, D. 2007. "Without Mercy: The Immediate Impact of Group Size on Lynch Mob Atrocity." *Personality and Social Psychology Bulletin* 33 (10): 1340–1352. https://doi.org/10.1177/0146167207303951.

Liebst, L. S. 2019. "Exploring the Sources of Collective Effervescence: A Multilevel Study." *Sociological Science* 6 (2): 27–42. https://doi.org/10.15195/v6.a2.

McDonald, M. G., Wearing, S., and Ponting, J. 2009. "The Nature of Peak Experience in the Wilderness." *The Humanist Psychologist* 37 (4): 370–385. https://doi.org/10.1080/08873260701828912.

Mears, A. 2020. *Very Important People: Status and Beauty in the Global Party Circuit.* Princeton University Press.

Mizrahi-Werner, J., Liebst, L. S., and Demant, J. (2024). "Beyond Bodily Co-Presence: A Micro-Sociological Study of Online Interaction Rituals." *Symbolic Interaction* 48 (1): 46–68.

Myers, W. A. 1979. "Imaginary Companions in Childhood and Adulthood." *The Psychoanalytic Quarterly* 48 (2): 292–307.

Olaveson, T. 2004. "Non-stop Ecstatic Dancing: An Ethnographic Study of Connectedness and the Rave Experience in Central Canada." Ph.D. diss., University of Ottawa.

Páez, D., Rimé, B., Basabe, N., Wlodarczyk, A., and Zumeta, L. 2015. "Psychosocial Effects of Perceived Emotional Synchrony in Collective Gatherings." *Journal of Personality and Social Psychology* 108 (5): 711–729. https://doi.org/10.1037/pspi0000014.

Rimé, B., and Páez, D. 2023. "Why We Gather: A New Look, Empirically Documented, at Émile Durkheim's Theory of Collective Assemblies and Collective Effervescence." *Perspectives on Psychological Science* 18 (6): 1306–1330. https://doi.org/10.1177/17456916221146388.

Shils, E. 1975 [1968]. The Concentration and Dispersion of Charisma. In *Center and Peripliery: Essays in Macrosociology*, edited by E. Shills. University of Chicago Press.

Singleton, T., Gerken, T., and McMahon, L. 2023. "How a Chatbot Encouraged a Man Who Wanted to Kill the Queen." *BBC Online News*, October 14. https://www.bbc.com/news/technology-67012224.

Smith, P. 2020. *Durkheim and After*. Polity Press.

Stefansen, K., Solstad, G. M., and Tokle, R. 2023. "What Happened to Me? Ambiguity and Surety in Narratives of Intoxicated Sexual Assault." *Sociology* 58 (3). https://doi.org/10.1177/00380385231209243.

Thumala Olave, M. A. 2018. "Reading Matters: Towards a Cultural Sociology of Reading." *American Journal of Cultural Sociology* 6 (3): 417–454. https://doi-org.ludwig.lub.lu.se/10.1057/s41290-017-0034-x.

Tutenges, S. 2023. *Intoxication: An Ethnography of Effervescent Revelry*. Rutgers University Press.

Tutenges, S., Sandberg, S., and Pedersen, W. 2020. "Sexually Violent Effervescence: Understanding Sexual Assault among Youth." *Sexualities* 23 (3): 406–421. https://doi.org/10.1177/1363460719830342.

Vandenberg, F., Berghman, M., and Schaap, J. 2020. "The 'Lonely Raver': Music Livestreams during COVID-19 as a Hotline to Collective Consciousness?" *European Societies* 23 (1): 141–152. https://doi.org/10.1080/14616696.2020.1818271

Wagoner, B. (ed.) 2009. *Symbolic Transformation: The Mind in Movement through Culture and Society*. Routledge.

Watkins, M. 2000. *Invisible Guests*. Spring Publishing.

Wellman, J. K., Corcoran, K. E., and Stockly-Meyerdirk, K. 2014. "'God Is Like a Drug . . .': Explaining Interaction Ritual Chains in American Megachurches." *Sociological Forum* 29 (3): 650–672. https://doi.org/10.1111/socf.12108.

Winchester, D., and Pagis, M. 2022. "Sensing the Sacred: Religious Experience, Semiotic Inversions, and the Religious Education of Attention." *Sociology of Religion* 83 (1): 12–35. https://doi.org/10.1093/socrel/srab004.

1

An Essay on *la Fête*

History of Collective Effervescence in Twentieth-Century French Thought

Romulo Lelis

Collective effervescence is gaining momentum and popularity within the twenty-first-century social sciences. Randal Collins's *Interaction Ritual Chains* (2004), has been the flagship of this renewed interest, inspiring new interpretations and developments among various scholars (Draper 2019; Liebst 2019; Case 2021; Vandenberg 2022; Mizrahi-Werner et al. 2024). The contemporary literature views the concept from a microinteractionist perspective that reduces collective effervescence to an emotional level based on individual psychology; notwithstanding its merits, this understanding largely deviates from the Durkheimian original sense.[1] In contrast, this chapter will foreground a Durkheimian perspective and, by rewriting the history of collective effervescence, argue that Durkheimian insights are themselves generative grounds for further research.

The concept of collective effervescence was created by the Durkheimian *Année Sociologique* group at the turn of the twentieth century but remained largely ignored by mainstream Durkheim-inspired theories afterward. Nonetheless, the concept never truly disappeared from theoretical works, and it remained alive in a somewhat alternative, hidden Francophone lineage of thought concerning festivals—*la fête*—throughout the twentieth century. This chapter delves into this stream of theories that focus on *la fête* as a way of shedding light on the enduring, if hidden, reflection on collective effervescence over the past century.

The first section of this chapter begins with a discussion of the creation of the concept among the *Année Sociologique* group, specifically Émile

Durkheim, Henri Hubert, and Marcel Mauss. The second section examines how the concept is utilized in the works of Mauss and his closest students, Marcel Granet and Robert Hertz. The third section focuses on the contributions of Georges Bataille, Roger Caillois, and Frantz Fanon. The fourth section explores the writings of Jean Duvignaud, Henri Lefebvre, Mona Ozouf, and Michel Maffesoli. By showing how the understanding of festivals and collective effervescence has been intertwined across these explorations, the final section of this chapter discloses the aesthetic, epistemic, and political dimensions of collective effervescence—dimensions that have been largely overlooked in its twenty-first-century applications.

The First Wave (1892–1912)

It is commonplace to say that Durkheim created the concept of collective effervescence. This is, however, a misleading statement of a more complicated story. Collective effervescence emerged in tandem with theories of nineteenth-century French crowd psychology. In Durkheim, it appeared for the first time in his *Leçons de Sociologie Criminelle*, a course taught at Bordeaux in 1892–1893, where he says that homicide, assault, and battery are "born of a certain collective effervescence" (Durkheim 2022, 128).[2] Effervescence appears again in his 1895–1896 lectures *Le Socialisme* (1928) and in *Le Suicide* (1897), but also as a pathological phenomenon concerning a state of maniac agitation due to the deregulation of people's desires in modern life. Thus, in its beginning, Durkheim's collective effervescence held a negative connotation, being considered a modern malaise. In this early context, its meaning aligned more closely with Gabriel Tarde's view of criminal crowds (Tarde 1886; Tarde 1901) and Gustave Le Bon's (1895) irrationality of the crowds than to what it would come to mean in *Les Formes Élémentaires de la Vie Religieuse* (Durkheim 1912). The question, then, is what happened between 1897 and 1912 that led to this shift in the conceptualization of collective effervescence? The answer lies in the creation of the *Année Sociologique* and, more precisely, the works of Hubert and Mauss, who served as editors of the sociology of religion section during this period.

Hubert and Mauss explored the positive aspects of collective effervescence by studying ecstatic rituals and festivals worldwide in ancient and Indigenous societies. In addition to using the term "effervescence," they referred to these states as "collective excitement"—their preferred term. In an 1899 review of a book about the origins of Christianity, Mauss highlights the mutual and "inner effervescence" in early Christian communities (Mauss 1899, 270). However, the states of collective excitement took their full potential only in the Hubert and Mauss essay "Esquisse d'une Théorie Générale de la Magie" (1904), wherein they argue that the idea-force *mana* was collectively produced in Malayo-Polynesian public festivals. They note:

> The whole social body comes alive with the same movement. There are no more individuals. In a manner of speaking, they all become parts of a machine or, better, spokes of a wheel: the magical round dance, performed and sung, becomes the ideal image of the situation. . . . The rhythmic movement, uniform and continuous, is the immediate expression of a mental state in which the consciousness of each individual is overwhelmed by a single sentiment, a single hallucination, a common objective. All the bodies sway the same swing, all the faces wear the same mask, all the voices utter the same cry; we have the terrific impression produced by the rhythm of the music and singing. To see all these figures masked with the image of the same desire, to hear all mouths uttering proof of their certainty—everyone is carried away by the convictions of the whole group, where there is no possibility of resistance. All the people are merged in the excitement of the dance: in their feverish agitation, they become but one body, one soul. Then, society's body genuinely manifests itself because each different cell, each individual, is closely merged with that of the next, like the cells that make up a single organism. In such circumstances . . . a feeling of universal consensus may create a reality. . . . Here, the laws of group psychology break the laws of individual psychology. A whole series of sequential phenomena—volition, idea, muscular movement, the satisfaction of needs—becomes completely simultaneous in this case. It is because society gesticulates that magical beliefs are imposed, and it is because of magical beliefs that society gesticulates. (Hubert and Mauss 1904, 134–135)

The image of the wheel illustrates the process of collective effervescence. In this context, the dramatic dance denotes the repeated, rhythmic, and synchronous agitation of gestures, voices, and sounds, producing a ritual setting separate from everyday life, in which there is a kind of hallucinatory alignment of all participants around a common idea-force of *mana*, that breaks their psyche and merges them as a way to create a single collective subject that, as a subject, can think and act on its own. In other words, collective effervescence is the culmination of this fusion of aesthetically oriented performances, sentiments, and ideas that overwhelms each person's psyche to the extent that they partake of the greater society's body and consciousness.

The next step in Hubert and Mauss's theorization was to link these public festivals with the modulation of time and space categories. In "Étude Sommaire de la Représentation du Temps dans la Religion et la Magie" (Hubert 1905), while analyzing German traditions, Hubert noted that these periodic festivals and their intervals endow the notion of time with a rhythm that gives birth to the calendars as a way of measuring this cyclical notion of time.[3] Then, Mauss and Henri Beuchat, in "Essai sur les Variations Saisonnières des Sociétés Eskimos" (1906), further explored how the spatial variation between periods of a festival's heightened sociality, followed by periods of disaggregation and dispersion, dictated the rhythm of collective life. When the whole society is held together to celebrate its festivals, Mauss and Beuchat characterized it as a "chronic state of effervescence and hyperactivity," during which the group "has a greater sense of itself and also holds a greater place in the consciousness of individuals" (Mauss and Beuchat 1906, 125). So, according to Hubert and Mauss, collective effervescence shapes how we conceive of and count time, as well as our morphological patterns of concentration and dispersion in space. For the *Année* team, the public festivals thus became the collective effervescence's core unit from which everything originates and evolves.

In a sense, Durkheim's perspective on collective effervescence in *Les Formes Élémentaires de la Vie Religiuse* (1912, 310–311) is thus a byproduct of Hubert and Mauss's concept rework. What does Durkheim add to that? He connects these Indigenous festivals to a discussion about the role of crowds in modern society. In his 1911 article "Jugements de Valeur et Jugements de Réalité," Durkheim introduces his renewed concept of collective effervescence for the first time:

> It is, in fact, at such moments of effervescence that the great ideals upon which civilizations rest are born. Creative or innovative periods are precisely those in which, under the influence of various circumstances, men are led to come closer together, when meetings and assemblies are more frequent, relationships better sustained, and the exchanges of ideas most active: such was the great Christendom crisis, the movement of collective enthusiasm which, in the 12th and 13th centuries, drew the scholars of Europe towards Paris and gave birth to Scholasticism, the Reformation and the Renaissance, the revolutionary era, the great Socialist upheavals of the 19th century. At such times, this higher life is actually lived with such intensity and exclusiveness that it monopolizes all minds to the more or less complete exclusion of egoism and commonplace. The ideal then tends to become one with reality; this is why men have the impression that the time is very close when it will become a reality itself and the kingdom of God will be established on earth. . . . Nevertheless, these ideals would quickly fade if they were not periodically revived. This

> is what festivals, public ceremonies, whether religious or secular, preaching of all kinds, those of the Church or those of the school, dramatic performances, and artistic manifestations are for—in a word, whatever draws men together into an intellectual and moral communion. These are like partial and weakened rebirths of the effervescence of creative eras. (1911, 448–449)

Here, Durkheim links the collective effervescence seen in Indigenous festivals to those large-scale transformative movements in European history, such as the Crusades, the Reformation, the Renaissance, the French Revolution, and the socialist movements. What links these disparate circumstances is their "dynamogenic function" (Mauss and Durkheim 1913, 98), meaning that states of collective effervescence trigger collective action. Treating all of these movements as festival-like phenomena, Durkheim connects them with minor festival-like phenomena, such as church, school, and arts participation, local festivals, demonstrations, and public ceremonies, arguing that these smaller iterations partially revive those larger ones. On the one hand, partial effervescence has something to do with the movement from a fragmentation of the sacred in modern societies, followed by the chronic difficulty of having regular large-scale events at which all society members can gather. And yet such distinction between high-end transformative festivals and low-end reproductive ones is a Durkheimian insight into how their alternation may still dictate the seasonal variations in modern life.

The Second Wave (1913–1930)

The second conceptual wave of collective effervescence theorization was carried out by Mauss and his junior colleagues, who extended the analysis of festivals to new historical and geographical contexts. Robert Hertz, a student of Durkheim and Mauss and a later member of the *Année*, explored collective effervescence while studying popular religion in Europe. In his 1913 article "Saint Besse: Étude d'un Culte Alpestre," Hertz investigates the persistence and transformations of an ancient religious peasant tradition in a rural Christian cult in the Italian Alps. The annual festival of Saint Besse takes several days and has a procession as its major event. The festival is central to maintaining the very existence of the saint, in the sense that, without the festival, it would simply seem that Saint Besse did not exist. The festival brings that sacred energy to its peak: "The assembled people, the rites, and the procession, the pious offerings bring the holy energy that emanates from the sanctuary to its highest point and put it into full activity" (Hertz [1913] 1928, 143). With the unreserved joy of being together comes the possibility of rising, "if only for a few moments, above the limited horizon of their daily life—to joyfully take upon their shoulders the heavy burden of the ideal" (Hertz [1913] 1928, 187). In addition, Hertz's posthumously published review essay discusses Russian sects born out of Orthodox Christianity around the seventeenth century. These popular Christian sects reintroduced ecstasy as a central feature of religious renovation, wherein the combination of dance, chant, and prophecies aimed to invoke the descent of the Holy Spirit. "These rhythmic dances, which last for hours and culminate in collective hallucinations and prophetic trances," in addition to the "impersonal force, which circulates through people and things," all point to striking similarities between Australian religion, early Christianity, and Russian sects since "they all stem from a 'society in effervescence'" (Hertz 1928, 248). To Hertz, then, collective effervescence is thus more prominent where the social organization is diffuse and collective life more intense, and less likely in societies wherein social organization is more hierarchical, rigid, and centralized.

Marcel Granet published *Fêtes et Chansons Anciennes de la Chine* (1919) following the trend of identifying the central role of the seasonal festivals,[4] but set in ancient China. As a protégé of Durkheim and Mauss, Granet placed great importance on poetry as the solemn public language created to be sung and performed at festivals. Additionally, he employed the category of rhythm as a way of articulating the dances, chants, exchanges, marriages, work, and feasts in Chinese life. Those festivals were marked by dances, drums, music, and ritual masquerades that mimicked cats and leopards forming a "holy orgy" with "a strange power of excitement." He notes: "How intense must have been the feelings that animated the crowd then! . . . They could not find their expression in the poor language of everyday life: these solemn feelings required a solemn language, poetry, to translate them" (Granet 1919, 224–225). Moreover, Chinese festivals connect these aesthetic and orgiastic practices with the exchanges and political alliances that bind local groups, forming and maintaining a political federation that would lead to the idea of a Chinese nation. According to Granet,

> *The festivals of ancient China are large assemblies that mark the seasonal rhythm of social life. They correspond to brief periods of assembly—where social life is intense—and alternate with prolonged periods of dispersing—where social life is almost non-existent.* During these assemblies, the alliance pact that binds small local groups in a community receives a new consecration in an orgy regulated by tradition. *The orgy, fueled by collective excitement, diminishes the barriers between typically closed groups, allowing for potential exchanges:* these exchanges, primarily involving people but also things, result in each group obtaining pledges, especially hostages, which

> are enduring assurances of loyalty to their fundamental pact. *The system of guarantees between federated groups is based on marriage alliances:* the ancient festivals are then characterized by sexual orgies that enable matrimonial exchanges. (238–239; italics in original)

Granet's argument about the role of ancient Chinese seasonal festivals in some ways follows the style of Mauss and Durkheim, but it also adds a clear connection between collective effervescence and its political role in organizing marriage and intergroup alliances. The orgy allows the initiation of young males and females through exogamy as a way of connecting local groups; it also gives birth to yin and yang, two elemental categories of thought in Chinese cosmology representing "male" and "female" as an opposite, but interconnected, self-perpetuating cycle. In this sense, Granet points out that because the festivals seem to bring peace, connection, and harmony among people, participants are led to imagine that their power goes beyond human affairs and that the stability and harmony of nature and the world are the result of the social stability and harmony achieved during these festivals.

Finally, perhaps the most important and influential publication of that period is Mauss's (1925) article "Essai Sur le Don." In it, he presents what he calls *systems of total prestations*, that is, generalized exchanges that could still be seen in North American potlatch and Melanesian kula: the massive seasonal festivals during which all the main events of collective life take place, together with dances, chants, and dramatic performances, what Mauss would later call a *total social fact*. The lengthy gatherings that characterize the dual morphology of these Indigenous nations are where one can see collective effervescence at work. According to Mauss,

> during the whole period of this concentration, they remain in a state of perpetual effervescence. Social life becomes extremely intense there.... It consists of a sort of perpetual agitation. There are regular visits from one tribe to another, from one clan to another, and from one family to another. These festivals occur repeatedly and often last for a long time. On the occasion of weddings, various rituals, and promotions, one spends without counting all that has been amassed during the summer and autumn with great industry. (1925, 90)

For Mauss, then, collective effervescence marks these periods of high-intensity festivals, and, as a consequence, all sorts of exchange, spending, and destruction can take place. In addition, it is due to collective effervescence that the notion of economic value is born and can circulate in everyday life. But there is also another significant move that Mauss makes in his essay: he points to the inherent instability between festival and war. In this regard, he observes how people involved in those festivals can suddenly pass from celebration to bellicosity in a moment:

> Buleau, a chief, had invited Bobal, another chief, and his people to a feast, probably the first of a long series. They began to rehearse the dances all night long. In the morning, all of them were excited by the night of vigil, dancing, and singing. After a simple observation by Buleau, one of Bobal's men killed him. And the troop massacred, pillaged, and carried off the women from the village. (Mauss 1925, 184)

In his example, Mauss identifies an intimate connection between festival and war, viewing them as two sides of the same coin. Indeed, the system of total prestations is developed as a way of mitigating conflict and increasing social bonds between friendly but always potentially rival groups. Thus, Mauss discloses here how festivals concentrate power into action, a momentum that can lead to radical political changes. He argues that collective effervescence is the core mechanism that triggers feasts, exchanges, and warfare. Ultimately, he concludes that politics emerges as a skill developed to manage the outcomes of these periods of effervescence.

The Third Wave (1931–1961)

Collective effervescence's third theoretical wave can be characterized by direct appropriations, reactions, and further elaborations from Mauss's work on festivals, while also addressing the primary political concerns of the time. First, there is the work of the Collège de Sociologie, developed by Roger Caillois and Georges Bataille. Bataille generated one of the most creative readings of Mauss's essay on the gift through his theory of a general economy. In his seminal essay "La Notion de Dépense" ([1933a] 1970), Bataille observes that classical economy is based on very narrow principles of production and conservation, leaving aside the greater role of economy in social life. Instead, the idea of unproductive spending rules the general economy; that is, something that exists as an end in itself therefore does not serve as a means to production. Drawing on the potlatch model, Bataille argues that it is the world of the archaic festivals that rule the general economy, and this provokes giant losses and catastrophes, which are ultimately characterized by "a certain orgiastic state" ([1933a] 1970, 303). However, since the bourgeoisie's raison d'être is rooted in their aversion to unproductive spending, those large forms of archaic festivals have shrunk. In the essay "La Structure Psychologique du Fascisme," Bataille ([1933b] 1970) defines bourgeois society as having a *homogeneous* character, in which everything moves around utility, and it is opposed to the *heterogeneous* forces that result from unproductive spending. Because of the "general laws of the heterogeneous social region in which effervescence takes its positive form" (Bataille [1933b] 1970, 343), these heterogeneous forces are precisely the transgressive, tumultuous, festival-like forces of collective effervescence. Although the homogeneous bourgeois society avoids contact with its heterogeneous elements, the latter often erupts to the surface due to the severe economic contradictions of the former. In this regard, Bataille points out Nazifacist and socialist movements as the two main heterogeneous upsurges of his time that, although opposed to each other as right- and left-wing movements, they have both challenged the very utilitarian nature of bourgeois society. Regarding Nazifacism, Bataille affirms that

> the fascist leaders undoubtedly belong to a heterogeneous existence. Opposed to the democratic politicians, who represented the inherent flatness of homogeneous society in various countries, Mussolini or Hitler stood out as entirely distinct. . . . it is impossible not to recognize the power that sets them apart from men, parties, and even laws: a power that breaks the regular course of things, the peaceful but tedious homogeneity, powerless to maintain itself (the fact that legality is broken is only the most obvious sign of the transcendent, heterogeneous nature of fascist action). ([1933b] 1970, 348)

On the Right, having all the traits that characterize collective effervescence, Nazifacism is discussed as a movement that presented itself as a transcendent force by connecting military power and charismatic leadership to carry out *total oppression*. On the Left, working-class movements became the most grandiose form of unproductive expenditure to the extent that they threatened the very existence of the bourgeoisie. In exploring these parallel if politically divided effervescences, Bataille draws attention to the subversive character of the "effervescent revolted masses" ([1933b] 1970, 369). In this scenario, an unprecedented dual effervescence emerges, in which two distinct, heterogeneous movements simultaneously challenge the existence of the same homogeneous society despite their hostility toward each other.

As a former Mauss student, Caillois was responsible for introducing Durkheim and Mauss's ideas to his generation. His 1939 paper "Le Sacré de Transgression: Théorie de la Fête," first presented to the Collège de France, and then published in his book *L'Homme et le Sacré* ([1939] 1963), was a theoretical landmark in this regard. In decoupling the sacred between the institutional sacred and transgressive sacred, Callois attributes the latter to the creative, destructive character of Indigenous festivals, where collective effervescence is translated into the notion of *paroxysm*. As Caillois points out, "in its complete form, the festival must be defined as the paroxysm of society, purifying and renewing it simultaneously" ([1939] 1963, 160). The institutional sacred is then characterized by the role of institutions in conserving the life created during festivals and ordering society. However, in modern societies, more complex hierarchical forms such as nation-states dominate and are less likely to accept any interruptions to the ordinary course of life. Since everything must continue the same way in perpetuity, states overcontrol seeking to minimize the role of festivals in modern societies. Caillois wonders, then, what could possibly trigger such a transgressive-creative collective effervescence in a modern society ruled by nation-states. According to his 1949 paper "Guerre et Sacré," war is the only event that breaks the institutionalized tranquility of everyday life in modern societies and works with the same intensity and significance as an archaic festival. Both inaugurate a period of intense socialization and concentration of various sources. In modern societies, he argues, "war represents the only moment of concentration and intense absorption in the group. . . . This is why it calls for comparison with the ancient season of collective effervescence" (Caillois [1949] 1963, 219). As a total phenomenon, war requires all the energies available and acquires a sacred status: it distinguishes itself from mere murder since it has more to do with human sacrifice, has no immediate utility, and the ultimate goal is destruction. Caillois declares that

> when war loses all measure, it mobilizes people's energies and spends the resources of a great nation without restraint. When it violates all rules and laws, and it has ceased to be on the scale or in the resemblance of anything human, it is then that it appears with the most luminous halo. Crushing generations under massive ruins, shining with the dark glow of an immense blaze, it appears as the dreadful paroxysm of collective life. Nothing can dispute its sinister glory of being the only event in modern society that tears individuals away from their particular concerns and suddenly throws them into another world where they no longer belong to themselves. ([1949] 1963, 231–232)

According to Caillois, war is characterized by radically suspending everything considered mundane. It violates the current laws and expends all resources, including human lives, if necessary. It demands the most brutal sacrifices from individuals without giving them anything in return. In a war, there are no longer individual rights, individual concerns, or individuals per se; they become subsumed into their nation's actions and decisions. In the modern period, war thus becomes a milestone for time division, creating a conceptual before and after, and inaugurating a new era when it bursts forth. For Caillois, war triggers the most vigorous collective effervescence state possible in modern life.

The third scholar of this period was Frantz Fanon,[5] who theorized the role of collective effervescence in the African decolonial revolutions of his time, primarily based on the emergent Algerian liberation war. In a 1957 article he characterized the Algerian revolution as an "effervescent phase of alignment of forces and organization of the armed struggle of the colonized people" (Fanon [1957] 2001, 86). In his last masterpiece, *Les Damnés de la Terre* ([1961] 2002), he then theorized decolonization as a moment of a violent and creative effervescence that led to a radical transformation of men: the creation of a new conception of humanity due to this sudden awakening of a community. "In a true collective ecstasy," he says, the once disinherited people put aside their rivalries, and proceed "in a solemn atmosphere, to the washing and purification of the local face of the nation" (Fanon [1961] 2002, 128). He then considers the roots of a violent-transformative power such as he had observed in Algeria and elsewhere. A similar energy can be found in those festival gatherings where the colonized meet periodically to perform sacred ecstatic dances. Indeed, Fanon argues that a study of the colonial world must focus on those festival gatherings. As he says:

> On the other side, we will see the affectivity of the colonized exhaust itself in more or less ecstatic dances. . . . The relaxation of the colonized is precisely this muscular orgy during which the most acute aggressiveness and the most immediate violence are channeled, transformed, and concealed. . . . At fixed times, on fixed dates, men and women meet in a given place and, under the serious eye of the tribe, launch into a pantomime that appears disordered but is in reality very systematized, where, through multiple channels, denials of the head, curvature of the spine, throwing the whole body back, the grandiose effort of a community to exorcise itself, to free itself, to tell itself is decoded like an open book. . . . Everything is permitted because, in reality, we only meet to let the accumulated libido and the prevented aggression volcanically flow. Symbolic killings, figurative rides, multiple imaginary murders, all this must come out. (Fanon [1961] 2002, 57–58)

In this quotation, Fanon argues that repressed violence and aggressiveness are transformed into mimes and figurative performances that, like lava, volcanically overflow and destroy everything that resists its power. It is this same energy that is channeled into and fuels decolonization. Once triggered, it created not only a violent reaction against colonialism but, with that, even if only for that moment, a whole reorganization of gender roles, with female revolutionary protagonism (Fanon [1959] 1972, 93), as well as the creation of a national character through the arts (Fanon [1961] 2002, 231–232).

The Fourth Wave (1962–1999)

The fourth wave of collective effervescence theory was carried out by scholars who mainly dealt with and expanded the reflections of the past generation.[6] First, there was Jean Duvignaud, a pioneer in the sociology of theater and a former assistant of Georges Gurvicth. In *Sociologie du Théatre*, Duvignaud (1965) argues that theater was born from festivals, and that both carry a permanent orientation against the established order. In *Fêtes et Civilizations* ([1973] 1991), Duvignaud points out that the rise of intellectuals that live in urban areas—as in, contemporary academics—has distorted our understanding of festivals to the extent that their meaning was degraded to a mere orderly celebration. Against this view, Duvignaud contends that festivals are subversive, antiestablishment events that reveal the power that acts upon people outside the institutions that structure social order. One of the most vivid examples of his perspective is his essay from May 1968, where Duvignaud analyzes the civil unrest in Paris. As he narrates:

> Doctrines become blurred: . . . Mao rubs shoulders with Trotsky, Stalin with the Jews, and the latter with the Arab activists. The incredibly rapid movement of these boys and girls . . . stirs this crowd to make it an animated, quivering figure, arouses a warm communication, a reciprocal opening of consciousness where emotion and sentimentality have no place. . . . Nothing is fixed here, nothing is established: effervescence is at its peak, which is to say that the groups are not organized around a common project, that no leader is recognized. Behind Proudhon, we discern Rousseau: dissolve the established links, . . . do not constitute oneself as a "State," as an "institution" . . . the story's plot is marked by explosions of this kind, unique, unpredictable, a kind of synthesis of disparate and contrary elements brutally brought together, mixed, and transformed. The people who are there have never really seen each other. . . . The police hunt down the "gangs of youths," but it is the present arrangement of our houses, our lives, and our institutions that gives rise to these marginal groupings. (Duvignaud [1973] 1991, 184–185)

In this excerpt, the author downplays the role of doctrines and emotions—at least the ones that people can feel in regular situations. Instead, the effervescence he articulates involves a strong sense of uprooting, of turning the world upside down as we used to know it. Moreover, Duvignaud points out civil unrest, riots, and demonstrations as emergent forms of modern festival-like events that can trigger collective effervescence. As he observes, the very manner in which postwar bourgeois society is organized fosters these crowd movements. Unlike traditional festivals, these riot-effervescent movements are carried out by people who have never seen or talked to each other and, not infrequently, have just met on the street. Notably, May 1968 marked the beginning of the so-called new social movements.

Another Gurvicth assistant who engaged with collective effervescence was Henri Lefebvre, who gave pride of place to festivals in his sociological studies of everyday life. For instance, in his revisionist study of the Paris Commune, *La Proclamation de la Commune*, Lefebrve argues that the Commune was the spring festival of the people of Paris, perhaps one of the greatest of modern times: "A spring festival in the city, a festival of the destitute people and the proletarians, a revolutionary festival and a festival of the Revolution; a total festival" (1965, 21). Lefebvre considers the structure of a festival to resemble that of a drama, noting that the Commune developed in the genre of a tragedy—an immense and bloody festival that sacrificed its leading actor, the underprivileged, to fulfill its fate. He pays particular attention to the poor as an emerging urban group and their relation to city festivals. Their constrained lives and lack of time and space drive them to engage in and enjoy the time-space amplification of festivals. As he states, "Grafted onto the peasant festival, the city festival amplifies rural traditions. The street, the café, and the festival constitute the social space of the poor" (Lefebvre 1965, 124). The series of insurrections from March to May of 1871 was marked by spontaneous gatherings that triggered a "volcanic effervescence" against the State and "metamorphosed itself into a community, a communion within which work, joy, leisure, fulfillment of needs . . . are no longer separated" (Lefebvre 1965, 390). Consequently, the Commune festival abolished political representation as a specialized task and merged politics with civil society. As Lefevebre concluded, as long as it lasted, the Paris Commune taught us how such effervescent crowds could "spontaneously turn themselves into a festival" (1965, 24).

In the May 1968 aftermath, Mona Ozouf published a revisionist study of the role of festivals in the French Revolution, *La Fête Révolutionnaire 1789–1799* (1976). In the book, she attacks the conflation between the French Revolution's riots and actual festivals, arguing that violence played only a marginal and figurative role in the latter. Such a distinction is necessary because the revolutionary festivals aimed to filter and neutralize the uncontrolled explosion of violence of the revolutionary *journées* by masking and dissimulating them with the virtuous values of the Enlightenment. As a manifestation of the Enlightenment, these revolutionary festivals should hide the violence and horror that have made them once possible. Ultimately, the festival organizers were trying to distance themselves from popular festivals, which they considered to be the opposite of enlightening reasoning. Ozouf says, "the popular festival is the unintelligible din of fire shovels and cauldrons; the hustle and bustle that clogs the streets and public squares; . . . In short, it is an effervescence that disconcerts reason or, worse, 'offends' it" (1976, 9–10). In this regard, rather than a wild collective effervescence, the organizers used the festivals as a way to control, educate, and please the crowds, driving them toward the realization of the First Republic. Despite their differences, the varied revolutionary festivals intertwined desire with knowledge, the education of the crowds with joy, politics, and aesthetics. They were also about collective effervescence of a controlled variety that resembled those traditional Catholic festivals that revolutionaries were trying to set themselves apart from. Indeed, Ozouf observes that the French Revolution replaced the Old Regime by mimicking its festivals and allowing a "transfer of sacredness" from the latter to the former (1976, 322). The fatherland replaced the church altar; the Declaration of Human Rights took the place of the Bible; the national anthem was substituted for prayer; civic days replaced holy days; revolutionaries replaced saints. At the very moment when the Revolution claimed innovation and gave rise to modernity, in actuality, there was an imitative return to past practices. As Ozouf puts it, "One would hesitate to call the festivals of the French Revolution 'revolutionary,' given how much emotional and subversive charge we have invested in the adjective of social turbulence" (1976, 339). In short, to Ozouf, the festivals of the French Revolution sought to neutralize subversion through ritual, continually attempting to domesticate and direct the crowd's effervescence.

Last but not least, perhaps the most famous and controversial contemporary scholar who has dealt with collective effervescence is Michel Maffesoli. Picking up the discussion where Duvignaud left off, he developed a theory of festival orgiastic states in his *L'Ombre de Dionysos* ([1982] 1985). In the book, Maffesoli argues that the Dionysian orgiastic states of collective effervescence constitute the most elemental form of sociality: "It is an effect of the domestication of morals to make us forget that effervescence is necessary for any social structuring whatsoever" ([1982] 1985, 26). Even modern society, which has always tried to efface collective effervescence, cannot escape the periodic return of those repressed forms of amorphous collectives that constitute society's underground power beyond the contemporary binary of individual agency and totalitarian State structure. "The individual, the 'I think,' etc., and the monopolized state structure are only two sides of the same phenomenon" (Maffesoli [1982] 1985, 148). Like his predecessors, Maffesoli points out the dissolution of the self into a more viscous, confusing collective subject. The festival is a crystallizing moment of collective power with a strong charge of excess, which by mimicking disorder through the ecstatic confusion of bodies, Dionysian effervescence periodically establishes a new order. What is most remarkable about collective effervescence is its unleashed passions that trigger collective action. These passions are difficult to control because "they call upon all the elements that are most of the time hidden in the social structure; it is in this sense that they are subversive" (Maffesoli [1982] 1985, 147). Indeed, as he would observe later in his *Le Temps des Tribus* ([1988] 2000), popular festivals worldwide, particularly in southern countries, would create a new wave of effervescence in reaction to northern dominance. According to Maffesoli, although the modern bourgeoisie has done everything "to control or sanitize possession dances and other forms of popular effervescence," one may see in those popular festivals "the fair revenge of the values of the South over those of the North, the 'choreographic epidemics'" ([1988] 2000, 181). In this sense, Maffesoli points out the rebirth of the Dionysian effervescence through the rise of new movements that advocate the resistance of traditional ways of life amid modernity, a clash that has been updated and revitalized by decolonial critique. As he articulates toward the conclusion, "It cannot be concluded; the Dionysian adventure has only just (re)begun" (Maffesoli [1988] 2000, 239).

Conclusion

This chapter has demonstrated that theorizations about collective effervescence have infused twentieth-century French thought. In doing so, it has disclosed a structured lexicon of aesthetically oriented terms linking collective effervescence to festivals that, since their Durkheimian genesis, have been assimilated and propagated through the intergenerational work of scholars across subjects, disciplines, and traditions over a century—sometimes with no reference to Durkheim.

In addition, the chapter has revealed an image of collective effervescence that contrasts with its twenty-first-century version. Within its theorizations in the festival context, collective effervescence is a mechanism that enables crowds to coordinate sentiments, thoughts, and actions so that they become a collective subject, able to carry out challenges and navigate situations that no one could cope with alone. Individuals are turned into parts of a wheel, and their self is diluted into a higher form of consciousness. Since such a mechanism is often triggered at critical moments, it also has a political character that allows the collective subject to act toward the realization of societal needs whether they may be the creation of cosmological categories, gift exchanges, wars, revolutions, riots, and all sorts of political unrest. Indeed, the most famous large-scale transformations of modern France were conceptualized under the rubric of "festival." Whether in a carnival parade or at war, collective effervescence interconnects the serious and joyous sides of life, demanding people for the sum of their energy—and sometimes even their lives—to achieve societal ideals. Moreover, the most salient outcome in tracing the connections between effervescence and festivals is the understanding that any crowd or gathering can be a potential site for aesthetically oriented performances (James 2014). Indeed, rhythm is a meta-aesthetic category that allows synchronization and, thus, collective action. Ultimately, because "effervescence" literally means a "bubbling solution," collective effervescence is, therefore, a Durkheimian figure of speech that captures the way a crowd behaves as if it were a bubbling solution, that is, an outward action of collective rhythmic agitation rather than a situatedness within the inward realm of emotions.

Finally, because the festival approach discloses a continuity between traditional and modern groups, collective effervescence has been used since Durkheim as a tool for critiquing modern, bourgeois, capitalist, and colonial society. By applying the same model to understand Indigenous and Western festivals, Durkheimian sociology created a reverse methodology that ponders, rather than affirms, modernity's self-image. As Duvignaud once concluded, this approach to the festival "pierces the discourse and suggests an image of the man in the world that contradicts the 'great *épopée* of the machine'" ([1977] 2012, 213). Since social scientists are becoming increasingly aware of modernity's bias, this chapter has indicated how applying the same inquiries to ourselves that we typically direct toward "others" is a keen insight rooted in Durkheimian tradition that can be highly generative for twenty-first-century scholarship.

FUNDING

This research has been funded by the Sao Paulo Research Foundation (21/10138-6).

NOTES

1. Apart from Collins's perspective, there are also studies using collective effervescence in different ways, such as those of Graeber and Wengrow (2021), Páez et al. (2026), Rimé and Páez (2023), Steiner (2023), and Tutenges (2023).

2. This and other quotes from the French sources cited in this chapter are directly translated from the source by the author.

3. For a detailed take on Hubert's contribution to the Durkheimian sociology of religion, see Lelis (2024).

4. Similarly, seasonal festivals were analyzed by Stefan Czarnowski (1919) on the Irish, Georges Dumézil (1924) regarding the Indo-Europeans, Louis Gernet (1928) concerning the ancient Greeks, and Nguyen Van Huyen (1934) on the Vietnamese.

5. Fanon was a colleague of Michel Leiris, well-acquainted with the Collège de Sociologie and Maussian scholarship.

6. Collective effervescence was introduced in the Anglophone world only in the fourth wave through Victor Turner's work. For a comparison between Durkheim's collective effervescence and Turner's *communitas*; see Olaveson (2001).

REFERENCES

Bataille, Georges. [1933a] 1970. "La Notion de Dépense." In *Oeuvres Complètes*. Tome I. Gallimard.

Bataille, Georges. [1933b] 1970. "La Structure Psychologique du Fascisme." In *Oeuvres Complètes*. Tome I. Gallimard.

Caillois, Roger. [1939] 1963. "Le Sacré de Transgression: Théorie de la Fête." In *L'Homme et le Sacré*. Leroux. Originally published in 1939 by Leroux.

Caillois, Roger. [1949] 1963. "Guerre et Sacré." In *L'Homme et le Sacré*. Leroux. Originally published in 1939 by Leroux.

Case, Benjamin S. 2021. "Contentious Effervescence: The Subjective Experience of Rioting." *Mobilization* 26(2): 179–196.

Collins, Randall. 2004. *Interaction Ritual Chains*. Princeton University Press.

Czarnowski, Stefan. 1919. *Le Culte des Héros et Ses Conditions Sociales: Saint Patrick Héros National de l'Irlande*. Alcan.

Draper, Scott. 2019. *Religious Interaction Ritual: The Microsociology of the Spirit*. Lexington Books.

Dumézil, Georges. 1924. *Le Festin d'Immortalité: Étude de Mythologie Comparée Indo-Européene*. Paul Geuthner.

Durkheim, Émile. 1897. *Le Suicide*. Alcan.

Durkheim, Émile. 1911. "Jugements de Valeur et Jugements de Réalité." *Revue de Métaphysique et de Morale* 19(4): 437–453.

Durkheim, Émile. 1912. *Les Formes Élémentaires de la Vie Religieuse*. Alcan.

Durkheim, Émile. 1928. *Le Socialisme*. Alcan.

Durkheim, Émile. 2022. *Leçons de Sociologie Criminelle*. Edited by Matthieu Béra. Flammarion.

Duvignaud, Jean. 1965. *Sociologie du Théatre: Essai sur les Ombres Collectives*. PUF.

Duvignaud, Jean. [1973] 1991. *Fêtes et Civilizations*. Actes Sud. Originally published in 1973 by Weber.

Duvignaud, Jean. [1977] 2012. *Le Don du Rien: Essai d'Anthropologie de la Fête*. Téraèdre. Originally published in 1977 by Stock.

Fanon, Frantz. [1957] 2001. "Les Intellectuels et les Démocrates Français Devant la Révolution Algérienne." In *Pour la Révolution Africaine: Écrits Politiques*. La Découverte. Originally published in 1964 by Maspero.

Fanon, Frantz. [1959] 1972. *Sociologie d'Une Révolution (l'An V de la Révolution Algérienne)*. Maspero. Originally published in 1959 by Maspero.

Fanon, Frantz. [1961] 2002. *Les Damnés de la Terre*. La Découverte. Originally published in 1961 by Maspero.

Gernet, Louis. 1928. "Frairies Antiques." *Revue des Études Grecques* 192:313–359.

Graeber, David, and David Wengrow. 2021. *The Dawn of Everything: A New History of Humanity*. Allen Lane.

Granet, Marcel. 1919. *Fêtes et Chansons Anciennes de la Chine*. Leroux.

Hertz, Robert. [1913] 1928. "Saint Besse: Étude d'un Culte Alpestre." In *Mélanges de Sociologie Religieuse et Folklore*. Alcan.

Hertz, Robert. 1928. "Les Sectes Russes." In *Mélanges de Sociologie Religieuse et Folklore*. Alcan.

Hubert, Henri. 1905. "Étude Sommaire de la Représentation du Temps dans la Religion et la Magie." *Annuaires de l'École Pratique des Hautes Études, Section des Sciences Religieuses 1904–1905*: 1–39.

Hubert, Henri, and Marcel Mauss. 1904. "Esquisse d'une Théorie Générale de la Magie." *Année Sociologique* 7: 1–146.

James, Wendy. 2014. "Human Life as Drama: A Maussian Insight." *Journal of Classical Sociology* 14(1): 78–90.

Le Bon, Gustave. 1895. *Psychologie des Foules.* Alcan.

Lefebvre, Henri. 1965. *La Proclamation de la Commune: 26 Mars 1871.* Gallimard.

Lelis, Romulo. 2024. "The Great Transformation: The Durkheimian Sociology from Émile Durkheim to Henri Hubert." *Anthropological Theory* 25(1): 97–117. https://doi.org/10.1177/14634996241248518.

Liebst, Lasse Suonperä. 2019. "Exploring the Sources of Collective Effervescence: A Multilevel Study." *Sociological Science* 6:27–42.

Maffesoli, Michel. [1982] 1985. *L'Ombre de Dionysos: Contribution à une Sociologie de l'Orgie.* Méridiens. Originally published in 1982 by Méridiens.

Maffesoli, Michel. [1988] 2000. *Le Temps des Tribus: Le Déclin de l'Individualisme dans les Sociétés Postmodernes.* La Table Ronde. Originally published in 1988 by Méridiens.

Mauss, Marcel. 1899. "Review of L. Duchesne, Origines du Culte Chrétien." *Année Sociologique* 2:269–271.

Mauss, Marcel. 1925. "Essai Sur le Don: Forme et Raison de l'Échange dans les Sociétés Archaïques." *Année Sociologique* nouvellle série 1:30–186.

Mauss, Marcel, and Henri Beuchat. 1906. "Essai sur les Variations Saisonnières des Sociétés Eskimos." *Année Sociologique* 9:39–130.

Mauss, Marcel, and Émile Durkheim. 1913. "Review of J. Frazer, Totemism and Exogamy; E. Durkheim, Les Formes Élémentaires de la Vie Religieuse." *Année Sociologique* 12:92–98.

Mizrahi-Werner, Jonatan et al. 2024. "Beyond Bodily Co-Presence: A Micro-Sociological Study of Online Interaction Rituals." *Symbolic Interaction* 48(1): 46–68. https://doi.org/10.1002/symb.1206.

Olaveson, Tim. 2001. "Collective Effervescence and Communitas: Processual Models of Ritual and Society in Emile Durkheim and Victor Turner." *Dialectical Anthropology* 26:89–124.

Ozouf, Mona. 1976. *La Fête Révolutionnaire 1789–1799.* Gallimard.

Páez, Darío, Bernard Rimé, Pierre Bouchat, et al. 2026. "Perceived Emotional Synchrony: A Social Psychological Perspective on Collective Effervescence." In *Collective Effervescence*, edited by Sébastien Tutenges and Philip Smith. Temple University Press.

Rimé, Bernard, and Darío Páez. 2023. "Why We Gather: A New Look, Empirically Documented, at Émile Durkheim's Theory of Collective Assemblies and Collective Effervescence." *Perspectives on Psychological Science* 18(6): 1306–1330.

Steiner, Philippe. 2023. *Faire la Fête: Sociologie de la Joie.* PUF.

Tarde, Gabriel. 1886. *La Criminalité Comparée.* Alcan.

Tarde, Gabriel. 1901. *L'opinion et la Foule.* Alcan.

Tutenges, Sébastien. 2023. *Intoxication: An Ethnography of Effervescent Revelry.* Rutgers University Press.

Vandenberg, Femke. 2022. "Put Your 'Hand Emotes in the Air': Twitch Concerts as Unsuccessful Large-Scale Interaction Rituals." *Symbolic Interaction* 45(3): 325–491.

Van Huyen, Nguyen. 1934. *Les Chants Alternés des Garçons et des Filles en Annam.* Paul Geuthner.

2

Cultivating a Crowd

Cultural Tools of Protest Action

Brady Wagoner and Sarah H. Awad

> Society cannot make its influence felt unless it is in action, and it is action only if the individuals that comprise it are assembled and acting in common. It is through common action that society becomes conscious of and affirms itself; society is above all an active cooperation.
>
> —(Durkheim, 1912 [1995], p. 421)

Anyone who has ever been a member of an emotionally engaged and physically active crowd knows how energizing it can be. Such experiences are accompanied by thrill and excitement, as well as a feeling of togetherness with others in a seamless flow of emotions and movements. In this chapter, we will explore these feelings in the context of crowd protests and how they fuel social movements. We will describe how the psychology of crowds has been theorized as either an irrational force or as normatively linked to identity concerns. The former position was adopted by the late nineteenth-century crowd theorists (most notably Gustave Le Bon, Gabriel Tarde, and Sigmund Freud) while more recently, accounts from extended social identity theory have gained ascendency (e.g., in the work of Stephen Reicher, John Drury, and Clifford Stott). We argue that Émile Durkheim's theory of collective effervesence provides us with an intermediate position and a helpful starting point to develop an account of protest crowds that both highlights embodied feelings and actions as well as their normative regulation. The distinct form of consciousness of being submerged in a group is phenomenologically real and consequential, but it is by no means automatic and guaranteed. Our argument is that it must be *cultivated* through various cultural devices to form an effective protest crowd and channel its energies beyond the event itself so as to sustain a social movement. After reviewing the different theoretical traditions of crowds and Durkheim's position within them, we go on to outline three cultural devices that work to this effect. These range from the most concrete and situated (viz. synchronized movement) to those that are more general and abstracted from the direct context of action (viz. symbols and narratives). Our primary example to illustrate these cultural devices and their effects are the Arab uprisings (esp., in Egypt), but we will supplement this with a broader set of examples to show that the principles generalize beyond the specific case.

Foundations of Crowd Psychology

Psychology inherited two different models of the social from nineteenth century thought: a community and individualist understanding (Greenwood, 2003). On the one hand, the social was understood as the identification with a particular community and its distinctive cultural forms and traditions that mediate thought. A person was social by virtue of growing up in a specific group and incorporating its language, customs, and values into him or herself. Thus, Robinson Crusoe was still operating within a social mold even while alone on his desert island; he brought society with him in an internalized form. This notion of the social as membership within a community was advanced by several early forerunners in psychology. For example, Wilhelm Wundt (1897) saw it as the "higher" branch of psychology (*Völkerpsychologie* or cultural psychology), which would study the cultural products of different communities to interpret their mentality. This was to be distinguished from a "lower" branch of psychology (physiological psychology), which would study individual psychological processes through experimental methods. The first textbooks of social psychology (McDougall, 1908; Ross, 1908) adopted the community conception but it was gradually displaced by another approach.

The second concept of the "social" came from crowd psychology. It emphasized how individuals in the presence of others become emotional, instinctive, and destructive. Here individuals are conceived according to Enlightenment ideas of a rational and autonomous self that is contaminated by the sway of other people. As Le Bon famously put it, "By the mere fact that he forms part of an organized group, a man descends several rungs in the ladder of civilization. Isolated, he may be a cultivated individual; in a crowd, he is a barbarian that is, a creature acting by instinct" ([1895] 2002, p. 8). According to Le Bon, individuals lose all sense of self and responsibility in the crowd. His book *The Crowd: A Study of the Popular Mind* ([1895] 2002) has had enormous impact on societies, inspiring leaders across the political spectrum but most notoriously Adolf Hitler and Benito Mussolini (Moscovici, 1981). Crowd psychology grew out of urbanization in which people are uprooted from traditions and brought together in centers of political power as a mass of strangers, which Le Bon thought threatened the social order: "Civilizations have yet only been created and directed by a small intellectual aristocracy, never by crowds. Crowds are only powerful for destruction" ([1895] 2002, p. 80). Le Bon had the French Revolution and the Paris Commune of 1871 in mind, as well as general aristocratic concerns about democracy, labor unions, trial by jury, and universal suffrage. As societies entered "the age of the crowd," he thought political leaders would have to find new means of taming them, much like Niccolo Machiavelli's playbook had done for an earlier epoch.

The guiding metaphor of crowd theory was hypnosis, where a hypnotizer "suggests" an idea that the hypnotized carries out (Wagoner, 2018). People in a crowd were thought of as being in a kind of hypnotic trance, in which individuals become "submerged" into a form of group consciousness. As Tarde (1890, p. 87) famously put it, "Society is imitation and imitation is a form of somnambulism." Le Bon ([1895] 2002) claimed that crowds in fact "demand illusions, and cannot do without them. They constantly give what is unreal precedence over what is real; they are almost as strongly influenced by what is untrue as by what is true" (Le Bon, [1895] 2002, p. 77). Freud (1922) similarly argued that crowds weaken the superego and drive individuals to a state similar to hypnosis. This state is not exactly irrational in the usual sense of the word but is rather an altered form of consciousness that obeys laws different from individual reasoning. It is brought on in the physical presence of others by emotional contagion and the power of vivid images planted in people's minds through suggestion. To quote Le Bon,

> Whatever strikes the imagination of crowds presents itself under the shape of a startling and very clear image, freed from all accessory explanation, or merely having as accompaniment a few marvelous or mysterious facts: examples in point are a great victory, a great miracle, a great crime, or a great hope. Things must be laid before the crowd as a whole, and their genesis must never be indicated. ([1895] 2002, p. 37)

Thus, crowd consciousness is dominated by images and affect rather than rational discursive thought, which draws on the cultural distinction between female and male forms of thinking. Leaders do not win over a crowd by reasoning with them, but by presenting spectacular images, slogans, and "lofty words" that excite people's passions. "The power of words is bound up with the images they evoke, and is quite independent of their real significance. Words whose sense is the most ill-defined are sometimes those that possess the most influence" (Le Bon, [1895] 2002, p. 61). Words like "democracy," "freedom," and "equality" are vague but precisely because of this, they have a "magical power" in the mind of the crowd that contains the solution to all problems. The most effective communicative style of a leader is thus *suggestion*, *assertation*, and *repetition* without proof and argumentation. It is difficult in today's day and age not to point to Donald Trump's statements like "build a (beautiful) wall," "crooked Hilary," and "the dishonest media" as examples. In short, crowds have a distinctive mentality analogous to a hypnotic trance and must be controlled by the manipulation of suggestive images and the emotions they evoke.

The Debate between Durkheim and Tarde

Durkheim visited Wundt's laboratory in Leipzig and developed the distinction between individual and collective representations, paralleling Wundt's "lower" and "higher" psychological processes. The former was thought to be universal across societies and grounded in the individual organism; the latter by contrast varied as a function of the cultural forms such as language that mediate thought. Cultural forms are generated through "the mutual interaction of the many" and are thus not reducible to the individuals that make them up. Durkheim made the analogy with the molecule H_2O: hydrogen and oxygen on their own are highly flammable, but the molecule H_2O can be used to extinguish a fire. In Durkheim's terms cultural forms are "collective representations" that stand above individuals and operate on them as a *constraint*. He describes human beings as *homo duplex*, as individuals with a basis in a physical body, and as social beings participating in collective representations that are the result of cooperation that has accumulated over generations. This places him squarely in the community notion of the social (Greenwood, 2003).

The two concepts of the social came to a head in a public debate between Tarde and Durkheim. To understand this, we need to first outline some of the features of Tarde's theory, which though similar was more nuanced and academically sophisticated than Le Bon's. The key concept for Tarde was *suggestion-imitation* through which collective behavior is dynamically constituted in role-creating and role-following. "Imitation" may occasionally lead to "opposition" and rarer still "invention," whereby novelties are then spread: this tripart distinction echoes Georg Hegel's thesis, antithesis and synthesis. Thus, in contrast to Le Bon's idea of civilized individuals becoming primitive in a group, Tarde conceived crowds as a dynamic network of semiconscious imitative interactions that could involve the production and spread of novelties. Moreover, he made a distinction between *crowds* (a physically anchored group) and *publics* (a dispersed group). With the advent of newspapers and other print media, Tarde (1989) thought we were in fact entering the "age of publics" (not an "age of crowds"), where thought could be instantly transmitted and imitated at a distance. In contrast to the deindividuating force of crowds, publics had at least the potential for rational deliberation, when different points of view were counterbalanced by, for example, reading different newspapers.

While Tarde's sociology was grounded in (social) psychology, Durkheim advocated a sharp split between the disciplines, famously saying, "Every time a social phenomenon is directly explained by a psychological phenomenon, we may rest assured that the explanation is false" (1895 [1982], p. 129). A good example of this principle is Durkheim's (1897) study *Suicide* where he explained differences in suicide rates between Catholics and Protestants, the married and unmarried, and a host of other social distinctions as a failure of social integration. Society is the stable source of our vitality and rationality; elucidating its structure and impact on individuals is the proper object of sociology. In contrast, Tarde saw society as a dynamic network of interactions in which new ideas, opinions, and fashions could emerge and quickly spread. While Durkheim represented a rationalist approach (updated to ground rationality in society rather than the individual), Tarde embodied the romantic spirit of invention placed into social interactions. After commenting on each other's work in print for over a decade, the two agreed to a public debate in 1903. Jaap Van Ginneken describes it as follows:

> Tarde reproached Durkheim that his self-contained world of social facts and collective representations was a reification, and excluded social conflict. Durkheim retorted that Tarde's concept of imitation and his psychological reductionism were vague and contradictory. In a way, it was the age-old discussion over the relation between continuity and change, the whole and the parts. (1992, p. 203)

In terms of its consequences, Durkheim was the clear winner: his approach to sociology won out and became institutionalized while Tarde's approach fell out of favor (though there has been a recent revival—Candea, 2016). However, there is a twist to the story: despite his explicit disavowal of psychological explanation, in the *Elementary Forms of Religious Life* Durkheim (1912) adopts crowd semantics and with it psychological concepts when describing collective effervescence. Thus, while Durkheim institutionally tried to keep psychology and sociology strictly separate, he could not avoid using notions from psychology to do justice to his phenomena of interest (Moscovici, 1991). In the next section, we will outline his approach and set up how it can be adapted to explore the dynamics of protest crowds.

Collective Effervesence in Light of Crowd Psychology

There is scholarly debate over to what extent Durkheim (1912) took over concepts from crowd psychology. Many have pointed out that he tended to use the word "assemble" (*assemblée*) or "gathering" (*rassemblement*) rather than "crowd" (*foule*), even if English translations have muddled the terms. The former is said to refer to a group of people who have intentionally gathered for a specific purpose, whereas the latter concerns accidental copresence of people such as in a city square. But in practice there is no clean division here and common examples were used by Le Bon and Durkheim, such as the French Revolution and Paris Commune. Borsch (2012, p. 72ff) has argued that in fact a distinction cannot be maintained and goes on to outline a list of commonalities between crowd psychology and Durkheim's (1912) theory. The semantics of crowd psychology is hard not to see in Durkheim's famous description of "collective effervescence":

> Once the individuals are gathered together, a sort of electricity is generated from their closeness and quickly launches them to an extraordinary height of exaltation. Every emotion expressed resonates without interference in consciousnesses that are wide open to external impressions, each one echoing the others. The initial impulse is thereby amplified each time it is echoed, like an avalanche that grows as it goes along. And since passions so heated and so free from all control cannot help but spill over, from every side there are nothing but wild movements, shouts, downright howls, and deafening noises of all kinds that further intensify the state they are expressing. (Durkheim, 1912 [1995], pp. 217–218)

Heightened emotional energy that contagiously spreads through a group and leads to individuals' loss of control is an apt description of crowd theory. And like Le Bon before him, Durkheim draws attention to the violence unleased by this energy: "The passions moving them are of such an intensity that they cannot be satisfied except by violent and unrestrained actions, actions of super-human heroism or of bloody barbarism" (1912 [1995], pp. 210–211). This is particularly clear in his vivid description of mourning rituals: "Men and women, seized by a veritable frenzy, were rushing about cutting themselves with knives and sharp-pointed sticks, the women battering one another's heads with fighting clubs, no one attempting to ward off either cuts or blows" (pp. 390–391). In contrast to Le Bon, however, Durkheim wants us to recognize that even in these cases there is strong normative regulation. Individuals feel obliged to go along with the collective expressions regardless of how they felt about the deceased, and in so doing come to feel the emotions of grief being expressed by others. Thus, this seemingly irrational frenzy of movement and emotions actually serves to stitch the social order together after a loss and reaffirm the group's identity. Durkheim has an implicit psychology here: individuals require social contact to build solidarity and revitalize their energies, which grow weak alone. In this sense, collective effervescence does not take us "below" our rational selves to our instinctual biological urges, as Le Bon or Freud had argued, but rather "above" ourselves to society, its ideals, and spiritual existence.

Thus, the concept of "collective effervescence" contains both the overflowing, embodied and emotional energies described by crowd psychology *as well as* a community focus linking it to higher psychological processes, norms, and ideals. The ritual's social and psychological function can also be seen in the way that symbols emerge from them, serving as "emblems" of the group and helping carry some of the energies experienced in it beyond the event itself. Australian aboriginal's totems, just like modern national flags and religious symbols, become profaned if they fail to be renewed through collective effervescence. These are sacred symbols of society that embody its vital forces. What Durkheim does not do is to show how these processes might be *harnessed* for purposes of social change, a topic that is generally neglected in his oeuvre. His emphasis remains focused on processes involved in creating the stable consensus that holds society together, but he also gave room for a "creative effervescence" that generates new ideas rather than simply re-exciting them (see Pickering, 2009). This is also for Durkheim the source of our categories of thought (e.g., time, space, and causality) and thus rationality (cf. the crowd as an irrational force). Durkheim's approach does not take on board Tarde's focus on social innovations and interpersonal interactions but does affirm the creativity of the crowd against the image of its regressive nature. Before moving on to our own extension of Durkheim's concept it is worth briefly reviewing the recent research on the psychology of crowds, which brings in normative dimensions that interested Durkheim as well as conflict and specific interaction dynamics that he neglected.

Crowds, Change, and Identity

Contemporary social psychology has been greatly influenced by the notion of the social coming from traditional crowd psychology (Greenwood, 2003). This is most obvious in deindividuation theories (Zimbardo, 1969), but its impact runs much deeper. Through the mediating role of Walther Moede's (1920) "experimental crowd psychology" and Floyd Allport's (1920) work, the social became reduced to *the short-term effects (usually negative) of interpersonal interactions among strangers in experimental settings* (Danziger, 2000). This is a far cry from the broader concept of the social as constitutive of human thought, which Wundt and Durkheim developed. Since the 1970s, there has been a number of calls to renew the broader concept of the social.

Moscovici (1976 [2008]), for example, aimed to revisit the "lost concept" of Durkheim's collective representations but in a guise that highlights issues of social conflict and change (i.e., as "social representations"). Moscovici (1972) also called out social psychology's "conformity bias" and advocated for developing a science of "movement" rather than a science of "order"—a critique that could also be leveled at Durkheim. These critiques have been echoed by social psychologists coming from a social identity tradition, who aim to highlight forms of agency, resistance, and solidarity in relation to social processes (Reicher and Haslam, 2013; Smith and Haslam, 2017).

Their "elaborated social identity" model sees crowds as integral to meaningful social and political participation (Drury and Stott, 2011). In the place of deindividualization, they highlight how crowds are spaces for mobilizing and creating social identities. Their research is rooted in historical analyses and protest-related field research, emphasizing larger societal contexts and the purposeful motivations underlying protests. Thus, similar to Durkheim's theory, they explore how group solidarity and specific norms are developed in crowds (Drury and Reicher, 2009). Along these lines, Reicher (2001) outlined different attributes of crowds and how they influence potential norms and actions. These include (a) the number and density of people in space, (b) whether the crowd is organized and planned or emerges in the moment, (c) the social significance of the crowd's goal (e.g., a civil rights movement or a theft mob), (d) whether the crowd has an institutional or authority dimension (e.g., the army or church), and finally (e) whether the crowd has a shared collective identity. At root, crowd behavior is here understood in terms of identity categorization, norm regulation, and strategic expression of identity in relation to outgroups (Klein, Spears, and Reicher, 2007; Reicher, Spears, and Postmes, 1995). The transition from a peaceful crowd to a riot is conceived in terms of a clash of social identities, understandings of legitimacy, and shifts in collective power (Reicher, 1996; Stott and Drury, 2000).

Their fieldwork details how crowd dynamics evolve in relation to (mis) identification of perceptions and actions between police and protestors, all happening within broader social and economic conditions. Police can misconstrue peaceful protestors as a homogeneous threat, which in turn leads to mutual escalation. Crowds spread to new locations where there is a critical mass of individuals who identify with the original crowd and share the same outgroup "enemy" (e.g., the police). The original crowd becomes a symbol of empowerment for the ones that follow by demonstrating the vulnerability of the outgroup (Drury et al., 2020). Thus, crowd events may grow and spread from one location to another, not so much by simple contagion but in terms of activating shared social identities. This contrasts sharply with Le Bon's portrayal of the senselessness of crowd behavior but also minimizes the embodied and imagistic form of thought that early crowd theorists brought to the fore. The energy and euphoria experienced in crowds are explained here through the development of a new empowering social identity (for an explicit reinterpretation of "collective effervesence" in a social identity approach see Hopkins et al., 2016). While there is some truth to this, explaining everything through self-categorization seems one-dimensional, reducing vitality to something ultimately very cognitive. Interactions with police do not simply enhance a discursive sense of identity but the heightened emotions of conflict work directly to bond the group and fuel a sense of efficacy in it. In the face of an approaching line of police, there is an increase of sound and movement, protestors come closer together, chants may begin, the group feels as one and becomes conscious of itself as a force. Our own approach in this chapter aims to highlight the affective and embodied dimensions of crowd interactions, even in language use. Thus, we will retain some of the earlier focus on imagistic and affective thought as well as the embodied dimensions of interactions as fundamental to understanding protest crowds.

Cultural Tools of Protest Action

In the remaining space of this chapter we will extend Durkheim's theory with concepts from contemporary psychology and further afield. Using the framework of cultural psychology, we will argue that group solidarity and emotion are *cultivated* through various cultural tools. This idea can be traced back to Vygotsky (1987) who, drawing on Durkheim, argued that "higher mental functions" are taken over from society. They begin as actual relationships *between* people (*intermentally*) and only gradually become internalized to operate (*intramentally*). Analytically, we must analyze both the process and consequences of this mediating activity. Focusing on mediators as joint tools of action also helps to not reify society nor to neglect conflict and social change, as Tarde had accused Durkheim of doing. To use contemporary terminology, action is *distributed* on the one hand between members of a group and on the other between people and cultural tools (Wertsch, 2002). What techniques and devices can be employed once people are assembled in order to foster bonds of solidarity and commitment to a shared cause? In what follows we will highlight and extend dimensions of Durkheim's theory to arrive at a typology of cultural devices that function to this end. This typology will progress from the most concrete and embodied to devices distanced and abstracted from the context of action. They are (a) rhythm and synchronized movement, (b) space, and (c) symbols and narrative. These parallel Durkheim's focus on time, space, and symbols but in contrast to his approach we highlight how they play out within social conflict and aspirations of social change.

Rhythm and Synchronized Movement

Rhythm is a cross-modal occurrence that taps into a fundamental experiential relation to the world and other people. In this way, it is much more than a private temporal duration. In a broader theory of rhythm analysis, Henri Lefebvre (1992) argues that our social world is organized through an interaction between individual rhythms (daily routines, biological functions, etc.), social and collective rhythms (cultural practices, traditions, social happenings, etc.), and environment rhythms (day and night, seasons, nature changes etc.). Though stability is never guaranteed in the interaction between these rhythms, there is a certain sense of continuity when they follow expected everyday norms. It is typically only when a disruption in these rhythms occurs that people become focally aware of them. Lefebvre refers to certain *moments*, such as in revolutions, in which existing orthodoxies are open to challenge, where there is the potential for things to be overturned or radically altered. Those ruptures introduce new rhythms in the place of the old ones. For example, the 2011 Egyptian revolution was planned to begin on National Police Day, which commemorates the police's role in resisting British colonial rule. This was done in order to draw attention to the brutality and corruption of the police force of today in comparison to the past. Protestors thus inserted new values into this period of "sacred" time, arguing the former no longer applied. January 25 is now the living memory of the 2011 revolution rather than National Police Day.

In Durkheim's (1912) theory time is socially ordered into periods marked by the profane and the sacred. In profane time people go about their lives to fulfill the basic necessities of life, while sacred time functions to bring to consciousness a community's ideal aspirations and moral values through collective rituals that generate effervescence. Religious and national celebrations are examples of sacred times set apart from our working lives. In modern societies, protests often aim to intentionally disrupt profane, everyday urban routines by occupying a square or blocking entrance to institutions. The idea here is to draw attention to a set of sacred values by rupturing our profane rhymes. In their place, new microrhythms are introduced that function both to highlight the change and create affective bonds among group members. Many of us are familiar with the chants, drums, marches, and songs that so often accompany protests, not to mention a variety of other crowds such as at sporting events. Why do these kinds of rhythms, widely found around the world and through history, function to create solidarity within a group?

Rhythms play a key role in synchronizing movements that seem to generate collective emotions. Anthropologist Victor Turner (1982) used to say that one can dance all night to the right music but find it difficult to do so for fifteen minutes without music (and we might add without the presence of other co-dancers). Turner, in fact, was said to have had his students perform Native American dances all night, to explore how fatigue could be transformed into an ecstatic and unconscious flow of movements and emotions. Durkheim himself pointed out that the collective expression of emotion, even in its most intensified and wild forms, requires "some order that permits harmony and unison of movement, [where] gestures and cries tend to fall into rhythm and regularity, and from there into songs and dances" (1912 [1995], p. 218). While this statement seems to suggest spontaneous synchronization, we will highlight the more deliberate use of this cultural device.

Military historian William McNeil (1995) has drawn our attention to cultivation of, what he calls, "muscular bonding" in human evolution and the development of societies, which occurs in dance, drill, and other activities in which movements are synchronized through rhythm. McNeil's firsthand encounter with muscular bonding traces back to the marching he experienced as a military recruit. Despite its seemingly impractical nature for battle skills, McNeil emphasizes its indispensable psychological impact on group formation and cohesion. Military leaders utilize such tactics, including drill, to instill a sense of commitment among recruits facing poor treatment and low pay while performing a dangerous job. The effect of this device is what Jonathan Haidt (2012), following Durkheim (1912), called the "hive switch," shifting human beings predominantly selfish orientation toward group altruism. Similar to Durkheim's notion of being homo duplex, Haidt says we are 90 percent chimpanzee and 10 percent bee. While the rhythms in miliary organization are planned and structured by military leaders, rhythms in a protest tend to be more improvised and emerge as the groups form together and use different forms of chants, songs, drumming, and dance.

Chants in particular synchronize protest group members in both movement and sound. During the 2011 Egyptian revolution, several chants emerged along the way, such as "*Bread, freedom, social justice*" and "*The people want the fall of the regime.*" The significance of those chants was not only in bringing people across cities in Egypt under one rhythmic movement and one aim, but it was also in how it connected the protests to other protest movements. The chant "*The people want the fall of the regime*" (الشعب يريد إسقاط النظام) traveled to Egypt from the earlier protests in Tunisia. The chant was in Modern Standard Arabic, which made it easily transferable across different local dialects, making its way to Syria, Libya, Bahrain, Lebanon, and Sudan, and it became part of many revolution songs across the region (Peeva, 2022). The chant also resonated with global protest culture, following the rhythms of many protest chants around the world: "clap, [rest], clap, [rest], clap, clap, clap." The same rhythm is present in the "Hell, no, we won't go!" of the anti-Vietnam movement or the famous Latin American chant "*¡El pueblo, unido,* *jamás será vencido!*" ("The people, united, will never be defeated!") (Center for Strategic International Studies, 2011).

The chanting in the Egyptian revolution created an immersive and synchronized group experience for participants that was crucial in the formation of political subjects; they became a multitude of equal voices calling for the same goals (Galeev, 2021). Additionally, it was the chanting and the sounds of the protestors marching that often attracted more people to join. The chants were part of a euphoric group experience that also make protestors presence in Tahrir Square loud and clear for all to hear, and further helped circulate the message of the protest beyond its physical limits (Galeev, 2011). In short, the chants were microrhythms that build community while simultaneously disrupting the established economic rhythms of Tahrir Square as a space of circulation for people, cars, and vendors (Gregory, 2013), transforming it into the voice of protest (Galeev, 2011). Collective chants and slogans are not only used as tools for unifying a group and energizing it against authorities, but also as tools of normative regulation that, for example, constrain the use of violence (Butler, 2011).

Space

We have just seen how protests create new temporalities that on the one hand bind a protest group together and on the other disrupt established temporal rhythms and divisions of time to be replaced with new ones. This simultaneously happens with space, which Durkheim (1912) also saw as socially organized into sacred and profane worlds. In protests, public spaces like squares, streets, parks, and governmental buildings become "sacred" spaces, in the sense of being sites for collective emotions and putting society's values on display. The Occupy Wall Street movement, for example, camped out in the epicenter of economic (profane) activity to highlight the contrast of values—one of their key slogans was "the 99% and 1%," pointing to the high wage earners with undue politic influence. The act of occupation disrupts the profane use of the space and elevates it to a symbol of collective dissent and aspiration, much like a religious festival transforms a site into a sacred gathering place. It redefines the meaning and behaviors deemed appropriate therein, investing them with protestor's identity and practices that gain high public visibility.

During the 2011 Egyptian revolution, the occupation of Tahrir Square visibly demonstrated the magnitude of the movement, representing a direct challenge to the authorities in a reclamation of the citizen's right to those spaces and control over them (Awad and Wagoner, 2018). This "sacred" gathering place was created through sit-ins, street art murals that filled the surround walls, protest performances, songs, and even a makeshift museum of the revolution. Through these interventions the square became both the physical and symbolic epicenter of the movement, projecting an image of inclusiveness beyond social differences or "communitas" (Olaveson, 2001) as well as utopian aspirations for the future, especially clear in songs produced in and about the square (Valassopoulos and Mostafa, 2014). Furthermore, it was a space of high visibility, located in the center of the city next to key government and cultural institutions. From the center of Tahrir one would see a mass of news cameras pointed down from the surrounding buildings, broadcasting events taking place there to the world. Protestors also developed the habit of pointing lasers at cameramen of TV stations that they perceived to be in league with the ruling regime. The significance was obvious in counterrevolution measures by subsequent governments to erase traces of the revolution from the square (Awad, 2017), which brings us to the issue of collective memory.

Often the same urban spaces are repeatedly used for protests as they carry a memory of what went before, linking new causes to old ones. These spaces become profane as practical activities of everyday life become dominant there again, but their latent symbolism can be rekindled in protest to give off additional opportunities for effervescence. Séamus Power (2018) describes how the 2015 antiwater tax protests in Dublin were choreographed to move through sites associated with the Irish rebellion against British rule, beginning in the "Garden of Remembrance" for "Irish Freedom" and ending at the headquarters of the 1916 rebellion of Irish revolutionaries. Similarly, Tahrir Square carries a memory of protest and struggle; its very name "tahrir" means "liberation" in Arabic. The name was first given to the square following the 1919 anticolonial revolution and become its official name after the 1952 revolution or coup d'état that changed the country from a monarchy to a republic (Awad, 2017). Many other examples could be given of anchoring new protest in old causes through place, such as "Martyrs Square" in Beirut. The key principle at work here has been known since the ancient art of memory tradition (Yates, 1966): familiar spaces are powerful carriers of memory. Halbwachs (1950 [1980]) also gave a central role to space in creating the social frameworks that hold groups together. Following Durkheim, he argued that every group develops a social framework that both helps it to "locate" its memories and represent its identity and values to itself as a model to be followed in the future. Squares like Tahrir remind groups of sets of values and significant events that took place there.

The role of spaces in cultivating crowds today also extends beyond physical spaces. The role of digital media and online spaces in developing solidarity and cultivating protest crowds has been increasingly evident (Castells, 2015; Harlow, 2012; Wojcieszak, 2009). For example, Laura Smith, Jeffery Gavin, and Elise Sharp (2015) have showed how the development of the Occupy Wall Street movement was preceded by online discussion that cultivated shared attitudes about common social and economic grievances. This extends the notion that psychological crowds emerge out of physical crowds' shared experiences, emotions, and cognitions (Neville et al., 2022) to also account for collective identities that are cultivated through online spaces that then move into occupying physical spaces. The relationship between online and physical spaces is very much interconnected in today's social movements in a way that also facilitates the traveling of ideas and solidarity movements across the globe (Greijdanus et al., 2020).

Online mobilization played a key role in both the 2011 Egyptian and earlier 2010 Tunisian revolutions. Both sharing photos showing oppression through the years and from local protests through mobile phones helped form an opinion-based social identity collective in online and physical spaces (McGarty et al., 2014). The online spaces also expanded the protest group to a broader segment of the population, where active technological-savvy young Egyptians utilized social media platforms to coordinate meeting points and plan the different protests (Castells, 2012). This networked form of communication enabled organizers of the Egyptian revolution to overwhelm the police by meeting out many locations at the periphery of Cairo and moving toward Tahrir Square in the center. The police were spread too thin to crack down on all the initial protest locations, which could have been done if things had started at Tahrir. The march toward the center also helped gather additional protestors as they moved through the city. Furthermore, Tahrir Square became in itself a verbal and visual image that traveled from one geographical space to another during the Arab uprisings and beyond the Arab region. Whether it was Zuccotti Park in the United States or Change Square in Sana'a, or Taksim Square in Turkey, or Tahrir Square in Sudan, all of these share similar decentralized forms of organization, where the urban spaces becomes the focal point for unity and assembly (Mitchell, 2012). This brings us to the notion of symbols, which was key to Durkheim's theory.

Symbols

In the excitement of effervescent activity, Durkheim described how people fixate on a common symbol that gives a concrete form to the euphoric emotions and vital energy that is linked to participation in society. A totemic animal or plant of the clan or a flag can become powerful emblems of the group that are capable of containing the experience after the dispersal of the crowd gathering. They are what make us focally aware of our existence as members of society and in fact represent a group to itself. Moreover, these symbols help to regenerate effervescence at the next gathering by rekindling the energy of the earlier one, as Tahrir Square did for different waves of protest. Without such symbols the experiences of such events would quickly dissipate in individual minds and the social ties that were forged in them would dissolve. To quote Durkheim: "That an emblem can be useful as a rallying point for any sort of group requires no argument. By expressing the social unit tangibly, it makes the unit itself more tangible to all . . . the emblem is not only a convenient method of clarifying the awareness of the society of itself: It serves to create—and is a constitutive element of—that awareness" (1912 [1995], p. 234).

This vital energy can be seen in protest symbols. Their iconic images or slogans (or even "hashtags" on digital media) condense collective meanings, histories, and goals of a movement into a concrete form (Awad and Wagoner, 2020). For example, the symbol of the hammer and sickle for the communist movement, or slogans such as "*Me Too,*" "*Black lives matter,*" or "*We are the 99%*" express in tangible form a protest narrative, which in turn channels the feelings of a group. Those symbols emerge in certain moments of collective events and take on a life of their own, generating energies for further collective identities and protests. Protest symbols as such need to be condensed and catchy, yet familiar to the group in a way that they can become part of larger narratives that help fortify their relevance. Visual symbols and narratives of a protest can help bring in the social and historical significance of the cause, provide an affective anchor point for a group identity, and therefore mobilize further solidarity and transferability of the cause to new contexts. As Durkheim (1912) argued, symbols give a group both an identity as well as a direction and motivation for action.

Many of the protest symbols of the Egyptian revolution emerged from the street art that was produced while occupying different squares. One example is a graffiti stencil of the ancient Egyptian queen Nefertiti with a gas mask, a symbol that combines a local historical meaning with a global protest symbol. The graffiti lived on as a famous iconic image of the revolution that took a life of its own traveling to online spaces and to other geographical locations, with its meaning elaborated and appropriated for further causes (Awad, 2020). Investigating protest symbols opens different questions about their meaning. We can ask how and why do certain symbols emerge from these events to represent the movement to both itself and the wider society. What are the constraints on appropriate symbols? How do they spread both within a social movement and between protest contexts? Are any symbols sufficient to become emblems of the group? One argument is that symbols must connect with existing values, identities, and grievances (Wagoner and Brescó de Luna, 2021) and embody multiple meanings that give the symbol its stability, appeal, and effectiveness. These are often symbols that vividly condense broad meanings of injustice into one personalized affective story (Awad and Wagoner, 2020). While in Durkheim's account any specific object that a group invests its energy into becomes a symbol, this process is further complicated here in how symbols also make an *appeal* to wider audiences.

Conclusion

> The former gods are growing old or dying, and others have not been born. . . . A day will come when societies once again will know hours of creative effervescence during which new ideals will again spring forth and new formulas emerge to guide humanity for a time. (Durkheim, 1912 [1995], p. 429)

As we have seen, Durkheim elaborated a kind of creative crowd psychology in his concept of collective effervescence. While similar in its semantics to the work of Le Bon, Tarde, and Freud, Durkheim drew a different set of consequences from the description of these events. For the former, immersion in crowds represented a lowering to instinctive biological forms of functioning, while for Durkheim they raised us to the higher realm of society, its values, and ideal aspirations. The idea of the social as leading to irrationality in traditional crowd theory (wherein only the individual standing alone is rational) becomes the very origin of rationality and morality in Durkheim's account (wherein it is located in society). Furthermore, whereas the crowd was a *destructive* force in Le Bon, Tarde, and Freud, Durkheim saw it as a *constructive* or creative force, necessary for social solidarity as well as moral renewal. Durkheim did not, however, systematically analyze the way in which collective effervescence was produced, though he provided some suggestive ideas that have been analyzed and validated by contemporary research (Rimé and Paez, 2023). We have followed Vygotsky's (1987) elaboration of Durkheim's theory to emphasize the *mediation* of (common) action through various cultural devices, and outlined an interrelated typology of mediators that help to intensify interactions toward effervescence. Our account highlights their role in constructing new moral orders in *conflict* with established ones. Protest crowds not only juxtapose their ideas to those currently holding sway, but also disrupt the everyday rhythms and spaces of a society to make these ideas visible. Furthermore, our analysis aimed to bring collective effervescence into the twenty-first century by exploring the spread of protest through new technologies that rapidly extend space, communication, and the spread of symbols to new contexts and digitally archive them for the future.

REFERENCES

Allport, F. H. 1920. "The Influence of the Group upon Association and Thought." *Journal of Experimental Psychology* 3:159–182.

Awad, S. H. 2017. "Documenting a Contentious Memory: Symbols in the Changing City Space of Cairo." *Culture & Psychology* 23, no. 2: 234–254.

Awad, S. H. 2020. "The Social Life of Images." *Visual Studies* 35, no. 1: 28–39. https://doi.org/10.1080/1472586X.2020.1726206.

Awad, S. H., and B. Wagoner. 2018. "Image Politics of the Arab Uprisings." In *The Psychology of Radical Social Change: From Rage to Revolution*, edited by B. Wagoner, F. M. Moghaddam, and J. Valsiner. Cambridge University Press.

Awad, S. H., and B. Wagoner. 2020. "Protest Symbols." *Current Opinion in Psychology* 35:98–102. https://doi.org/10.1016/j.copsyc.2020.03.007.

Borch, C. 2012. *The Politics of Crowds: An Alternative History of Sociology*. Cambridge University Press.

Bruner, J. 1990. *Acts of Meaning*. Harvard University Press.

Bruner, J. 2001. "Self-Making and World-Making." In *Narrative and Identity: Studies in Autobiography, Self and Culture*, edited by J. Brockmeier and D. Carbaugh. John Benjamins.

Butler, J. 2011. "Bodies in Alliance and the Politics of the Street." *Transversal* (blog), September 2011. http://transversal.at/transversal/1011/butler/en.

Candea, M., ed. 2016. *The Social after Gabriel Tarde: Debates and Assessments*. Routledge.

Castells, M. 2012. *Networks of Outrage and Hope: Social Movements in the Internet Age*. John Wiley & Sons.

Center for Strategic and International Studies. 2011. "The People Want the Fall of the Regime!" Center for Strategic and International Studies Newsletter, May 17. https://www.csis.org/analysis/rhythm-revolution-protest-chants-egypt-ecuador.

Danziger, K. 2000. "Making Experimental Social Psychology: A Conceptual History, 1920–1970." *Journal of the History of the Behavioral Sciences* 36, no. 4: 329–347.

Drury, J., and S. D. Reicher. 2009. "Collective Psychological Empowerment as a Model of Social Change: Researching Crowds and Power." *Journal of Social Issues* 65:707–725.

Drury, J., and C. Stott. 2011. "Contextualizing the Crowd in Contemporary Social Science." *Contemporary Social Science* 6, no. 3: 275–288.

Drury, J., C. Stott, R. Ball, et al. 2020. "A Social Identity Model of Riot Diffusion: From Injustice to Empowerment in the 2011 London Riots." *European Journal of Social Psychology* 50, no. 3: 646–661. https://doi.org/10.1002/ejsp.2650.

Durkheim, É. 1897. *Le Suicide: Étude de Sociologie*. Félix Alcan.

Durkheim, É. 1982. *The Rules of Sociological Method*. New York: The Free Press. Originally published in 1895 by Félix Alcan.

Durkheim, É. 1995. *The Elementary Forms of Religious Life*. George Allen. Originally published in 1912 by Félix Alcan.

Freud, S. 1922. *Group Psychology and the Analysis of the Ego*. Translated by James Strachey. The International Psycho-Analytical Press.

Galeev, O. 2021. "Construction of Protest Space through Chanting in the Egyptian Revolution (2011): Musical Dimensions of a Political Subject." In *Musical Spaces*, edited by J. Williams and S. Horlor. Jenny Stanford Publishing.

Greenwood, J. 2003. *The Disappearance of the Social in American Social Psychology*. Cambridge University Press.

Gregory, D. 2013. "Tahrir: Politics, Publics, and Performances of Space." *Middle East Critique* 22, no. 3: 235–246.

Greijdanus, H., C. A. de Matos Fernandes, F. Turner-Zwinkels, A. Honari, C. A. Roos, H. Rosenbusch, and T. Postmes. 2020. "The Psychology of Online Activism and Social Movements: Relations Between Online and Offline Collective Action." *Current Opinion in Psychology* 35:49–54.

Haidt, J. 2012. *The Righteous Mind: Why Good People Are Divided by Politics and Religion*. Pantheon Books.

Halbwachs, M. 1980. *The Collective Memory.* Harper and Row. Originally published in 1950 by Presses Universitaires de France.

Harlow, S. 2012. "Social Media and Social Movements: Facebook and an Online Guatemalan Justice Movement That Moved Offline." *New Media & Society* 14, no. 2: 225–243.

Hopkins, N., S. D. Reicher, S. S. Khan, S. Tewari, N. Srinivasan, and C. Stevenson. 2016. "Explaining Effervescence: Investigating the Relationship Between Shared Social Identity and Positive Experience in Crowds." *Cognition and Emotion* 30:20–32.

Klein, O., R. Spears, and S. Reicher. 2007. "Social Identity Performance: Extending the Strategic Side of SIDE." *Personality and Social Psychology Review* 11, no. 1: 28–45. https://doi.org/10.1177/1088868306294588.

Le Bon, G. 2002. *The Crowd: A Study of the Popular Mind.* Dover. Originally published in 1895 by Félix Alcan.

Lefebvre, H. 1992. *Rhythmanalysis: Space, Time, and Everyday Life.* Bloomsbury Academic.

McDougall, W. 1908. *An Introduction to Social Psychology.* John W. Luce & Co.

McGarty, C., E. F. Thomas, G. Lala, L. G. E. Smith, and A.-M. Bliuc. 2014. "New Technologies, New Identities, and the Growth of Mass Opposition in the Arab Spring." *Political Psychology* 35:725–740. https://doi.org/10.1111/pops.12060.

McNeil, W. H. 1995. *Keeping Together in Time: Dance and Drill in Human History.* Harvard University Press.

Mitchell, W. J. T. 2012. "Image, Space, Revolution: The Arts of Occupation." *Critical Inquiry* 39, no. 1: 8–32.

Moede, W. 1920. *Experimentelle Massenpsychologie.* Hirzel.

Moscovici, S. 1972. "Society and Theory in Social Psychology." In *The Context of Social Psychology*, edited by J. Israel and H. Tajfel. Academic Press.

Moscovici, S. 1976. *Social Influence and Social Change.* Academic Press.

Moscovici, S. 1981. *The Age of the Crowd: A Historical Treatise of Mass Psychology.* Cambridge University Press.

Moscovici, S. 1986. "Discovery of the Masses." In *Changing Conceptions of Crowd Mind and Behavior*, edited by C. F. Grauman and S. Moscovici. Springer.

Moscovici, S. 1991. *The Invention of Society: Psychological Explanations for Social Phenomena.* Polity.

Moscovici, S. 2008. *Psychoanalysis: Its Image and Its Public.* Polity. Originally published in 1976 by Presses Universitaires de France.

Neville, F. G., D. Novelli, J. Drury, and S. D. Reicher. 2022. "Shared Social Identity Transforms Social Relations in Imaginary Crowds." *Group Processes & Intergroup Relations* 25, no. 1: 158–173. https://doi.org/10.1177/1368430220936759.

Olaveson, T. 2001. "Collective Effervescence and Communitas: Processual Models of Ritual and Society in Emile Durkheim and Victor Turner." *Dialectical Anthropology* 26:89–124.

Peeva, Y. 2022. "Rhythms of Protest." *The Gazelle*, November 13. https://www.thegazelle.org/issue/234/rhythms-of-protests.

Pickering, W. S. F. 2009. *Durkheim's Sociology of Religion Themes and Theories.* James Clarke.

Power, S. 2018. "Economic Inequality and the Rise of Civic Discontent: Remembering and Deprivation in the Republic of Ireland." In *The Psychology of Radical Social Change: From Rage to Revolution*, edited by B. Wagoner, F. M. Moghaddam, and J. Valsiner. Cambridge University Press.

Reicher, S. 2001. "The Psychology of Crowd Dynamics." In *Blackwell Handbook of Social Psychology: Group Processes*, edited by M. A. Hogg and R. S. Tindale. Blackwell.

Reicher, S., and S. A. Haslam. 2013. "Towards a 'Science of Movement': Identity, Authority, and Influence in the Production of Social Stability and Social Change." *Journal of Social and Political Psychology* 1, no. 1: 112–131.

Reicher, S. D. 1996. "The Battle of Westminster: Developing the Social Identity Model of Crowd Behaviour in Order to Explain the Initiation and Development of Collective Conflict." *European Journal of Social Psychology* 26, no. 1: 115–134. https://doi.org/10.1002/(SICI)1099-0992(199601)26:13.0.CO;2-Z.

Reicher, S. D., R. Spears, and T. Postmes. 1995. "A Social Identity Model of Deindividuation Phenomena." *European Review of Social Psychology* 6, no. 1: 161–198. https://doi.org/10.1080/14792779443000049.

Rimé, B., and D. Paez. 2023. "Why We Gather: A New Look, Empirically Documented, at Emile Durkheim's Theory of Collective Assemblies and Collective Effervescence." *Perspectives on Psychological Science* 18, no. 6: 1306–1330.

Ross, E. A. 1908. *Social Psychology.* Macmillan.

Smith, J. R., and S. A. Haslam. 2017. *Social Psychology: Revisiting the Classic Studies.* Sage Publications.

Smith, L. G. E., J. Gavin, and E. Sharp. 2015. "Social Identity Formation During the Emergence of the Occupy Movement." *European Journal of Social Psychology* 45, no. 7: 818–832. https://doi.org/10.1002/ejsp.2150.

Tarde, G. 1889. *L'opinion et la foule.* Presses Universitaires de France.

Tarde, G. 1890. *Les lois de l'imitation.* Ressources.

Turner, V. 1982. *From Ritual to Theatre: The Human Seriousness of Play.* Performing Arts Journal Publications.

Valassopoulos, A., and D. S. Mostafa. 2014. "Popular Protest Music and the 2011 Egyptian Revolution." *Popular Music and Society* 37, no. 5: 638–659. https://doi.org/10.1080/03007766.2014.910905.

Van Ginneken, J. 1992. *Crowds, Psychology and Politics, 1871–1899.* Cambridge University Press.

Vygotsky, L. S. 1987. *The Collected Works of L. S. Vygotsky. Vol. 4, The History of the Development of Higher Mental Functions.* Plenum Press.

Wagoner, B. 2018. "From the Age of the Crowd to the Global Age." In *The Psychology of Radical Social Change: From Rage to Revolution*, edited by B. Wagoner, F. M. Moghaddam, and J. Valsiner. Cambridge University Press.

Wagoner, B., and I. Brescó de Luna. 2021. "Collective Grief: Mourning Rituals, Politics, and Memorial Sites." In *Cultural, Existential, and Phenomenological Dimensions of Grief*, edited by A. Køster and E. Kofod. Routledge.

Wertsch, J. V. 2002. *Voices of Collective Remembering.* Cambridge University Press.

Wojcieszak, M. 2009. "Carrying Online Participation Offline: Mobilization by Radical Online Groups and Politically Dissimilar Offline Ties." *Journal of Communication* 59, no. 4: 564–586.

Wundt, W. 1897. *Outline of Psychology.* Translated by C. H. Judd. Williams and Norgate; Wilhelm Engelmann. https://doi.org/10.1037/12908-000.

Yates, F. 1966. *The Art of Memory.* University of Chicago Press.

Zimbardo, P. G. 1969. "The Human Choice: Individuation, Reason, and Order vs. Deindividuation, Impulse, and Chaos." In *Nebraska Symposium on Motivation*, edited by W. J. Arnold and D. Levine. University of Nebraska Press.

3

Perceived Emotional Synchrony

A Social Psychological Perspective on Collective Effervescence

Darío Páez, Bernard Rimé, Pierre Bouchat,
Silvia da Costa, and José J. Pizarro

Since the turn of this century, the social sciences and humanities have shown renewed interest in the study of collective emotions, with frequent reference to the ideas developed in this regard by Émile Durkheim (1912 [1915]) (for review see von Schève and Salmela, 2014). From the outset, the contributions of our research group on collective emotional processes have drawn on this author's views (e.g., Martin-Beristain et al., 2000; Páez et al., 2007; Rimé, 2007). This work rests on social psychological research based on quantitative methods. In this context, it quickly became apparent that we needed an indicator of the "collective effervescence" described by the French sociologist as the climax of collective gatherings. To this end, we have developed a self-report measure we call "Perceived Emotional Synchrony." This measure is proposed to respondents after participation in a collective assembly for assessing the extent to which they experienced the emotions inherent in collective effervescence. In this chapter we examine the development and characteristics of this instrument. Before delving into this, we focus on what Durkheim meant by the notion of "collective effervescence." In particular, we stress the existential significance that the author attributed to participation in a collective assembly. Next, we examine the successive moments in collective assemblies that contribute to the emergence of collective effervescence among participants. We then describe our self-report measure of Perceived Emotional Synchrony. The subsequent sections consider the moderating role of this variable as well as its relationship to other variables. We conclude by considering the dispositional and situational antecedents of Perceived Emotional Synchrony.

Collective Effervescence: Concept and Scope

The pairing of the words "effervescence" and "collective" is an original creation by Durkheim. He introduced it in *The Elementary Forms of Religious Life*, the book in which he analyzed traditional religious gatherings in an effort to develop a general model for collective assemblies (Durkheim, 1912 [1915]). "Collective effervescence" is mentioned sixteen times in this work. Curiously, at no point did the French sociologist provide a precise definition of what he meant by this concept. A systematic examination of the context surrounding the various appearances of collective effervescence in the text has enabled us to propose the following synthesis (Rimé and Páez, 2023). Collective effervescence refers to a state of high intensity excitement that combines exaltation and exuberance. It results from the amplification of emotions shared by participants in collective assemblies. In this state, participants are transformed. They experience both a surge of power and an out-of-self transport resembling a mystical experience that involves a feeling of being part of something bigger than oneself. As all participants experience the same state in synchrony, a sense of communion, fusion, or unity arises.

The broader theoretical context in which Durkheim placed this analysis indicates that this feeling of communion with the group is indeed the essential component of collective experiences. Durkheim believed that individuals cannot cope with human existence on their own. They must draw on the collective beliefs and representations that previous generations have accumulated. When individuals participate in collective life and share these beliefs and representations, they are able to face the world with confidence and energy. However, in daily life, existence takes place away from the collective and in relative isolation. As a result, individuals' collective resources are gradually eroded. A revitalization of beliefs becomes necessary. For Durkheim, this is precisely the function of collective assemblies in which individuals regularly take part. In communion with others, individuals revitalize their faith, for it is the sharing of a faith that makes it a reality. For Durkheim, this is why all groups, be they political, economic, or professional, hold periodic meetings at which their members can revitalize their common faith. In sum, to strengthen sentiments, which left to themselves, quickly weaken, people should be brought into closer and more active contact with one another.

In this theoretical frame, the key importance of the emotional experience of collective effervescence becomes self-evident. Among participants in a collective assembly, this experience results in a sense of communion or unity with the community. The more participants personally experience collective effervescence, the more they become aware of the outcomes of their participation in the collective process. We now turn to the successive phases of a collective assembly outlined in Durkheim's work, and how each of them contribute to the emergence of a collective effervescence.

A Sequential Model of Collective Effervescence

Durkheim's (1912 [1915]) analysis sought to identify the essential elements of any form of collective gathering. To this end, he drew on the facts available regarding the most primitive and simplest religion that could be accessed. He found such sources in anthropologists' accounts of religious events among Australian aborigines and so-called North American Indians, which at the time, were viewed as simple and primitive. However, Durkheim did not propose a linear exposition of a theory, and his writings are not easily accessible. His essential ideas are scattered throughout lengthy descriptions of anthropological observations. As a result, references to his views today often come from second- or thirdhand sources. In a review article, we have sought to extract from Durkheim's classic book the essential elements of his conception of collective processes and to relate them to currently available empirical data (Rimé and Páez, 2023).

From our analysis of Durkheim's account, we deduced that effervescence results from the cumulative effects of five successive moments occurring in collective assemblies. They involve (1) participants' initial co-presence and interactions, (2) their display of homogeneous manifestations, (3) emergence of a group consciousness, (4) participants' transmission and amplification of emotions, and (5) collective effervescence. Our literature review (Rimé and Páez, 2023) shows that each of these moments are largely supported by recent empirical research. Hereafter, we give an overview of the five moments and the related findings.

Moment 1—Co-presence and interactions. As soon as participants come together, their co-presence has the effect of changing the content of their consciousness. Everyday concerns give way to contents shared by the group, such as shared beliefs, traditions, and ideals, which promotes the emergence of a common mindset within the assembly. This phenomenon was extensively documented in studies conducted in the context of social identity theory (e.g., Drury and Reicher, 2005, 2009). These studies illustrate that when people take part in a group with whom they share features, purposes, or fate, they engage in a cognitive transformation. Participants redefine their identity, switching from an individual-level identity to a group identity. They categorize themselves with the other participants in terms of context-relevant features (e.g., "We are all drummers" or "We are all antiracist demonstrators"). Once identified with the group, participants then act in accordance with this group's norms in such a way that a shared mindset emerge (for reviews see Drury, 2018, 2020).

Moment 2—Homogeneous manifestations. Durkheim noted that "homogeneous manifestations then develop in the assembly. By emitting same cries, words and gestures, participants nourish the group feeling" (1912 [1915], p. 212). By performing such homogeneous actions, participants inform one another that they share the same internal states, and they thus become conscious of their moral unity. Contemporary studies conducted in two distinct fields confirmed that the practice of homogeneous movements indeed brings participants closer together. The first of these observations comes from the study of behavioral mimicry, in which one person unintentionally and effortlessly copies another person's posture or body movements (Chartrand and Lakin, 2013). A meta-analytic review of such studies concluded that being mimicked indeed enhances openness to others (Hale and Hamilton, 2016). The second observation stems from studies of interpersonal synchrony, in which the actions of two or more people overlap in time (Bernieri et al., 1988). Two meta-analytic reviews consistently demonstrated that involvement in interpersonal synchrony leads participants to develop prosocial behaviors, perceived social bonding, and positive affect (Mogan et al., 2017; Rennung and Göritz, 2016).[1]

Moment 3—Group consciousness. According to Durkheim, co-presence and homogeneous actions lead participants to stop acting as separate individuals. They abandon their personal goals and concerns and align instead according to common goals and norms. Participants then further perceive their similarity with others and experience the blurring of individual differences, which fosters a sense of "we-ness," or group consciousness. Empirical support for this third moment of the sequential process is well illustrated by a study comparing people who did and did not participate in a parade across nine nations (Zumeta et al., 2020). Participation was found associated with a feeling of non-differentiation or togetherness, as measured by an identity fusion scale.

Moment 4—Transmission and amplification of emotions. According to Durkheim, the collective expression of affects generates a transmission of emotions from mind to mind. Furthermore, as in an echo chamber, emotions expressed in common are amplified. The collective sharing of emotions thus feeds an upward spiral. It fosters similar emotions of ever-increasing intensity in the participants that further enhances their perception of oneness. These proposals are now well documented by research. Notably, several studies demonstrated that experiencing affective conditions together with others, even without communication, has the effect of amplifying the experience (e.g., Martin et al., 2015; Nahleen et al., 2019).

Moment 5—Collective effervescence. At the climax of the gathering, a state of overexcitement pervades all participants. Durkheim considered this state to induce two major subjective outcomes. On the one hand, all participants feel a surge of energy that translates into feelings of power and self-confidence accompanied by positive affects. On the other hand, they experience a sense of collective communion that feeds their feeling of social integration and makes them momentarily open to others, receptive and deeply socialized. How does this affect the return to ordinary life? If we follow Durkheim's observations, participants who leave a collective assembly should, at least temporarily, show measurable effects on several psychosocial variables. In particular, they should show an enhanced sense of belonging to a cohesive social entity, as well as an increase in positive affect, in self-confidence, and in adherence to the beliefs and values involved in the event.

These predictions have barely been empirically tested with quantitative measurement tools since Durkheim formulated them. We conducted the first series of studies designed to fill this gap (Páez et al., 2015). In this context, we felt the necessity of developing a variable that could assess the extent to which the participant had experienced collective effervescence. Such a variable is indeed likely to be a key mediator in the effects people draw from their participation in the collective assembly. As said earlier, it is expected that the more they experienced effervescence, the more they would manifest the psychosocial consequences from participation. With this in mind, we developed the Perceived Emotional Synchrony self-assessment scale.

Perceived Emotional Synchrony: Concept and Measurement

The concept of Perceived Emotional Synchrony stems from the view that, for participants, the experience of their mutual synchronization is essential in fueling effervescence. Collective effervescence can be seen as the result of a multifaceted process of synchronization (Páez et al., 2015). Thus, in a collective assembly, participants converge together in a special place and at a specified moment: they share concerns, intentions, and goals; they share cognitive and emotional responses to the context (e.g., flags, emblems, leaders, or icons); they focus on the same target (podium, stage, altar, speaker, leader, priest, etc.); they synchronize their behavior by displaying homogeneous gestures and movements (acting, moving, and marching together); and they synchronize their expressive manifestations (singing together, yelling, saying particular words or sentences, playing music, dancing, etc.). These various elements all stimulate participants' emotional arousal in such a way that they experience similar emotional states. Their reciprocal emotional stimulation and the collective amplification of these emotions fuel a growing experience of emotional synchronization involving perceptions of similarity and unity: "We feel the same, we are the same, we are one." Collective effervescence is thus largely made up of shared emotions and is itself experienced by participants as a powerful emotion.

A Perceived Emotional Synchrony measurement was introduced in the first of the four studies published in the article by Páez and colleagues (2015). It consisted of eighteen items that explored in various formulations the experience of synchronization, shared emotions, unity, fusion, similarity, or social integration. This version of the scale soon gave way to shorter forms more convenient for data collection on large numbers of respondents. Wlodarczyk and colleagues (2020) have devoted a body of work to the psychometric testing of the scale. A content analysis of the long version indicated that the Perceived Emotional Synchrony scale assesses two main aspects of the collective experience: emotional communion or intense sharing of emotions and feelings of unity. An analysis of the structural validity of the scale was conducted on data collected from 550 volunteer participants at a folk festival. A principal component analysis confirmed that the advised number of dimensions composing the scale is one. The value of unidimensional congruence was near maximal (0.998). The value of explained common variance was also very high (0.954), confirming that the data can be treated as essentially unidimensional. The one-factor model was then tested for a short version involving only six items. Several considerations guided the construction of this short form. In addition to considering item-total correlations, the decisions regarding inclusion of items were also based on a thorough examination of their content. Three items of felt unity (e.g., *We all acted as one person*) and three of shared intense emotionality (e.g., *We felt a strong shared emotion*) that had the highest coefficients with the latent variable were adopted for this short version. The test of the one-factor model showed excellent fit to the data.

In addition to its reliability and structural validity, Wlodarczyk and colleagues (2020) also tested the incremental validity of the short version of the scale. The relevant criterion adopted here was participants' well-being. The study examined whether Perceived Emotional Synchrony was incrementally valid beyond alternative variables proposed to explain the effects of collective gatherings, such as social identification, arousal, and rumination (Whitehouse and Lanman, 2014; Hopkins et al., 2016). The scale's incremental validity against such variables was tested and consistently supported in data collected on two different collective gathering events. In sum, it can safely be concluded that the shortened version of the Perceived Emotional Synchrony scale satisfies the essential psychometric criteria.

The Mediating Role of Perceived Emotional Synchrony in the Outcomes of Participation in Collective Assemblies

In the previous sections, we examined the steps that lead to collective effervescence and how we measure the emotional experience of unity with other participants at collective gatherings via a self-reported scale of Perceived Emotional Synchrony. Having focused on this central mechanism of the gathering experience, we now turn our attention to the effects of participation. According to Durkheim (1912 [1915]), the survival and well-being of individuals rest on their social integration, and collective assemblies are key to it. Participation in collective gatherings revivify the individuals' faith in collective representations, strengthen their feeling of group belonging, and help them face daily life with a sense of power and meaning (Rimé and Páez 2023). Perceived Emotional Synchrony is, in our view, the main predictor of the effects of participation in collective gatherings.

The first set of empirical studies testing these effects involved participants in gatherings that had either positive emotional connotations (festive folk events) or negative ones (sociopolitical protest demonstrations) (Páez et al., 2015). The dependent variables targeted the main effects predicted by Durkheim's model: social integration, empowerment, positive emotions, and endorsement of socially shared beliefs and values. These variables were measured before and after participation in the event, both in participants and in control respondents who did not take part in the event. In addition, after participation, respondents completed the Perceived Emotional Synchrony scale. In each of these studies the results largely confirmed the expected effects. Respondents who had taken part in the event subsequently showed a highly significant rise in their sense of social integration, their positive affect, their self-esteem, and their adherence to the event's beliefs and values. In the frame of the present chapter, the key observation lies in the confirmation of the mediator's role played in these effects by Perceived Emotional Synchrony. In each of the four studies, as expected, the more participants experienced emotional synchronization in the collective situation, the more pronounced were the various predicted effects.

These initial results have since been confirmed by a series of studies: Perceived Emotional Synchrony was found to be positively correlated with positive affect (e.g., Bouchat et al., 2020; Zumeta et al., 2020), social integration (e.g., Pizarro et al., 2019; Zumeta et al., 2020), identity fusion (Bouchat et al., 2024; Zabala et al., 2024; Zumeta et al., 2020), well-being (Pizarro et al., 2017; Wlodarczyk et al., 2020), and ingroup commitment (Zumeta et al., 2016). These results are in line with Durkheim's initial observations and suggest that collective gatherings help to cement societies and individuals face daily life once recharged. Further, a meta-analysis conducted by Pizarro and colleagues (2022) confirmed Perceived Emotional Synchrony to predict longitudinally the relevant outcomes: social integration, empowerment, positive emotions, and endorsement of socially shared beliefs and values.

Beyond these effects, Perceived Emotional Synchrony has also been studied in relation to a set of variables not directly tackled, or not tackled at all, in the first set of empirical studies mentioned above. Thus, other studies addressed Perceived Emotional Synchrony in relation with variables such as self-transcendence (da Costa, 2024; Pizarro et al., 2022; Zabala et al., 2024), perceived emotional climate (Páez et al., 2013; Pelletier, 2018; Pizarro et al., 2022), creativity (Castro-Abril et al., 2021; da Costa et al., 2015), and prosocial behaviors (Castro-Abril et al., 2021; da Costa et al., 2023; Zlobina and Davila, 2022).

First, Perceived Emotional Synchrony was found to be correlated with self-transcendence indicators. Feelings of self-transcendence are especially important for the gathering experience in that they momentarily blur the sense of oneself, orient participants toward outward social concerns, and induce feelings of oneness with others. In this respect, they are key to many gatherings, including those involving the element of the sacred. In their meta-analysis, Pizarro and colleagues showed that collective effervescence was linked with self-transcendent beliefs ($r = 0.45$) as well as with values such as Schwartz's universalism and benevolence values, which emphasize concern for the well-being and interests of others. Further, a study carried out by Zabala and colleagues (2023) in the context of a relay race across the Basque Country, showed that Perceived Emotional Synchrony was closely linked with self-transcendent emotions and with *kama muta*, an emotion referring to being moved by love of others (Fiske et al., 2017; Zickfeld et al., 2019).

Beyond the feeling of transcendence, several studies have investigated the relationship between the gathering experience and perceived emotional climate. In their meta-analysis, Pizarro and colleagues (2022) showed that collective effervescence is associated with a positive emotional climate ($r = 0.25$) (see also Pizarro et al., 2021b). However, as Durkheim pointed out, emotional valence matters little in explaining the positive effects of gatherings, with negatively valenced emotions having just as much impact as positively valenced ones. For instance, a study showed that participants in the Indignados movement in Spain perceived an emotional climate characterized by greater anger compared to nonparticipants (Páez et al., 2013). Another study, conducted during collective gatherings following the March 2016 terrorist attacks in Brussels, showed that Perceived Emotional Synchrony mediated the relationship between positive personal emotions and the perceived positive socioemotional climate in Belgium (Pelletier, 2018). These results suggest that Perceived Emotional Synchrony act as a regulatory mechanism between individual-level emotions and the emotional climate perceived within the society.

In addition to recharging individuals, participation in collective gatherings also seems to influence their creativity, that is, their creation of new, different, and useful ideas (Castro-Abril et al., 2021). Indeed, two meta-analyses found that high-arousal positive affect during participation in social movements is positively associated with creativity (da Costa et al., 2015). Further, creativity's relationship with Perceived Emotional Synchrony was highlighted in a study conducted during the 2019 antigovernment protests in Chile (Castro-Abril et al., 2021). The results of this study showed that Perceived Emotional Synchrony predicted both self-reported cognitive creativity and individuals' proposals for societal improvement and mediated the influence of participation on creativity.

Finally, several studies showed that Perceived Emotional Synchrony was linked with specific behaviors. For instance, the results of two studies by Zlobina and Davila (2022) conducted in Spain during the COVID-19 pandemic showed that active participation in collective applause was linked to more intense emotional synchrony and indirectly predicted self-reported preventive behaviors. These results are in line with a set of findings that suggest that Perceived Emotional Synchrony is related to collective behaviors because it reinforces factors that facilitate participation in demonstrations (da Costa et al., 2023). These results also point to the persuasive potential of participation in gatherings. Although the question of the persuasive power of gatherings has been addressed by illustrious predecessors (Freud, 1921; Le Bon, 1895), its empirical study remains in its infancy. In a context of rising populism, the study of this aspect constitutes an interesting research prospect (see the chapter by Wagoner and Awad in this volume).

The results of these studies therefore support the central role of Perceived Emotional Synchrony in explaining the effects of participation in collective gatherings (see Figure 3.1 for a summary of the model). However, one of the characteristics of these studies is that the effects of participation were measured, for the most part, soon after the individuals had taken part in the gathering. The question then arose as to the medium- or even long-term effects of participation in collective gatherings. Two studies have attempted to address this aspect. The first was carried out in the context of a large-scale girl and boy scouting event (twenty-five thousand participants). Using a quasi-longitudinal design with three measures taken over two-and-a-half months, Bouchat and colleagues (2020) found that participation in this collective gathering led to an increase in the scouts' levels of social integration and well-being after their participation. Further, higher Perceived Emotional Synchrony during the gathering was associated with stronger identity fusion, pride of being a scout, openness to experience, self-esteem, positive affects, and adherence to specific scouting values, even after ten weeks.

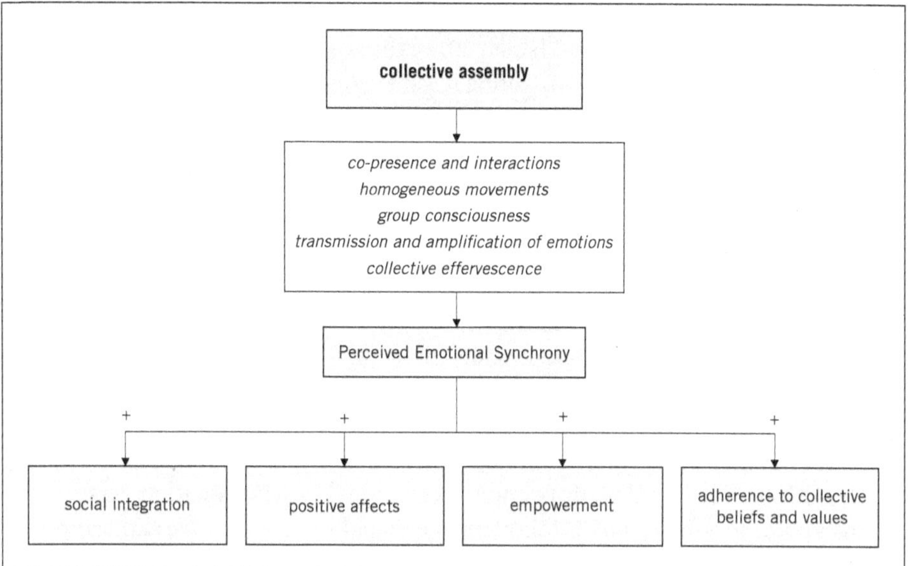

Figure 3.1 The successive moments of collective assemblies, their contribution to the emergence of Perceived Emotional Synchrony, and the mediating role of Perceived Emotional Synchrony in the effects of participation.

Another study was carried out in the context of an eleven-day relay race across the Basque Country involving up to six hundred thousand participants. Using a three-stage measurement design, Zabala and colleagues (2023) showed that participation led to an increase in the levels of social integration, remembered well-being, and collective empowerment. Further, they showed that Perceived Emotional Synchrony during the relay race was positively linked with social integration, social acceptance, and social actualization after six to seven weeks. The results of these two studies suggest that the effects of participation in particular large-scale gatherings are relatively long-lasting. These results echo findings in the field of collective action that showed that participation in such actions is followed by long-lasting positive effects on psychological well-being, self-esteem, fostering of collective identity, and concern for social justice (for a review see Vestergren et al., 2018).

Relations between Perceived Emotional Synchrony and Other Explanatory Mechanisms

In the previous section, we highlighted the important role played by Perceived Emotional Synchrony in explaining the effects of participation in collective gatherings. However, this mechanism is not the only one to have been studied in the context of social gatherings and rituals. A series of studies investigated the emotional convergence at play during and following specific rituals (von Scheve, 2011; von Scheve and Ismer, 2013); the positive, moral, and transcendent emotions elicited by participation in gatherings (Van Cappellen and Rimé, 2014; Yaden et al., 2017; Corcoran, 2015; Pizarro et al., 2019); and the links from these experience to a sense of sacredness, spiritual connection, or morality (Gabriel et al., 2017, 2020; Fiske, 1992; Rai and Fiske, 2011). Another major set of studies examined the behavioral aspects at play during the gatherings. These consider gatherings from the angle of interpersonal coordination (Mogan, Fischer, and Bulbulia, 2017; Rennung and Göritz, 2016) and imitation (Chartrand and Lakin, 2013).

A series of studies have empirically investigated the relationships between Perceived Emotional Synchrony and other explanatory mechanisms. Bouchat and colleagues (2024) have explored the relationship between situated social identity and Perceived Emotional Synchrony across thirteen studies ($N = 2260$). The social identity and the emotional synchronization perspectives point to similar effects following participation in collective gatherings: An increase in perceived intimacy and a reinforcement of shared identity switch from an individual frame of reference to a frame based on the group values and norms, empowerment, and positive affect. However, both perspectives diverge on the main explanatory mechanism of the effects of participation in gatherings. On the one side, the feeling of sharing a common identity within the crowd is the determining factor of most of the effects of collective gatherings (e.g., Hopkins et al., 2016, 2019), on the other it is emotional synchronization, and both perspectives have strong evidence to support them. To contrast these two perspectives, the thirteen studies (Bouchat et al., 2024) were conducted in highly varied contexts, using the same design and similar measures. The results of factor analyses and random model meta-analysis strongly support the idea that group identification and emotional synchronization constitute two differentiated constructs that are systematically positively associated. These mechanisms can even interact one with another, suggesting the existence of a sequential feedback of influence. At the aggregated level, results of multilevel models show that both group identification and emotional synchronization are significant predictors of key social-psychological variables. Overall, emotional synchronization and group identification during collective gatherings can be considered two facets of a multifaceted psychological convergence marked by temporal feedback. As such, it can explain transitions from gathered individuals to a unified group through participation in collective rituals and gatherings (Rimé and Páez, 2023). The systematic study of the relationships between the mechanisms that explain the effects of gatherings, using experimental designs and meta-analyses, seems to us to be both a promising and necessary line of work.

Antecedents of Perceived Emotional Synchrony

Two categories of antecedents of Perceived Emotional Synchrony can be distinguished: situational antecedents relating to the characteristics of the gatherings and dispositional antecedents relating to the personality of the participants.

In terms of situational antecedents, the frequency of collective gatherings seems to play a role in the experience of emotional unity felt by participants. Indeed, the results of a study conducted by Draper (2014) on 434 religious congregations in the United States show that emotional effervescence is positively correlated with ritual frequency. Cusi and colleagues (2022) also showed that frequency of participation in gatherings was positively correlated with Perceived Emotional Synchrony experienced during them (see also Pizarro et al., 2021a). Another situational antecedent concerns group size and density. Liebst (2019) showed, through a methodologically sound study, that crowd density or the number of co-present individuals physically gathered in a demarcated place, correlated with the intensity of emotions experienced at musical concerts. Furthermore, in line with Durkheim's insights, the presence of symbols during the gatherings seems to influence the experience of emotional communion between individuals. For instance, Wlodarczyk and colleagues (2023) showed that participants in religious rituals reported higher transcendence beliefs and Perceived Emotional Synchrony compared to participants in collective leisure weekend activities. In their synthesis of thirteen studies, Bouchat and colleagues (2024) also showed that the highest levels of Perceived Emotional Synchrony were found in highly symbolically laden demonstrations and costly initiation rituals while the lowest levels were found in well-regulated and ritualized activities. In social psychology, interest in situational factors such as the characteristics of collective gatherings is still low. As such, and given the results of the few studies carried out on the subject, they deserve the greatest attention. It should be added that among situational antecedents, the attitude adopted by participants is to be considered. For instance, research on revelry suggests that people have to be "willing to let go." According to Gauthier (2004), one must "resist resisting" and willingly "surrender to body, crowd and sound." Moreover, it is important to come prepared for the ritual. As was stated by Tutenges, "If they have been to a similar ritual before—or if they have been informed about, trained in, or otherwise prepared for it—it will be much easier for them to tune into one another and work together according to the ritual protocol, thereby collectively pumping up the energy" (2023, p. 27).

Dispositional characteristics generally attract more attention in a discipline focused on individuals. In the case of collective gatherings, the most widely studied dispositional antecedent is personality. Pooled correlations of the studies by Gabriel et al. (2020), Pizarro et al. (2021a), and Cusi et al. (2022), showed that the experience of emotional communion during the gatherings was positively correlated with four of the five Big Five dimensions of personality: openness, agreeableness, extraversion, and consciousness. This effect, albeit small, shows that several dispositional variables appear to influence the individuals' experience of collective gatherings. Beyond the subjective experience of gatherings, it would also seem interesting to investigate the influence of personality factors on the Perceived Emotional Synchrony of gatherings in which individuals participate. Finally, what the results of studies conducted on the antecedents of Perceived Emotional Synchrony suggest is that situational factors have a much stronger impact on individuals' experience than dispositional factors, even if the weight of the latter is not negligible.

Conclusion

We attempted to formalize Durkheim's collective effervescence using the concept of Perceived Emotional Synchrony. The concept reflects the participants' experience of their equivalence in terms of identity, thoughts, motivations, behavior, expression, and emotions, an experience that gives rise to a feeling of unity and fusion. Theoretical perspectives converging with the present one are currently emerging, not only in the study of collective emotions but also in other fields. Thus, Chung and colleagues (2024) have concluded that collective emotions combine three basic characteristics: (1) a dynamic process of reciprocal interaction eliciting similar intertwined emotions, (2) feeling of togetherness in which individuals not only feel *as* other individuals do, but *with* others, and (3) mutual awareness, by which individuals represent both their own mental states and the mental states of those with whom they interact. In a similar vein, Shteynberg and colleagues (2023) have shown, in a review of shared attention studies, that when self and other converge in their experience, they develop a unified mental state, or shared mental perspective. These authors showed that such a collective mind has the effect of amplifying people's emotional, cognitive, and behavioral responses to jointly attended stimuli, of inducing relational bonds, and of enhancing the cooperation among attendees. These observations echo collective assemblies in which the perception that others share our emotions and that "we are a group" reinforces the entitativity of the collective. Thus, Perceived Emotional Synchrony might well be an emotional process fueling the unified mental state envisioned by Shteynberg and colleagues. In social psychology, the concept of perceived positivity resonance (e.g., Prinzing et al., 2023) refers to a high-quality interpersonal connection that can arise between romantic partners, longtime friends, coworkers, or even complete strangers. It occurs within social interactions, when multiple individuals show coordinated increases in shared positive affect, in caring nonverbal synchrony, and in biological synchrony. Episodes of positivity resonance are theorized as enhancing momentary other-focus, perspective taking, empathy, interpersonal understanding, feelings of togetherness and social closeness. Perceived positivity resonance thus describes an interpersonal equivalent of what Durkheim envisioned for collective situations. We note that the interpersonal process involved in perceived positivity resonance is also observed in situations of social sharing of emotions. There, in a dyad, one member shares an emotional experience with the other. Such situations have long been described as favoring the development of an interpersonal dynamic involving an upward emotional spiral leading to a closer bond between the participants (Rimé, 2009; Rimé et al., 2020). These studies also provide an interpersonal equivalent of Durkheim's collective assemblies.

This convergence of research suggests that synchronization, and particularly emotional synchronization, constitutes a subject in the zeitgeist. Altogether, these recent developments of psychological science demonstrate what a visionary Durkheim was in developing his concept of collective effervescence.

NOTE

1. Positive affect refers to a state of mind characterized by feelings of happiness, confidence, friendliness, vigilance, enthusiasm, and energy. Although positive affect overlaps to a significant degree with the concept of positive emotions, they are not identical. Whereas positive affect represents a mood state, positive emotion involves important bodily changes (facial expression, physiological arousal, nonverbal behavior, action tendencies). Positive affect is usually measured through a list of words describing this mood state (e.g., excited, strong, enthusiastic, vigilant, determined). Respondents are asked to rate each according to the extent that it describes them.

REFERENCES

Beristain, C. M., Páez, D., and González J. L. (2000). "Rituals, Social Sharing, Silence, Emotions and Collective Memory Claims in the Case of the Guatemalan Genocide." *Psicothema* 12:117–130.

Bernieri, F. J., Reznick, J. S., and Rosenthal, R. (1988). "Synchrony, Pseudosynchrony, and Dissynchrony: Measuring the Entrainment Process in Mother-Infant Interactions." *Journal of Personality and Social Psychology* 54:243–253. https://doi.org/10.1037/0022-3514.54.2.243.

Bouchat, P., Pizarro, J. J., Páez, D., Zumeta, L., Basabe, N., Wlodarczyk, A., Hatibovic, F., and Rimé, B. (2024). "The Contributions of Group Identification and Emotional Synchrony in Understanding Collective Gatherings. A Meta-Analysis of Thirteen Studies." *Group Processes & Intergroup Relations* 27:1931–1959. https://doi.org/10.1177/13684302231223897.

Bouchat, P., Rimé, B., Van Eycken, R., and Nils, F. (2020). "The Virtues of Collective Gatherings: A Study on the Positive Effects of a Major Scouting Event." *Journal of Applied Social Psychology* 50:189–201. https://www.doi.org/10.1111/jasp.12649.

Castro-Abril, P., da Costa, S., Navarro-Carrillo, G., Caicedo-Moreno, A., Gracia-Leiva, M., Bouchat, P., et al. (2021). "Social Identity, Perceived Emotional Synchrony, Creativity, Social Representations, and Participation in Social Movements: The Case of the 2019 Chilean Populist Protests." *Frontiers in Psychology* 12:764434. https://www.doi.org/10.3389/fpsyg.2021.764434.

Chartrand, T. L., and Lakin, J. L. (2013). "The Antecedents and Consequences of Human Behavioral Mimicry." *Annual Review of Psychology* 64:285–308. https://doi.org/10.1146/annurev-psych-113011-143754.

Chung, V., Grèzes, J., and Pacherie, E. (2024). "Collective Emotion: A Framework for Experimental Research." *Emotion Review* 16:28–45. https://doi.org/10.1177/17540739231214533.

Corcoran, K. E. (2015). "Thinkers and Feelers: Emotion and Giving." *Social Science Research* 52:686–700. https://doi.org/10.1016/j.ssresearch.2014.10.008.

Cusi, O., Alfaro-Beracoechea, L., Sánchez, M., and Alonso-Arbiol, I. (2022). "Frecuencia de Participación en Encuentros Colectivos, Sincronía Emocional Percibida y Emociones de Trascendencia en Una Muestra de Jóvenes de México" [Frequency of Participation in Collective Meetings, Perceived Emotional Synchrony and Emotions of Transcendence in a Sample of Young People in México]. *Revista De Psicología* 18:27–46. https://doi.org/10.46553/RPSI.18.36.2022.p27-46.

da Costa, S. (2024). *Positive Valence Collective Rituals in Spain 2023 and Their Effect in Collective Efficacy and Social Identification.* ISPP's 2024 Annual Meeting 4–6 July 2023, Santiago, Chile.

da Costa S., Páez, D., Martí-González, M., Díaz, V., and Bouchat, P. (2023). "Social Movements and Collective Behavior: An Integration of Meta-Analysis and Systematic Review of Social Psychology Studies." *Frontiers in Psychology* 14:1096877. https://www.doi.org/10.3389/fpsyg.2023.1096877.

da Costa, S., Páez, D., Sánchez, F., Garaigordobil, M., and Gondim, S. (2015). "Personal Factors of Creativity: A Second Order Meta-Analysis." *Revista de Psicología del Trabajo y de las Organizaciones* 31:165–173. https://doi.org/10.1016/j.rpto.2015.06.002.

Draper, S. (2014). "Effervescence and Solidarity in Religious Organizations." *Journal for the Scientific Study of Religion* 53:229–248. https://doi.org/10.1111/jssr.12109.

Drury, J. (2018). "The Role of Social Identity Processes in Mass Emergency Behaviour: An Integrative Review." *European Review of Social Psychology* 29:38–81. https://doi.org/10.1080/10463283.2018.1471948.

Drury, J. (2020). "Recent Developments in the Psychology of Crowds and Collective Behavior." *Current Opinion in Psychology* 35:12–16. https://doi.org/10.1016/j.copsyc.2020.02.005.

Drury, J., and Reicher, S. D. (2005). "Explaining Enduring Empowerment: A Comparative Study of Collective Action and Psychological Outcomes." *European Journal of Social Psychology* 35:35–58. https://doi.org/10.1002/ejsp.231.

Drury, J., and Reicher, S. D. (2009). "Collective Psychological Empowerment as a Model of Social Change: Researching Crowds and Power." *Journal of Social Issues* 65:707–725. https://doi.org/10.1111/j.1540-4560.2009.01622.x.

Durkheim, E. (1915). *The Elementary Forms of Religious Life.* Translated by J. D. Swan. George Allen & Unwin. Originally published in 1912 by Presses Universitaires de France.

Fiske, A. P. (1992). "The Four Elementary Forms of Sociality: Framework for a Unified Theory of Social Relations." *Psychological Review* 99:689–723. https://doi.org/10.1037/0033-295x.99.4.689.

Fiske, A. P., Seibt, B., and Schubert, T. W. (2017). "The Sudden Devotion Emotion: Kama Muta and the Cultural Practices Whose Function is to Evoke It." *Emotion Review* 11:1–13. https://doi.org/10.1177/1754073917723167.

Freud, S. (1921). *Massenpsychologie und Ich-analyse.* Internationaler Psychoanalytischer Verlag.

Gabriel, S., Naidu, E., Paravati, E., Morrison, C. D., and Gainey, K. (2020). "Creating the Sacred from the Profane: Collective Effervescence and Everyday Activities." *The Journal of Positive Psychology* 15:129–154. https://doi.org/10.1080/17439760.2019.1689412.

Gabriel, S., Valenti, J., Naragon-Gainey, K., and Young, A. F. (2017). "The Psychological Importance of Collective Assembly: Development and Validation of the Tendency for Effervescent Assembly Measure (TEAM)." *Psychological Assessment* 29:1349–1362. https://doi.org/10.1037/pas0000434.

Gauthier, F. (2004). "Rave and Religion? A Contemporary Youth Phenomenon as Seen Through the Lens of Religious Studies." *Studies in Religion/Sciences Religieuses* 33:397–413. https://doi.org/10.1177/000842980403300307.

Hale, J., and Hamilton, A. F. D. C. (2016). "Cognitive Mechanisms for Responding to Mimicry from Others." *Neuroscience & Biobehavioral Reviews* 63:106–123. https://doi.org/10.1016/j.neubiorev.2016.02.006.

Hopkins, N., Reicher, S. D., Khan, S. S., Tewari, S., Srinivasan, N., and Stevenson, C. (2016). "Explaining Effervescence: Investigating the Relationship between Shared Social Identity and Positive Experience in Crowds." *Cognition and Emotion* 30:20–32. https://doi.org/10.1080/02699931.2015.1015969.

Hopkins, N., Reicher, S., Stevenson, C., Pandey, K., Shankar, S., and Tewari, S. (2019). "Social Relations in Crowds: Recognition, Validation and Solidarity." *European Journal of Social Psychology* 49:1283–1297. https://doi.org/10.1002/ejsp.2586.

Le Bon, G. (1895). *Psychologie des Foules* [*The Crowd*]. Alcan.

Liebst, L. S. (2019). Exploring the Sources of Collective Effervescence: A Multilevel Study. *Sociological Science* 6:27–42. https://doi.org/10.15195/v6.a2.

Martin, L. J., Hathaway, G., Isbester, K., Mirali, S., Acland, E. L., Niederstrasser, N., Slepian, P. M., Trost, Z., Bartz, J. A., Sapolsky, R. M., Sternberg, W. F., Levitin, D. J., and Mogil, J. S. (2015). "Reducing Social Stress Elicits Emotional Contagion of Pain in Mouse and Human Strangers." *Current Biology* 25:326–332. https://doi.org/10.1016/j.cub.2014.11.028.

Mogan, R., Fischer, R., and Bulbulia, J. A. (2017). "To Be in Synchrony or Not? A Meta-Analysis of Synchrony's Effects on Behavior, Perception, Cognition and Affect." *Journal of Experimental Social Psychology* 72:13–20. https://doi.org/10.1016/j.jesp.2017.03.009.

Nahleen, S., Dornin, G., and Takarangi, M. K. (2019). "When More is Not Merrier: Shared Stressful Experiences Amplify." *Cognition & Emotion* 33:1718–1725. https://doi.org/10.1080/02699931.2019.1597683.

Páez, D., Basabe, N., Ubillos, S., and González, J. L. (2007). "Social Sharing, Participation in Demonstration, Emotional Climate, and Coping with Collective Violence after the March 11th Madrid Bombings." *Journal of Social Issues* 63:323–337. http://dx.doi.org/10.1111/j.1540-4560.2007.00511.x.

Páez, D., Javaloy, F., Wlodarczyk, A., Espelt, E., and Rimé, B. (2013). "El Movimiento 15-M: Sus Acciones como Rituales, Compartir Social, Creencias, Valores y Emociones" [15-March Movement: Their Actions as Rituals, Social Sharing, Beliefs, Values, and

Emotions]. *Revista de Psicologia Social* 28:19–33. https://www.doi.org/10.1174/021347413804756078.

Páez, D., Rimé, B., Basabe, N., Wlodarczyk, A., and Zumeta, L. (2015). "Psychosocial Effects of Perceived Emotional Synchrony in Collective Gatherings." *Journal of Personality and Social Psychology* 108:711–729. https://doi.org/10.1037/pspi0000014.

Pelletier, P. (2018). "The Pivotal Role of Perceived Emotional Synchrony in the Context of Terrorism: Challenges and Lessons Learned from the March 2016 Attack in Belgium." *Journal of Applied Social Psychology* 48:477–487. https://doi.org/10.1111/jasp.12526.

Pizarro, J. J., Alfaro-Beracoechea, L., Cusi, O., Ibarra, M. L., Zumeta, L. N., and Basabe, N. (2021a). "Eventos Locales, Efectos Globales: Emociones Trascendentes e Identificación con Toda la Humanidad" ["Local Events, Global Effects: Transcendent Emotions and Identification with All Humanity"]. *Revista de Psicología* 39:625–654. https://www.doi.org/10.18800/psico.202102.005.

Pizarro, J. J., Basabe, N., Amutio, A., Telletxea, S., Harizmendi, M., and Van Gordon, W. (2019). "The Mediating Role of Shared Flow and Perceived Emotional Synchrony on Compassion for Others in a Mindful-Dancing Program." *Mindfulness* 11:125–139. https://doi.org/10.1007/s12671-019-01200-z.

Pizarro, J. J., Basabe, N., Fernández, I., Carrera, P., Apodaca, P., Man Ging, C. I., Cusi, O., and Páez, D. (2021b). "Self-Transcendent Emotions and Their Social Effects: Awe, Elevation and Kama Muta Promote a Human Identification and Motivations to Help Others." *Frontiers in Psychology* 12:1–17. https://doi.org/10.3389/fpsyg.2021.709859.

Pizarro, J. J., Telletxea, S., Bobowik, M., and Zumeta, L. N. (2017). "Experimental Ritual: Humanizing Immigrants or Utilitarian Prejudice in Europe?" *Universitas Psychologica* 16:1–14. https://doi.org/10.11144/Javeriana.upsy16-5.erhi.

Pizarro, J. J., Zumeta, L., Bouchat, P., Wlodarczyk, A., Rimé, B., Basabe, N., Amutio, A., and Páez, D. (2022). "Emotional Processes, Collective Behavior and Social Movements: A Meta-Analytic Review of Collective Effervescence Outcomes during Collective Gatherings and Demonstrations." *Frontiers in Psychology* 13:974683. https://doi.org/10.3389/fpsyg.2022.974683.

Prinzing, M., Le Nguyen, K., and Fredrickson, B. L. (2023). "Does Shared Positivity Make Life More Meaningful? Perceived Positivity Resonance is Uniquely Associated with Perceived Meaning in Life." *Journal of Personality and Social Psychology* 125:345–366. https://doi.org/10.1037/pspi0000418.

Rai, T. S., and Fiske, A. P. (2011). "Moral Psychology Is Relationship Regulation: Moral Motives for Unity, Hierarchy, Equality, and Proportionality." *Psychological Review* 118:57–75. https://doi.org/10.1037/a0021867.

Rennung, M., and Göritz, A. S. (2016). "Prosocial Consequences of Interpersonal Synchrony: A Meta-Analysis." *Zeitschrift Fur Psychologie* 224:168–189. http://doi.org/10.1027/2151-2604/a000252.

Rimé, B. (2007). "The Social Sharing of Emotion as an Interface between Individual and Collective Processes in the Construction of Emotional Climates." *Journal of Social Issues* 63:307–322. http://dx.doi.org/10.1111/j.1540-4560.2007.00510.x.

Rimé, B. (2009). "Emotion Elicits the Social Sharing of Emotion: Theory and Empirical Review." *Emotion Review* 1:60–85. https://doi.org/10.1177/1754073908097189.

Rimé, B., Bouchat, P., Paquot, L., and Giglio, L. (2020). "Intrapersonal, Interpersonal, and Social Outcomes of the Social Sharing of Emotion." *Current Opinion in Psychology* 3:127–134. http://dx.doi.org/10.1016/j.copsyc.2019.08.024.

Rimé, B., and Páez, D. (2023). "Why We Gather: A New Look, Empirically Documented, at Émile Durkheim's Theory of Collective Assemblies and Collective Effervescence."

Perspectives on Psychological Science 18:1306–1330. https://doi.org/10.1177/17456916221146388.

Shteynberg, G., Hirsh, J. B., Wolf, W., Bargh, J. A., Boothby, E. J., Colman, A. M., Echterhoff, G., and Rossignac-Milon, M. (2023). "Theory of Collective Mind." *Trends in Cognitive Sciences* 27:1019–1031. https://doi.org/10.1016/j.tics.2023.06.009.

Tutenges, S. (2023). *Intoxication: An Etnography of Effervescent Revelry*. Bristol University Press.

Van Cappellen, P., and Rimé, B. (2104). Positive Emotions and Self-Transcendence. In *Religion, Personality, and Social Behavior*, edited by V. Saroglou. Psychology Press.

Vestergren, S., Drury, J., and Chiriac, E. H. (2018). "How Collective Action Produces Psychological Change and How that Change Endures Over Time: A Case Study of an Environmental Campaign." *British Journal of Social Psychology* 57:855–877. https://doi.org/10.1111/bjso.12270.

von Scheve, C. (2011). Collective Emotions in Rituals: Elicitation, Transmission, and a "Matthew-effect." In *Emotions in Rituals*, edited by A. Michaels and C. Wulf. Routledge.

von Scheve, C., and Ismer, S. (2013). "Towards a Theory of Collective Emotions." *Emotion Review* 5:406–413. https://doi.org/10.1177/1754073913484170.

von Scheve, C., and Salmela, M., eds. (2014). *Collective Emotions: Perspectives from Psychology, Philosophy and Sociology*. Oxford University Press. https://doi.org/10.1093/acprof:oso/9780199659180.001.0001.

Whitehouse, H., and Lanman, J. A. (2014). "The Ties That Bind Us: Ritual, Fusion, and Identification." *Current Anthropology* 55:674–695. https://doi.org/10.1086/678698.

Wlodarczyk, A., Zumeta, L., Basabe, N., Rimé, B., and Páez, D. (2023). "Religious and Secular Collective Gatherings, Perceived Emotional Synchrony and Self-Transcendent Emotions: Two Longitudinal Studies." *Current Psychology* 42:4754–4771. https://doi.org/10.1007/s12144-021-01826-0.

Wlodarczyk, A., Zumeta, L., Pizarro, J. J., Bouchat, P., Hatibovic, F., Basabe, N., and Rimé, B. (2020). "Perceived Emotional Synchrony in Collective Gatherings: Validation of a Short Scale and Proposition of an Integrative Measure." *Frontiers in Psychology* 11:721. https://doi.org/10.3389/fpsyg.2020.01721.

Yaden, D. B., Haidt, J., Hood, R. W., Vago, D. R., and Newberg, A. B. (2017). "The Varieties of Self-Transcendent Experience." *Review of General Psychology* 21:143–160. https://doi.org/10.1037/gpr0000102.

Zabala J., Conejero, S., Pascual, A., Zumeta, L. N., Pizarro, J. J., and Alonso-Arbiol, I. (2023). "Korrika, Running in Collective Effervescence through the Basque Country: A Model of Collective Processes and their Positive Psychological Effects." *Frontiers in Psychology* 14:1095763. https://www.doi.org/10.3389/fpsyg.2023.1095763.

Zabala, J., Vázquez, A., Conejero, S., and Pascual, A. (2024). "Exploring the Origins of Identity Fusion: Shared Emotional Experience Activates Fusion with the Group Over Time." *British Journal of Social Psychology* 63:1479–1496. https://doi.org/10.1111/bjso.12723.

Zickfeld, J. H., Schubert, T. W., Seibt, B., Blomster, J. K., Arriaga, P., Basabe, N., . . . and Fiske, A. P. (2019). "Kama Muta: Conceptualizing and Measuring the Experience Often Labelled Being Moved across 19 nations and 15 languages." *Emotion* 19:402–424. https://doi.org/10.1037/emo0000450.

Zlobina, A., and Davila, M. C. (2022). "Preventive Behaviours During the Pandemic: The Role of Collective Rituals, Emotional Synchrony, Social Norms and Moral Obligation." *British Journal of Social Psychology* 61:1332–1350. https://www.doi.org/10.1111/bjso.12539.

Zumeta, L. N., Castro-Abril, P., Méndez, L., Pizarro, J. J., Włodarczyk, A., Basabe, N., . . . and Pinto, I. R. (2020). "Collective Effervescence, Self-Transcendence, and Gender Differences in Social Well-Being during 8 March Demonstrations." *Frontiers in psychology*: 607538. https://doi.org/10.3389/fpsyg.2020.607538.

Zumeta, L. N., Oriol, X., Telletxea, S., Amutio, A., & Basabe, N. (2016) "Collective Efficacy in Sports and Physical Activities: Perceived Emotional Synchrony and Shared Flow." *Frontiers in Psychology* 6:1960. https://doi.org/10.3389/fpsyg.2015.01960.

4

Charisma and Collective Effervescence

Great Composers

Randall Collins

The theories of charisma and of collective effervescence are connected. A charismatic leader is someone who produces collective effervescence in an audience and generates enthusiastic followers by leading highly successful interaction rituals.

This is a more micro-sociological way of looking at charisma than the traditional analysis stemming from Max Weber (1922 [1968], 241–255, 1111–1156). In that perspective, charisma is one of the forms of political authority. It is historically important because it is the agent of rapid social change, chiefly by the eruption of a new religious movement or a political leader with a vision of a new social order. Here I shift the perspective to processes located on the level of social interaction: What does the charismatic person do that generates new social identities and ideals? After locating these micro-sociological patterns, we can apply the theory of charismatic leadership to a nonpolitical realm. I will sketch the charisma of the composers who changed the styles of music between 1700 and 1900 and recruited new kinds of audiences who became musical social movements.

Charisma operates by shaping collective emotions. The charismatic individual is an expert at leading highly successful interaction rituals, with collective effervescence as their outcome. The ingredients of interaction rituals were first spelled out by Émile Durkheim for religious and political activities. Applied to charisma, the ingredients are bringing a group of people together in bodily co-presence; galvanizing their attention onto a common focus, such as the words and gestures of the leader; and building an intense emotion, which propagates through the audience in a self-reinforcing spiral. The emotionally aroused crowd develops a shared bodily rhythm—chanting together, swaying, dancing, applauding, which increases their awareness of themselves as an entity, a feeling of intersubjectivity. The rhythmic coordination of bodily movements, especially as it grows more intense, is collective effervescence. Those who take part in it feel it as a peak experience, transcending mundane everyday life.

When an interaction ritual focuses upon a person who is the center of attention, that person becomes charismatic, imitated, and followed by others. This process has been studied primarily for religious and political movements. It also has an important effect for careers in entertainment, ranging from popularistic and violent (Tutenges 2023), to the most esoteric "high art" movements. Here I will apply it to classical composers.

Frontstage and Backstage Charisma: In Politics and in Music

Looking at charismatic composers from Ludwig van Beethoven to Sergei Rachmaninoff, we notice that they can be charismatic in two different ways. These can be called frontstage and backstage charisma. Frontstage charisma happens through the performance of their music. Their concerts are deeply absorbing interaction ritual, with all of its characteristics of shared focus of attention, rhythmic entrainment, building up a strong emotional mood in the audience. Great composers are experts at interaction rituals—not by making speeches as in the case of political and religious leaders—but in the musical performance itself. This does not mean the music must always be as thunderous as Beethoven; there are quiet forms of musical charisma, such as Franz Schubert's, similar to the quiet charisma of leaders of spiritual meditation and prayer. (It is no coincidence that the great musical expression of prayer is Schubert's *Ave Maria*.)

In Erving Goffman's terms, we can call this kind of musical performance frontstage charisma. It is a public performance, highly idealized, but it is prepared for by a great deal of private composing, revising, rehearsing, and getting the right people together in the right place. The latter is backstage charisma, which consists in leading and energizing people to do these mundane tasks. It is informal and personal; some people are good at it, others are not. In my research on historical charismatic persons (Collins 2020) frontstage charisma is the ability to make great speeches to rapt audiences (Jesus, Mohammed, Winston Churchill, Franklin D. Roosevelt).

Backstage charisma is the ability to impress people in small, intimate gatherings. He or she becomes the informal leader, swaying people by emotional dominance. They take the lead in the interaction ritual by generating emotional energy (EE). Some religious or political leaders had both frontstage and backstage charisma (Jesus, Jeanne d'Arc, Franklin D. Roosevelt). Some operated primarily through their backstage charisma (Cleopatra, Lawrence of Arabia). Some had frontstage charisma but lacked backstage, personal dominance (Churchill, Adolf Hitler).

We find this also among composers. Some were charismatic in both frontstage and backstage (Richard Wagner with his musical spectaculars, plus his ability to charm supporters). Some had only frontstage charisma (Beethoven, who made an undistinguished presence in person).

Frontstage charisma is collective effervescence generated by an attention-galvanizing performance in a public place, building up as enthusiastic audiences attract increasing numbers of followers. Charisma gives a sense of belonging to a movement spreading beyond the horizon. A famous example is Franz Liszt, whose renown as an astonishing pianist preceded him in his tours across Europe, a network of followers rippling outward before he arrived. In this sense, charisma is a micro-mechanism that expands into a dynamic macro-process. (I owe this suggestion to Phil Smith.)

Backstage charisma is small-scale rhythmic/emotional entrainment in a face-to-face conversation, focused on an individual adulated by the group. Such a person is said to have charm, magnetism, chemistry. Their friends become a coterie. If they spread their enthusiasm to others, they set in motion a process of giving the charismatic individual a reputation that opens doors elsewhere. We shall see this process for musicians such as Schubert.

Applying Theory of Charisma to Composers

My current research is on what makes composers of music famous, not just in their lifetimes, but across the generations. It includes information on the trajectory of their careers, their audiences, networks with other composers, and styles of personal interaction. This is a good source of comparisons, since composers across several hundreds of years of history have varied greatly in how charismatic they were—how much collective effervescence was generated by their music. Charisma is one source of fame, but not all composers who became famous in historical hindsight were charismatic. Thus, the music of Antonio Vivaldi, Johann Sebastian Bach, and Wolfgang Mozart was created in an era when musicians were merely servants, providing background for ceremonies or social gatherings. In a later century, concert audiences might find their music inspiring—even "charisma at a distance." But in their time, the audience could go on chatting during the music, and composers were given little attention frontstage or backstage.

The social structure of performance changes can be seen in the careers of three of the most charismatic composers: Beethoven, Liszt, and Wagner. Beethoven was the first musician to become regarded as important as the highest rulers and nobility. At the height of his reputation, Beethoven was walking with Johann van Goethe, Germany's most admired writer. When the empress of Austria approached Goethe from the opposite direction, with her entourage of court nobles, Goethe stepped aside, doffed his hat, and bowed down. Beethoven continued without changing his stride, letting the empress and the nobles get out of his way. Beethoven told Goethe, "It is they who should yield precedence to us" (Hamburger 1951).

Beethoven's music was emotional and dramatic beyond anything that came before. He acquired a circle of admirers, first in the salons of Vienna nobles, playing his piano compositions, then in a series of rousing symphonies in commercial concert halls. Beethoven's charisma emerged at a time when the upper classes were competing with each other via their musical protégés and when middle-class concert audiences emerged. Audience behavior changed as well: previously (especially in opera houses) people gathered to chat and flirt during the performances. However, a new regime of public demeanor took hold: audiences were expected to be silent, pay respectful attention, and interrupt the music only for cheers and applause at breaks in the performance. Beethoven was the first composer to receive this deference. Applauding became a new collective social ritual, paired with the ritual of respectful silence. Charisma requires a receptive audience and thus a double-pronged causality converged: the new concert audience, and Beethoven responding to the opportunity by composing music of unprecedented collective effervescence.

We can observe whether a musical performance is a successful public ritual or a failure by whether it is enthusiastically applauded or not and if the audience is silently attentive or absorbed in their own private conversation. Composers like Giuseppe Verdi and Johannes Brahms suffered humiliating failures early in their careers. They learned to surmount these setbacks by improving their compositional techniques and pulling the audience into the musical flow.

Beethoven had frontstage charisma but not backstage. He made a shabby appearance, unkempt and careless of everything but his music. He was alternately jokey or contentious, unable to keep a housekeeper for long, constantly moving his residence as he wore out his welcome. His growing deafness did not hinder his ability to compose music, and he was able to converse with his many visitors and admirers by having them write penciled notes. Personally, he was neither graceful nor impressive, that was all in his music.

Liszt, in the generation after Beethoven, was the first full-fledged star musician, in the modern sense—the Beatles of his day. Audiences, especially young women, mobbed him at his concerts, snipping off pieces of his hair and clothes for souvenirs. Tall and slender, with an angelic face and hair rippling over his shoulders, he was a mesmerizing presence as he dropped his gloves and sat down at the piano. Fans watched his hands through opera glasses to see if he really had extra fingers; cascades of notes flowed from the piano while he seemed to go into a trance, head thrown back. Stories of his erotic affairs preceded him and added to his reputation. The 1830s and 1840s was the time when, as Beethoven prophesied, the musical genius really would outrank the nobility. Liszt toured Europe playing for kings and nobles who hushed to hear him.

Liszt's charisma was promoted by a new social medium: the piano. Pianos existed in the previous century, but now they were being manufactured as a mass consumer product. The growing middle class of the Industrial Revolution now could afford to have a piano in their home, setting off a boom in the music business. One no longer needed to attend a concert, which would have been largely the prerogative of the upper classes in major cities. Ordinary people could buy sheet music and play it on their piano. It was the predecessor of recorded music, which would arrive in the twentieth century and set off a wave of pop music stars. Liszt made his career composing music for this market. In his earlier years he performed other's compositions rather than his own: the latest popular opera songs, the symphonies of Beethoven and Hector Berlioz; themes from Wagner's new operas. Liszt acquired a reputation for piano music that captured the essence of other composers' music better than the originals. His tours and his sheet music sales went in symbiosis; it was like Elvis appearing on television in the 1950s or the Rolling Stones on tour in the 1960s. He was the first composer to make a lot of money—first by his tours, which still reached mainly the upper classes, and then by sales of his sheet music, which, like the stories about him, circulated among people who never heard him in person.

As he approached forty, Liszt cut back on his performances to concentrate on composing "the music of the future," hoping to become the next Beethoven. He eventually reconciled himself to his niche, promoting Wagner as the true genius of new music. His frontstage charisma was chiefly as a performer. He always had backstage charisma, charming almost everyone who met him. Liszt was unusually good-natured, encouraging those who approached him. Pyotr Tchaikovsky (who was personally uncharismatic and rather jealous of rivals) called Liszt a hypocrite because he praised so many different composers. But Liszt had no jealousy. From the beginning to the end of his life, he was the center of attention; different from most famous persons too, because he never put anyone down. He finally became a Catholic clergyman. At the center of the social networks of musicians during his day, Liszt is the odd case where his charisma surrounded him personally more than his compositions.

Wagner eventually acquired enormous fame; his music became the center of a veritable religious cult. By the 1870s, the music world was divided between the rival cults of Wagner and Brahms. This is in keeping with the social organization of charisma: it does not mean everyone joins in one reverberating network of collective effervescence; historically all charismatic figures had their enemies. Wagner had a slow start: his operas began to find successful audiences when he was around age thirty, but he was forced into exile for taking part in the failed revolution of 1849. During this period, we can say that Wagner had more backstage charisma than frontstage; he had trouble getting his operas performed, and they were mainly known by other composers who read the scores.

But his backstage charisma was considerable. He charmed people with his enthusiasm and his talk, articulating his vision of a new kind of musical theater. His aim was to break away from focusing on a soprano or tenor stopping the action to sing a four-minute song, showing off how long they could hold the high notes and improvising trills and arpeggios. The action of the opera was to be carried by the orchestra, using voices as just another instrument in the harmonic blend. Instead of a series of intermittent songs, the orchestra built to a huge, drawn-out crescendo much like a sexual orgasm. Wagner promised his audience an experience of overwhelming collective effervescence. In operas like *Tristan and Isolde* he carried it off.

Descriptions of how Wagner behaved face-to-face with musicians and singers are surprising. At rehearsals, he would enthusiastically embrace them if he liked their performance. He would also drop dramatically flat on the floor to show how he felt. When a friend visited, he would acrobatically climb up the side of a house in excitement. Wagner was a spendthrift who was always in debt, always living in a grand manner by borrowing from others. How could he keep on getting so many people to support him? He swept them up in his enthusiasm—making them disciples who conveyed his effervescence to others. Wagner's several love affairs—scandalous to conventional morality—were the result of his extraordinary personal magnetism. A rich admirer in Switzerland gave him a house adjacent to his own, where Wagner carried out an affair with that patron's wife. Later, he had a prolonged affair with Liszt's daughter Cosima—herself "illegitimate" since Liszt, too, lived a bohemian lifestyle and never married. Cosima was married to a young conductor, Hans von Bulow, who was a Wagner enthusiast and the principal conductor of his operas. The affair with Cosima was taken in stride; von Bulow continued to be Wagner's conductor. Wagner's backstage charisma in his own circle was extraordinary.

In the late 1860s, Wagner acquired a superconvert: the young King Ludwig of Bavaria, who built fantasy palaces like the Disneyland-ish Neuschwanstein Castle (named after the swan boat in Wagner's *Lohengrin*). Royal patronage enabled Wagner to build his own opera house at Bayreuth, and finally produce all his operas. The opening performance of *Der Ring des Nibelung* (the *Ring* cycle) in 1876 was attended by royalty from all over Europe, including the German emperor, and attracted composers like Tchaikovsky, and subsequently Claude Debussy. Wagner's new style of composing was influential throughout the early modern era. After his death, his followers included Gustav Mahler and Hugo Wolf—both were avid Wagnerians, although Jewish, undisturbed by Wagner's diatribes against Jewish influence in music. (Wagner had attacked what he considered the superficial light entertainment of Giacomo Meyerbeer and Jacques Offenbach.) The attitude of Mahler and Wolf, disturbing in today's hindsight, illustrates the strength of the Wagnerian movement's public charisma.

Composers Without Charisma

For quite some time composers lacked charisma and were viewed as merely servants or functionaries. Bach was a church organist who provided music for religious services; he was admired by other musicians but received no deference. Vivaldi was a priest who made a reputation in Venice by training girls in an orphanage to perform his compositions; when he decided later in life to try his luck in Vienna, he had little success and died in poverty, like Mozart fifty years later. Mozart was a child prodigy who toured the courts of Europe with his father, but his early fame was as a curiosity. He was extraordinary on the keyboard at age six. When he became a professional composer as a teenager his work attracted only modest attention, and he was remembered as a child has-been. He struggled to free himself from being the court musician for Prince-Archbishop Colloredo of Salzburg. But going out on his own was a hit-or-miss proposition at that time and even the successful operas of his last years did not save him. Joseph Haydn was a liveried servant almost his entire life who was appreciated by his music-loving lord who provided a house orchestra for him to try out his many compositions. In the 1790s, Haydn's music became popular when his sheet music was sold around Europe. In old age he was released from service and invited to present commercial concerts in London, which Beethoven was to take full advantage as an adult.

Earlier, around 1700, nearest to being a celebrity was George Handel. His father was the personal doctor to a German duke—a high-ranking position. He prohibited young Handel at first from learning music, a demeaning profession—his son was intended for a legal career and attended Halle

University. Nevertheless, Handel was allowed a gentlemanly grand tour of Italy, where he impressed the leading musicians with his skill at harpsichord and organ. He was popular with other visiting lords and was offered positions both in London and with the Prince-Elector of Hannover, who eventually inherited the English throne. For a while, Handel lived in the palace of an English lord and joined with other nobles in commercial ventures of running an opera house, for which Handel provided the music and recruited the players and singers. London was the epicenter of theater, just expanding into commercial music. Handel bridged the career of royal household entertainer and opera impresario. The theater had its dangers—investors collapsing in stock speculations, competition from rival companies—and Handel had to survive bankruptcy, but he had his day job with the king to fall back on. He reached a peak in 1742 when the king rose to hit feet during the Hallelujah chorus of the *Messiah*—a custom observed ever since. His performance of *Music for the Royal Fireworks* in 1749 caused the first known traffic jam as the audience overwhelmed London bridges. Toward the end of his life Handel was famous, but not charismatic. His professional life was conducted like a business. Personally he was gruff, not charming.

Is Charisma in the Music or in the Composer?

As long as a composer performs their own music, this question doesn't arise. Like Jesus making a sermon or Churchill making a radio speech, the speaker generates collective effervescence as the crowd becomes rapt with attention and carried away by the words. Churchill's rhythmic phrases are like a composer building their melodic trajectory. Beethoven had this effect on his audiences as a young pianist with the drama of the *Sonata Pathétique*, the hypnotic rocking of *Moonlight Sonata*. His style of building to a climax through a series of surprising chord changes. As he grew deaf, he no longer conducted the orchestra, but he was present to receive the audience's acclaim. Beethoven's frontstage charisma combines his personal appearance—a dramatic-looking individual with his shock of wild hair—with the tempestuous experience of hearing his music.

But does charisma continue to be the collective effervescence of a crowd when the music is propagated on printed scores and performed elsewhere by other conductors? This is inescapable for high levels of charismatic fame, since it is the spreading of disciples and followers across distant space and time that converts a local event into a social movement. The stretch becomes even greater when music is "recorded" on some kind of instrument. As indicated, pianos were permeating middle-class homes at the time when Liszt composed piano versions of symphonies and operas. Liszt not only generated almost hysterical collective effervescence in his in-person concerts but propagated a form of take-away charisma when amateurs could sit down at home to mimic the sounds of a performance as best they could. The end result was watered down charisma, an echo of collective effervescence. Great charisma radiates outward, felt at a distance by huge numbers of people who are no longer an assembled audience.

Let us examine several exemplary cases as music traveled from background music in aristocratic salons to peak experiences-of-a-lifetime for audiences hearing superstars.

Schubert had little personal charisma. His great symphonies were not performed until after his death. He started with excellent apprenticeship opportunities, attending a choir school that had its own student orchestra where he conducted currently published symphonies of Mozart and Beethoven, and eventually evolved his own style. As an adult, Schubert eked out a living composing songs—high art *lieder* setting the words of famous poets—which were performed in Vienna cafes by his singer friends while he accompanied on the piano. These Schubertiades, spread via word-of-mouth and extended into middle-class salons. Schubert's music and reputation would ride a wave of new sociability rituals: with home pianos and increasing wealth, the custom grew of hosting after-dinner gatherings to hear a small performance. Art songs, they were called, became distinguished from ordinary popular songs or traditional folk songs.

Popular music became a genre increasingly distinct from high art music, which became two different kinds of social rituals. The former could be happy sing-alongs with everyone joining in (such as drinking songs or marching songs). The latter were to be listened to with rapt attention and serious appreciation, the same emotional attitude as the exalted mood of the concert hall. What Schubert launched, and other composers extended, was transferring the public effervescence of the symphony hall to the small-scale private gathering. This created a further status differentiation within the middle class, not just in terms of money or ancestry, but a new social identity: the cultural elite. In the writings of critics like Robert Schumann and Matthew Arnold, people who did not appreciate high art music or painting were called philistines; whatever their money, their taste was vulgar. A war between high, serious music, and ordinary, popular entertainment—never of much concern in previous history—was now becoming a prominent claim to social status. This new dimension of social stratification was an unexpected by-product of the new charisma of the "great composer."

The extremely popular operas of Verdi make us confront another aspect of the question whether the charisma is in the music or in the composer. Attending a Verdi opera could be an enormous experience. During the nineteenth century, orchestras were huge, and composers knew how to create a dramatic range of sounds from a blend of many new instruments. A top composer like Verdi became an expert at picking a libretto, usually by a famous novelist or playwright. Preferably a melodramatic plot that could be turned into stage scenes featuring rousing choruses, anguished duets, and arias giving the Luciano Pavarottis and Kiri Te Kanawas of the time opportunity to hit the high notes with tremolos melting the audience in their seats. The collective effervescence is on the stage, not only in the music; the dramatic moments of the plot, the singers' transcendent voices, the supporting build-ups and hushes of the orchestra—all these are engineered to produce maximum audience effect.

Does the charisma of generating operatic collective effervescence cling to the composer or the performance? For this also becomes the era of the superstar opera singer, above all of the prima donna (in Handel's time the female parts had been sung by castrati), but also the famous tenor or baritone. From Enrico Caruso onward, at the turn of the twentieth century, when the composer of classic favorites was no longer alive, it was the singer who became the star, the repository of frontstage charisma.

Verdi had little personal charisma. He clawed his way to the top of the highly competitive world of Italian opera, where each city's opera house was its center of social life. The politics of the great institutions like La Scala at Milan revolved around cliques controlling funding for favorite composers. Verdi learned the formula for arousing audiences. His entering wedge was the chorus that carried political resonance: the Hebrew slaves under captivity in Babylon; "Patria oppressa!" in *Macbeth* could be sung as a protest against Austrian domination of Italy. The call to arms in medieval Spain from *Il trovatore* was so famous that the leader of the Italian national movement burst out singing it from his balcony when news arrived of Austria's defeat. Verdi fought ruthlessly to get the best librettist and best singers. He boycotted opera houses that didn't give him what he wanted. Verdi would lock his personal assistant in a room until he produced the desired musical effects. From a lower-middle class family, and working in a time before copyrights, Verdi squeezed maximum profit from his opera performances, making himself a respectable landowner. He became the archetype of the backstage slave driver who produces a wonderful frontstage product. Personally, Verdi was suspicious, obsessive, and abrasive. He acquired the nickname "the bear of Busetto" after the town where he holed up on his country estate.

Nevertheless, Verdi was applauded vociferously when called to the stage at the premiere of his most successful operas and carried on the shoulders of a cheering crowd on the streets back to his hotel. A great opera must have a wonderful aria, a catchy tune instantly memorable, so that people could sing it in the streets that same evening and for days thereafter. This is what Verdi trained himself to provideéhis greatest operas are those that have the most popular excerpts (as can be seen from recorded compilations). This created another twist to the backstage/frontstage relationship. Verdi was so concerned not to let his best tunes leak to the public before the premiere that he would leave out the peak aria during rehearsals and only unveil it just before the performance. This is manipulated collective effervescence at a high order of manipulation.

Composers Without Charisma: Modern Composers Behind the Scenes

The disjuncture between personal, frontstage charisma and the socially dispersed charisma (as we might call it) of famous musical compositions, is most on display where a composer receives little recognition during their career and is mainly famous posthumously. Schubert, as we have seen, is partially a case of this. His universally loved *Unfinished Symphony* was only rediscovered because his *lieder* continued to acquire admirers and build his fame beyond the grave. Berlioz set out to create the most stirring music ever, importing Beethoven's symphonies into France, and trying to go beyond them with bigger, louder orchestras and melodramatic effects, whose meaning was explained by a printed program (hence "program music"). Berlioz had a small coterie of enthusiasts in Paris; Wagner said everyone else regarded him as a madman. Berlioz was indeed capable of creating a buzz in the audience and eventually made his reputation as a touring conductor in Germany and Eastern Europe. He also had a great deal of personal backstage charisma. Felix Mendelssohn, who met him in Rome, said his ideas and music were crazy, but he was the epitome of the charming, witty Frenchman. Berlioz presents us with a case where a composer has no frontstage charisma during his lifetime but considerable backstage charisma. (Wagner went through this too but lived to reach the peak of both kinds of charisma.) This seems a paradoxical conception of charisma, but such is the social world of collective effervescences (plural!).

Robert Schumann was another admirer of Beethoven, who concluded that nothing further could be accomplished in that style, hence he spent his younger years as a music journalist trying to promote a new style of music. For much of his career, Schumann was better known as a journalist than a composer. He studied the great compositions of predecessors in various genres of music, from piano to opera to symphony, but didn't have a breakthrough into popularity until he began to publish books of piano pieces for children—exploiting a new market with a huge increase of pupils. His wife, Clara Schumann, renowned as the greatest woman pianist, was far more famous than himself. Schumann considered her repertoire too popularistic—she urged him to write something less esoteric. He was embarrassed accompanying her on tours, standing silent and unnoticed at the back of the room while she was the center of attention. Schumann lost whatever backstage charisma he once had as a young enthusiast; he became shy and withdrawn, eventually suffering such a crisis of confidence that he attempted suicide and died in an insane asylum. His recognition was almost entirely posthumous: the charisma was in the music as audiences came around to it, chiefly through the piano repertoire for the home market.

As modern music developed in the late nineteenth and into the early twentieth century, composers became backstage technicians. Brahms had a long struggle to work up the skill and confidence to write symphonies in the grand Beethoven tradition. By this time he had bigger orchestras with new combinations of instruments to work with. Tchaikovsky, who became a self-taught teacher of orchestration at the newly founded Moscow Conservatory, imitated European models and applied them to much more lushly orchestrated ballet, catapulting Russian ahead of tradition-bound French ballet. Although Brahms became touted as the idol of the anti-Wagnerian faction, the charisma was entirely in the music; Brahms himself was morose and insulting at fashionable evening parties of Vienna. Tchaikovsky's music could be delightful, but he was diffident about conducting it, as he considered his most famous orchestra piece, the *1812 Overture*, to be mere hackwork. His backstage personality contrasted strongly with the delightful impression given by his ballets; he was caustic about his rivals, both in Russia and in Europe.

Ballet turned out to be an ideal vehicle for avant-garde music at the turn of the century. Atonality, sudden shifts in rhythm, and choppy transitions from one mood to another made sense when audiences could see the action danced on the stage. Debussy and Maurice Ravel admired the Russians and collaborated with them. The *Ballets Russes* concerts in Paris featured ever more outrageous departures from traditional forms culminating in the *succès de scandale* of Igor Stravinsky's *Sacre de Printemps* in 1913. But the charisma attached more to the ballet dancers—in this case the famous Vaslav Nijinsky—than to the composers. Stravinsky was a hard worker who spent two years on the score and an unprecedented twenty rehearsals to make sure the players got it right (most ordinary orchestral performances get two or three rehearsals). Personally, Stravinsky appeared more like a dentist; he in turn called Ravel "a Swiss watchmaker." Ravel scored a big hit with *Bolero*, a tour de force repeating the same line of Spanish flamenco dance eighteen times—gradually building from near-silence to a crashing climax; the collective effervescence was orgasmic, but a frontstage effect of a very uncharismatic technician. Much the same can be said of the tone poems and operas of Richard Strauss who sound engineered the cosmic chord burst of *Zarathustra* (the opening scene of the film *2001*) and the erotic/sacrilegious *Salomé*, ending like *Sacre de Printemps*, with leading lady being killed on stage. Yet Strauss himself was quiet and sarcastic, preferring to conduct minimally with one hand in his pocket.

Like ballet, the tone poem and modern opera could incorporate as much dissonance and lack of a tone center as the avant-garde could create. The formal sequences and repetitions of the sonata and symphony in the era of Mozart and Beethoven had made it easy for the audience to follow the music, but this became unnecessary as the audience could read the program or see what was going on. What failed to win much acceptance was the extreme avant-garde in traditional sit-down concerts of abstract music. Arnold Schoenberg and his followers were admired only among a hyper-sophisticated elite; an audience of music technicians was necessary to appreciate the modernists. Nevertheless, ultramodern music found an unexpected home in film music—especially in film noir and suspense movies, where melody and chord resolutions were unnecessary for a few seconds of mood music, and atonality fitted well with the dark dramatics on screen. Film music could be emotionally effective, even with popular audiences who didn't even notice it was avant-garde but at the sacrifice of the composer who disappeared entirely behind the scenes.

In the classical world of the concert hall, the last frontstage charismatic composer was Rachmaninoff, a Russian exile who exploited the huge concert grand piano to the full range of its seven resonant octaves. His famous concertos and preludes mimicked the deep peals of heavy church bells at the bottom of the keyboard. Rachmaninoff was a flamboyant personality on stage; his morose personality—Stravinsky said he was "a six-and-a-half foot scowl"—fitting well with his combination of moody chord resonances and beautiful high-flowing melodies. In the 1955 film *The Seven Year Itch*, the comic hero tries to seduce Marilyn Monroe by putting on a record of Rachmaninoff's *Second Piano Concerto*. "It quakes them and shakes them," he says, "and makes you goose-pimply all over." Marilyn won't have any of it; she prefers the two-finger piano jingle "Chopsticks." The personal charisma of the composer is at an end. The same era of high-fidelity long-playing records introduced in the 1950s divorced classical music from the live audience in which collective effervescence is aroused. The era of the charismatic composer was over.

Where Does Charisma Come From?

Weber took the term "charisma" from the ancient Greek word for "gift." The charisma of the great religious leaders was a sudden break from tradition, and by extension a way that history takes great leaps in new directions. Does this mean that charisma sprang out of nowhere? But in fact, the historical instances of charismatic leaders happen in distinctive circumstances. The great "world-historical" religions all were created at times when a cluster of ancient states were winnowing down to a large-scale empire. In each case, ancient cults of local gods were transcended by the advocates of a new doctrine. Charisma appears when the social conditions are present for a big change. There is no charisma without an audience prepared to receive it. Charisma in music appears in a similar way, if on a smaller scale.

Charismatic composers coincided with a change in the social conditions for audiences, and with changes in techniques that made it possible to create new kinds of musical effects, new kinds of collective effervescence. Musical charisma does not come out of nowhere; the buildup of large-scale orchestra music was carried by personal networks of musicians, such as Haydn, Mozart, Beethoven and Schubert in Vienna. What do the network of composers get from each other? Learning the techniques that have aroused audiences thus far, hence a springboard for creating techniques to arouse audiences in a different way. They explore the possibilities of producing new music for aristocratic patrons, and the riskier careers of commercial concert halls. They learn what new instruments have what effects—Mozart hears about the clarinet; Beethoven shows what can be done with a more resonant piano; Wagner gives his melodies not to the high violins but to new valve horns in the middle octaves. Some composers come too early to survive independently on the market. A few benefit from the optimal combination of audiences, instruments, and techniques for writing music. It is where there is a distinctive combination of circumstances—the composer playing or conducting their own music on a commercial stage—that charisma adheres to the personality of the composer. The composer becomes indistinguishable from the collective effervescence of hearing their music.

But the process does not stop there. The music business grows beyond the charisma of the composer in the concert hall. The music publishing business makes it possible for other conductors to present famous music in absentia. The multiplication of concert halls and opera houses shifts charisma to famous singers, star conductors, and ballet dancers. The burgeoning business of home pianos creates private and intimate performances—by students, by children, for self-entertainment, for musical evenings after dinner. Composers become successful by producing niche music for these specialized venues. They become increasingly technicians behind the scenes, experts at the techniques of how to create musical effects in the audience—to produce highly-charged collective effervescence without feeling it oneself. By the time we reach film music, the charisma of the composer has almost entirely disappeared.

It is a myth that charisma is an eruption of inspiration, a sudden Amadeus-like gift of the gods. The important composers were always hardworking technicians. Of course this continued to be true at the time of Beethoven, Liszt, and Wagner, when the surrounding conditions of the market enabled them to feel that they were sharing with the audience their own experience of musical effervescence. In subsequent generations, composers became more calculating, self-conscious of the way their techniques could move their audience without being moved themselves. Across a half-dozen generations of composers, their success in creating musical effervescence diffused the charisma away from themselves personally. Charisma disappeared into a phenomenon of the market.

REFERENCES

Collins, Randall. 2020. *Charisma: Micro-sociology of Power and Influence.* Routledge.

Hamburger, Michael (ed.) 1951. *Beethoven: Letters, Journals and Conversations.* Thames and Hudson.

Tutenges, Sebastien. 2023. *Intoxication: An Ethnography of Effervescent Revelry.* Rutgers University Press.

Weber, Max. 1968. *Economy and Society.* Bedminster Press. Originally published in 1922.

5

Does It Need to Be Loud?

Religious Effervescence and Microlevel Sound

Scott Draper

Collective effervescence (CE), as conceived by Émile Durkheim (1912 [1995]) and supported in much subsequent research, is profoundly consequential in human life. It fuels social solidarity and the sense of moral purpose that comes with it (Collins 2004; Draper 2019; Froese 2016; Parker and Hackett 2012). This chapter pertains to how we generate it (i.e., CE as the dependent variable).

Inspired by the predictive theoretical model proposed by Randall Collins (2004), my research here and elsewhere considers how various properties of religious rituals tend to foster or inhibit CE. Collins (following Erving Goffman) centers social occasions as his units of analysis. He proposes a small set of microlevel interactional dynamics which, when proficiently managed, propel gathered humans into an effervescent emotional state: *bodily co-presence* refers to bodies in a shared physical space, *barriers to outsiders* refers to social cues of exclusion, and *shared mood-shared focus*[1] refers to mutually-attuned emotions and objects of attention. These concepts have steered me to the sacred implications of mundane features of religious occasions, such as seating capacity, acoustics, duration of sermons, greeting times, transitions, and other aspects of religious dramaturgy, framing, and stage-setting.

This chapter is an overture, if you will, to a line of study I'm proposing regarding the influence of sound, specifically volume, on CE in religious rituals. I've examined a wide range of scholarship, and examples from my own fieldwork,[2] to begin to clarify what we do and don't know about the relationship between auditory volume and CE. I offer novel questions, early conclusions, and testable propositions for microlevel research on religion.

Rapture Versus Hush

Durkheim's *The Elementary Forms of Religious Life* (1912 [1995]) presents CE as the emotional force, produced in successful rituals, that jolts individual consciousness into collective consciousness, enabling shared identities, morals, and truths. He gave religious rituals special attention due to their powerful and often unquestioned authority in social constructions of reality (Benzecry and Collins 2014; Rawls 2004).

We tend to associate the emotional jolt of CE with loud, rapturous occasions, as in this vivid description from Durkheim:

> From every side there are nothing but wild movements, shouts, downright howls, and deafening noise of all kinds that further intensify the state they are expressing. . . . The human voice is inadequate to the task and is given artificial reinforcement: Boomerangs are knocked against one another; bull roarers are whirled. . . . And by expressing this excitement, they also reinforce it. (1912 [1995], 218)

Based on this and other descriptions from Durkheim, there can be little question that rituals such as the following, an account of a contemporary evangelical service in Rwanda, would qualify as effervescent:

> Church members began lifting the white plastic chairs they had been sitting on into the air and dancing with them held high above their heads. The mood was nothing less than ecstatic. Women ululated, and a young man in the back pews of the church enthusiastically blew on a long horn. Around me several church members knelt on the floor and spoke in tongues, while others either sang along to the song lyrics or yelled exclamations such as "*Yesu ashimwe!*" ("Praise Jesus") with their eyes closed and hands held toward the ceiling. Church members smiled at each other and laughed, and those who were dancing particularly vigorously were caught on camera and projected onto the church's various television screens. (Mariko Grant 2018, 43)

But then consider this exchange between two American Buddhists, discussing their weekly sessions of quiet, collective meditation. Can what they're describing also be considered CE?

> MATT:[3] When you walk into that room and you sit there with that group of people who are also meditating and you're doing some-

thing completely solitary—you know, it's just you working on your own mind—but somehow being in a room full of other people doing it is empowering. I always find it easier to meditate here than at home.

STEVE: You pick up on the energy.

MATT: Yeah. It's some sort of energetic something.

Quiet rituals like what Matt described are common in many traditions, yet they feel fundamentally different from the exuberant occasions typical of research on religious CE (e.g., Heider and Warner 2010; Inbody 2015; Plancke 2014; Wellman et al. 2020). Do quiet, subdued rituals belong in a different category? If so, then what is the "energetic something" that often emerges from the hush?

Across and within religious traditions, and even within some religious persons, there is conflict between the merits of loud practices that feel more ecstatic versus quiet practices that feel more solemn. The following discussion occurred during a focus group with members of Ward 6, a Church of Jesus Christ of Latter-day Saints congregation located in a western U.S. state. They had been telling me about recent delicate conversations with certain parents whose kids get too noisy during Sunday morning sacrament meetings, which the focus group had agreed should feel "reverent" and "quieter":

KERRY: [We're] trying to make people more aware that, you know, your screaming child could affect somebody else trying to listen and feel the Spirit. Um, now . . . now I'm not saying that children really detract from that, 'cause we believe children are pure. But, you know, when you're trying to listen to the talk, and you have someone screaming in your ear, you know, it's best to probably take the child out to the foyer. Just trying to educate the folks.

TINA: Just tact, yeah, like—

KERRY: Yeah.

TINA: Respect and tact . . .

JOAN: We need to remember that the chapel . . . is a sacred place.

This and our ensuing discussion led me to ask about emotional expression during the meetings, yielding the following exchange:

SCOTT: Do you ever find yourself trying not to express something that you're feeling? Thinking like, "Maybe this is not the appropriate . . . "? People aren't speaking in tongues or shouting or anything like that.

JAROD: I think so.

JIMMY: I th—yeah.

JAROD: Recently there's been talk about overly-, overexpressing and trying to hold yourself back, or limit things and, you know you read the—It's a joyous place, and the gospel's a joyous thing. And you read in the scriptures where everyone shouted "Hosanna!" and did all these jubilant celebrations, and they were spontaneous. . . . And so, sometimes I f . . . I feel . . . a little inhibited. Like, we're trying to monitor the way everybody needs to feel something. I- I- I do feel that sometimes. And—

JOAN: I think that's a fine line between reverence and expressing, too. Like that's hard, and I think sometimes it's squelched. I was just thinking, we visited a [LDS congregation] in the South, where there was a very large Baptist um . . . influence. . . . And I loved it. They would say, "AMEN!" They'd go, "Amen!" [laughter from a focus group member] and I thought, "Oh! I'd love to hear that more!" And I'd love for our songs to maybe be a little more, you know, um. . . . I just feel like it's always a balance act. . . . Our hymns tend to be—Gladys Knight, was um baptized into our faith. And she has her own music that she's put out, 'cause she said, "I love everything about this gospel. Except for this dreary music."

[Laughter from focus group.]

What do decibels deliver to CE? To begin to answer this, I'll first draw attention to different types of CE, as a starting point for studying a type I'll call "quiet, religious CE." I'll offer three counterexamples to quiet, religious CE, and then many more positive examples. From there, to demonstrate applications of these concepts, I'll consider the impact of volume during sermons, chants, prayers, and other practices that heavily involve talking. These spoken practices exemplify a more general pattern where dynamic tension between loud and quiet sounds is built into the structures of religious rituals, and also extended *across* rituals, influencing traditions' "emotional rhythms" over time (Summers-Effler 2010). Building on these ideas, the final two sections of this chapter consider volume as an "effervescence accelerator" (Draper 2021), drawing on Collins's theory to make a general case for pumping up the volume.

Different Types of Effervescence

Although Durkheim centered action and noise in his descriptions of CE, he did not ignore quiet moments. In some of his examples, quiet seems to frame the commotion. He writes, "The very act of congregating is an exceptionally powerful stimulant" (1912 [1995], 217). Just gathering is intense in this description, as the corroborees he's considering are between families whose lives are normally more isolated from other groups (216–217). From there, as those gathered begin to move and make sounds together, building a rhythm, the ritual gets progressively louder and more intense: "The initial impulse is thereby amplified each time it is echoed, like an avalanche as it goes along" (218).

Durkheim's longer descriptions of rituals have sonic ebbs and flows, as in an all-night ritual of the Australian Warumungu people, where "from time to time, the singing would flag and almost die, then break out suddenly again" (219). In the following text, the violent climax of this ritual seems intense, but so does its hushed conclusion, expressed in the final sentence:

> At the first sign of day, everyone jumped to their feet; the fires that had gone out were relit; urged on by the Kingilli, the Uluuru furiously attacked the mound with boomerangs, lances, and sticks, and in a few minutes it was in pieces. The fires died and there was profound silence. (219)

The microsociological research tradition has taken Durkheim's insights into rituals and CE in new directions (Smith 2020). Goffman and Collins in particular have drawn attention to "interaction rituals" (IRs), which include not just rare, ecstatic ceremonies, but also everyday occasions where humans construct their realities via synchronized movements and sounds that rouse shared emotions in the presence of sacred symbols. Collins has referred to CE as "a condition of heightened intersubjectivity" (2004, 35) and advanced a testable theoretical model of its situational causes (bodily co-presence, barriers to outsiders, shared mood-shared focus) and effects (social solidarity, emotional energy [EE],[4] sacred objects, moral standards).

Tutenges (2023) has likewise shown how CE appears in different forms. In his study of intoxication, he points to a series of ideal types of CE, which are distinguished by their phenomenological qualities. Some of these types ("sad effervescence," "compassionate effervescence," and "equanimous effervescence"), like many of Collins's examples, call into question the noise usually associated with CE. Tutenges emphasizes that the degree of emotional intensity varies across effervescent occasions, and can even be subtle:

> Effervescence occurs not just in different forms but also in varying degrees. At its lowest degree, it is a subtle buzzing of increased interactivity and mutual awareness. At its highest pitch, it is a powerful rush of rhythmically synchronized actions and emotions that involves a sense of being overtaken by a collective force with its own agenda. (2023, 10)

Here, I'm considering two additional experiential types—religious CE and quiet CE—and their microlevel intersections. They are not mutually dependent but do frequently come together as a coupled type I'll refer to as "quiet, religious CE." Before pointing to examples of quiet, religious CE, I should clarify what I am *not* referring to.

Counterexamples: "Silence," Dispiriting Quiet, and Solo Effervescence

First, *literally silent IRs* cannot be effervescent, because IRs are not literally silent. Avant-garde composer John Cage's symphony *4′ 33″* helped demonstrate this point, as did his argument that even a visitor alone in a "soundproof" anechoic chamber can hear their own blood circulating. He understood silence as sounds that were not intended, which therefore are not heard (Cage 1966). In other words, regardless of what we may mean by the term, background noise is always occurring anyway beyond our conscious awareness.

Social interactions are full of sounds, even when no one is talking (Goffman 1986). As part of my fieldwork, I've listened to—while transcribing, with much rewinding and repetition—many hours of audio recordings of focus groups and other occasions, from urban, suburban, and rural settings. Unintended sounds are perpetual, even when no one is talking, including but not limited to traffic, music, birds, footsteps, air conditioners, shifting chairs, water bottles, and especially cleared throats. "Silent" meditation and prayer are not exceptions. Genuine silence is best understood as a social construction, albeit a consequential one, especially in religions. The emphasis here, though, is "quiet." This concept, like "loud," is comparative and context dependent.[5]

Quiet is mostly strenuously avoided in contemporary IRs, although there is cross-cultural variation in how much of it people will tolerate (Stivers et al. 2009). The second counterexample, *dispiriting quiet*, looms widely as a threat to effervescence. Lulls in conversation, profound misunderstandings, refusals to validate: "awkward silence" is alienating, causing shame and flight response. Modern people tend to feel moral pressure, once engaged in an IR, to maintain a flow of words (Goffman 1967, 1986; Stivers et al. 2009). Having nothing to say can be a symptom of outsider or marginal status, lacking the cultural capital to join in (e.g., novices, nonfluent speakers, children). Or we might possess the capital but withhold it during a conflict. "Cold silence" threatens or announces an expired social bond. To actively "silence" is to suppress or shun someone in a weaker position.

Collins (2020), in a microsociological analysis of biblical confrontations between Jesus and Jesus's critics, indicates how the dispiriting power of silent treatment can even be employed to defuse CE. In some of these narratives, Jesus responded to his antagonists by saying nothing at first, in one case simply crouching and writing something in the dirt with his finger. His use of strategic pauses helped establish his charisma, even pacifying angry mobs (Collins 2020, 7–10). CE can incite violence, but dispiriting quiet can intervene humanely and/or preemptively by "individualizing crowds" and deescalating emotionally heated conflicts.

Third, solitary religious experiences can only reach solitary ecstasy; as such, they are relevant but more tangential to this chapter. Collins (2004) theorizes three successive orders of ritual: a first order of collectively effervescent rituals where symbols become sacred, a second where participants refer to the symbols already sacralized in first-order rituals, and a third order of solitary rituals where individuals privately reflect on those same symbols. Here I'll suggest a new concept for IR studies: *solo effervescence*, a third-order solitary achievement, which depends upon the emotional charge of symbols first sacralized in collective contexts.[6] Solitary practice can still be "social," insofar as it includes nonhuman and/or non-copresent interactants such as God, Mary, ancestors, authors of texts, or a more generalized other (Cerulo 2009; Froese and Jones 2021; James 1902 [1961]; Luhrmann 2012; Mead 1934). Solitary practice and solo effervescence can be powerful, especially when extended over time as slow-burning, private ritual chains. The focus here, though, is on the first and second orders of collective IRs.

Effervescence Does Not Need to Be Loud

"Optimal" volume varies in IRs, based on many factors. Still, we can ascertain patterns in practice that tend to boost or forestall CE. Table 5.1 indicates practices and settings during which experiences of quiet, religious CE are likely—though not always, or even necessarily very often. The table is only a small sample, and the items are neither exhaustive nor necessarily mutually exclusive. For each one, there are numerous complexities to sort out. Also, the intensity of CE, if reached, will vary. Together, though, they do point to a unique type of CE often experienced in quiet, religious contexts.

Volume and Effervescence in Sermons, Chants, and Other Spoken Practices

To demonstrate potential microlevel applications of these ideas, in this section I'll consider a subset of religious practices that emphasize speech, including conversations, sermons, chants, liturgies, and prayers. Through the rest of this chapter, theoretical propositions are presented in bullets, as suggestions for future research.

TABLE 5.1. SAMPLE OF PRACTICES, SETTINGS, AND ASSOCIATED MOODS CONDUCIVE TO QUIET, RELIGIOUS COLLECTIVE EFFERVESCENCE		
Practice/Setting	**Example**	**Common Associated Mood (Many Possible)**
Quiet practices		
In speech	Dynamic tension in sermons Dramatic pauses Gathering serious thoughts	Captivation Suspense Gravity
In music	Dynamic tension in songs Evensong	Stimulation Sublimity
In collective prayer or meditation	Silent confession during corporate prayer Unprogrammed worship (Quakers) Quiet chants Moments of silence Collective meditation	Penitence Revelation Unity Community Empowerment
While working together	Monastic labor Teaching/modeling practices Flipping pages together to find a scripture	Cooperation Gratitude Proficiency
In intimate IRs	Prayer group IRs Religious lullabies	Motivation Love
During sacraments	LDS sacrament Right before "I do" in weddings Quiet moments during funerals	Reverence Support Muted sorrow
During trials/competitions	Waiting for verdict in a heresy trial	Dread
During sacrifices	Right before execution	Horror
Sotto voce mini-IRs	Whispering jokes during a sermon	Transgression
Copresence with a sacred person/at a sacred site	Sharing a meal with one's guru Fellow pilgrims arriving	Devotion Awe
Quiet settings		
Quieting venues	Confessionals	Contrition
Quiet cultures	Sign language religious IRs Introverted friends discussing religion	All moods Fellowship
Quiet media	Mentorship via text message	Encouragement
Following a cacophonous IR	Nursery volunteers relaxing after a service	Relief

How does volume impact CE during spoken religious practices? The field of musicology aids the sociology in this case, as it indicates how a dynamic tension between louder and quieter sounds in music rhythmically entrains listeners' collective absorption and emotional engagement (Egermann et al. 2013; Mannes 2011). Music considered "loud" overall contains not just loud sounds, but loud sounds in rhythmic exchange with quiet ones. Musicians set up patterns that they then modify or supplant, an "expectation violation" that engages listeners' emotions in a song. Writing about the sequence of tones in a song, but also applicable to volume dynamics, Schütz observed, "The consciousness of the beholder is led to refer what he actually hears to what he anticipates will follow and also to what he has just been hearing and what he has heard ever since this piece of music began" (1951, 88–89).

In speech, too, quiet moments contribute most to CE when in rhythmic sequence with louder ones. Quiet provides a framework for vocalization. Dauenhauer (1980) points to "fore-and-after silence" and "intervening silence" as the two primary uses of silence in speech. Fore-and-after silence sets the boundaries for a distinct "utterance," whereas intervening silence punctuates the words and sentences within it (Bakhtin 1986; Sim 2007). In conversation, an utterance occurs when one speaker "holds the floor," so each speaker's "turn" is framed, normally, by bursts of fore-and-after silence, often quite brief in solidary conversations (Collins, 2004; Sacks et al. 1974). There is some variation, but a norm of "minimal-gap-minimal-overlap" is found in friendly talk across many cultures, with differences in average response times tending to measure under half a second (Gregory 1983; Stivers et al. 2009).

Sermons and other spoken liturgies can be analyzed much like conversations, especially when the audience talks back, for example in call-and-response sermons, as well as recited creeds, litanies, chants, etc. (Loeb 2014). Speeches are not just speeches, but symbolic exchanges between a speaker's sounds and gestures and those of their audience. Collins (2004), based on Clayman (1993), analyzes the rhythm of an audience's claps, boos, and laughter in response to political speeches. Similar methods could apply to a congregation's shouts, preachers' requests ("Can I get an 'Amen'?") or replies ("Y'all are feeling the Spirit today!"), or to patterns in Pentecostal groups' utterances while speaking in tongues.

- Congregations who normalize engaged vocalizations during sermons will experience intense CE more frequently than congregations who normalize more passive listening.
- In congregations where spontaneous expression is normal, louder and more frequent engaged vocalizations will positively correlate with intense CE.

Sermons and other speeches contain fore-and-after pauses framing readings, stories, outline points, etc., with cadences that vary across traditions and speakers. Seasoned public speakers develop a sense of timing for comic beats, grave deliberations, or for the audience to reflect. A speaker holding the floor can pause to build suspense, or consciously moderate volume, as when orators or musicians start soft, enticing listeners to lean in, and then increase volume at strategic moments to amplify entrainment.

An effervescent public prayer should follow the same pattern, where dynamic tension between loud and quiet sounds helps convey and entrain strong emotions. Alongside the words and cadences of the person praying, others present might make sounds such as whispered affirmations ("Yes!"; "Mm."), side involvements, sighs, stirrings, and other "creature releases" (Goffman 1986). These sounds as well can be analyzed as elements of congregations' "prayer styles," shaping absorption and emotion in prayer rituals (Froese and Jones 2021).

- CE will be more common and intense in response to spoken rituals that contain a focused dynamic tension between louder and quieter sounds, in contrast to spoken rituals where volume is invariant or randomly variant.

Absorption is jeopardized, though, when pauses appear unintended and become "lapses" (Sacks et al. 1974). Listeners can become alarmed and situationally alienated by very brief gaps if they suggest poor preparation, technical glitches, etc. A speaker caught in stage fright cannot channel a rhythmic interactive flow with their audience. Efforts to save face, rather than the speech itself, become the object of attention. The audience may feel intense collective empathy, pity, or even scorn for the speaker. But their fixation on the occasion per se imperils shame and self-consciousness, and a discomforting awareness of the constructedness of their social reality (Garfinkel 1967; Goffman 1967).

- Pauses and gaps in oratory, when enhancing the speaker's focus and reflecting their emotional engagement, will generally promote CE.
- Pauses and gaps in oratory, when weakening the speaker's focus and reflecting emotional alienation, will generally impede CE.

Loudness as an Effervescence Accelerator

Based on several examples so far, CE does not always have to be loud. Close attention to music, conversation, and a range of spoken religious practices suggests that CE can appear in the hush as well as the noise, and in fact depends upon the dynamic interplay of both.

In the remainder of the chapter, though, I'll strongly qualify that conclusion by emphasizing that—when promoting intersubjectivity, and in rhythm with quieter moments within and across rituals—increasing volume generally *does* intensify CE. CE, like volume, is a matter of degree—more like a dial than a switch. Intersubjectivity can reach a point where it feels heightened and effervescent. Beyond that threshold, though, CE's intensity varies within and across rituals. Although loud volume is unnecessary, it is nonetheless a powerful stimulant to high-intensity CE.

Collins (2004) theorizes a small set of very generalizable social dynamics or "ingredients," which when built into social occasions reliably generate CE. I'll now consider each of these in turn, along with Collins's cross-situational concept of "ritual chains." Volume is a physiological stimulant that intensifies the impact of each ingredient, thus serving as what I've referred to as an *effervescence accelerator* (Draper 2021). Shared mood-shared focus seems to be the only ingredient in Collins's model that is always essential to CE. Barriers to outsiders, for example, are not always present; religious organizations who are so inclined can find ways to avoid building them (Wellman et al. 2020; Wollschleger 2017). Bodily co-presence, too, can be circumvented, at least in some phone calls, virtual meetings, and other non-copresent rituals (Brown 2021; Draper 2019). However, intersubjectivity somehow needs to be *heightened* to reach CE, or to intensify it, so barriers and co-presence, often in tandem, are nonetheless pervasive in contemporary religion. When situations demand more emotional fuel, religious organizations step on effervescence accelerators.

Bodily Co-presence

Sound is a physical encounter. When speaking, our vibrating vocal cords send invisible waves of pressure to eardrums nearby. When hearing, our eardrums stimulate chain reactions in the body, the brain, and the signals sent between body and brain. At any moment, our brains and nervous systems interpret sounds along with other sensory inputs. Our interpretations of these inputs are shaped by experience, including instances of pleasure and pain that our bodies effectively record, triggering physical and emotional responses and directing which of numerous competing incoming stimuli we're even likely to notice (Damasio 1994; Goffman 1986; Heinskou and Liebst 2016; Summers-Effler 2004). Hearing involves the whole body and can significantly shape a person or a scene. Sound's vibrations are not only captured by the ear canal, but—depending on the hearers' sensitivities, and also the volume—literally shake their bones, a physical bridge with the sound maker.

At Promised Land Baptist, a black church whose rituals I considered in Draper (2019), the congregation's sounds helped fill a sanctuary that, though only about 25 percent full, felt much more crowded. For one thing, the congregants shouted and clapped enthusiastically during worship, especially during the call-and-response sermon. For another, their organist rarely took breaks during the three-hour service. His organ, the ritual's loudest sound, was well-amplified, and the congregation had to "project" to be heard. Visually, co-presence was low, but the congregants' loud engagement, plus their organist, made the service feel crowded and full of action.

Many situational variables interact to mediate the effects of particular sounds, including, but not limited to, a venue's size and acoustics, the number of bodies present, the sound's source, and the hearers' locations. These factors combined can deeply shape practices, along with orthopraxy and sacred symbols (Baumann 2015; Goffman 1959, 124–125; Heider and Warner 2010; Tallon 2016). A tall cathedral, for example, might inspire awe during singing but reverberate during homilies, urging stillness, or a reticence to speak. A crying baby or coughing fit in this context can derail the focus, inspiring discipline in how parishioners manage and evaluate their sounds. Or a small room that requires less vocal projection might prompt subtle self-presentation and rhetoric, backstage emotional transparency, and likewise for media such as videos or podcasts recorded in small studios. An open-air meeting might compel speakers to project loudly and articulate sharply, making large gestures, sacrificing subtlety of argument to compensate for how their sound diffuses and competes with other stimuli for the audience's attention. Focused loudness is needed, and speakers to large crowds can get pretty authoritarian about the crowd's role, as well: "Is that the loudest you can get? I can't HEAR you! Make some NOOOOOISE!" (also see Tutenges 2013, 241).

Social settings require specific solutions to reach optimal sound dynamics for CE and can only be generalized so much. One generalization that does well under scrutiny is the requirement that sounds not derail intersubjective thought and emotion, or obscure sacred symbols. Sound, though, does more for those experiences than absence of sound, during which the heights of intersubjectivity are harder to reach, but more on this later.

Barriers to Outsiders

Although barriers to outsiders do not seem essential to CE, they still are powerful and pervasive stimulants to it (Draper 2021). Volume is a key way to cue exclusion. The loud sounds of rock concerts advance into their surrounding locales, reaching outsiders but not fully entraining them, signaling exclusion from the nearby action. Resentful outsiders often appeal to authorities to quiet the noise. Inside the venue, the loud sounds penetrate, forcing the revelers' attention upon themselves and their envelopment within the ritual.

Rock concerts and religious rituals have much in common. Religious congregations, revivals, and festivals can get raucous, and neighbors often call the police (Fowler 2020). As Ehrenreich observes, contemporary rock music cultures have simply "re-created carnival" (2006, 220), playing out a recurring historical conflict between the common people and the elites who try to control them. Her book *Dancing in the Streets* (Ehrenreich 2006) chronicles numerous such conflicts, mostly involving loud religious festivals. In medieval Europe, for example, Church authorities often strove to tamp down the carousing of the laity during holidays. Later, colonialism loomed large as "civilized" colonists echoed each other in associating the "noisy" rituals of colonized people with "primitive irrationality," and their own more reserved rituals with their presumed rationality.

The civilizing process (Elias 1978), together with the inner-worldly asceticism Weber (1904 [2001], 1922 [1968]) associated with Calvinism, prioritizes public orderliness, interpersonal distance, and the appearance of self-discipline. These same norms remain the basis of contemporary bourgeois presumptions regarding public and "personal" space. Accordingly, Collins highlights the discomfort and indignance common among middle- and upper-class Americans when "situationally stratified" in public by the loud music and "highly audible action" (2004, 275) of categorically excluded people, such as members of the black lower class or teenagers. The pattern repeats in relations between adults and kids everywhere, including those gathered for religious meetings: the less-powerful try to make noise and the more-powerful try to quiet them in the name of order.

Abstaining from sound, too, can be very exclusive, though it is generally easier than noise for outsiders to ignore. Monastic quiet has been related to barriers in a few ways. Monks and nuns are "religious virtuosi," historically often coming from upper-class communities, or recipients of state or upper-class patronage, and practitioners of extreme and highly disciplined lifestyles (Collins 1986; Lawrence 2001; Weber 1922 [1968]). Monasteries are sacred locations, often remote and cloistered, and novices must be initiated over time into special practices. Most monasteries are hierarchically organized. None of this rules out CE, as the allure of EE from exclusive-status IRs can help motivate the extreme lifestyle; spiritual pride is often discussed as a temptation that monks and nuns must learn to overcome (Benedict 1998; Trungpa 1973).

Opportunities for CE in monasteries are often constrained by norms requiring quiet, composed demeanor, as is common in high-status and upper-class communities. But CE is still likely, as in the following circumstances:

- During quiet, focused, collective practices (e.g., meditation, manual labor, low-volume chanting), low-intensity CE of co-presence, and shared commitment to the practice will occur frequently.

- Visitors encountering renowned monastics are likely to experience intense CE of rarefied co-presence with sacred individuals (Collins 1986; Lawrence 2001).
- Monastics are likely to experience CE during rituals of status or changes in status.

Mystic monastic traditions often emphasize the inadequacy of words and intellect. The practice of silence may seek, for example, union with, nearness to, or contemplation of the Divine; an experience of emptiness; salvation; mindfulness; or concentration. Apophatic theology holds that God transcends humans' concepts. Buddhist philosophies regarding meditation, of which there are many, often stress the need to spurn worldly attachments and illusions to become enlightened. "Silence" is often conceived not only as withholding physical sound but also as calming "noisy" inner monologues. Mystic quiet often involves an effort to detach from all things worldly and conventional, including one's own self, or profane speech (Collins 1986; Nārada 1993; Weber 1922 [1968]). These barriers with "the world" are shared by co-practitioners, heightening fellow-feelings during collective occasions of quiet meditation and similar practices.

Intersubjectivity/Shared Mood-Shared Focus

Volume is intrinsic to much of the intersubjectivity achieved during religious practices. One reason is that it legitimates the gathering and collectively confirms sacred symbols, signaling that the practice is a good investment of time and energy. Stark observed that "participation in ritual and prayer are . . . sources of confidence in religious expectations" (2001, 178). Especially, *co*-participation boosts confidence. Because the number in attendance increases total volume, volume and confidence should correlate as well in most samples of rituals.

- The degree of confidence in sacred symbols produced in IRs will positively correlate with their total volume.

Entrained vocalizations and instruments signal absorption and make it contagious. Explaining the phenomenology of music-making, Schütz writes, "It is . . . this mutual tuning-in relationship by which the 'I' and the 'Thou' are experienced by both participants as a 'We' in vivid presence" (1951, 79). To verify mutual attunement, we rely heavily upon each other's sounds.

Sound and music also cue and accompany dance and other synchronized movements. In this way as well, announcing which movements to make together, ritual sounds promote embodied intersubjectivity and CE. Shouts and percussions prompt the next moves or dances, as in many North American Indigenous rites. Sounds normally frame collective silent practices as well, as with the resounding bells or gongs that start and finish Zen meditation sessions, or speakers' instructions framing moments of silence.

Rituals that minimize sound give fewer movement cues, making mutual consciousness more challenging—but again, not impossible. As Michal Pagis has demonstrated, intersubjectivity can occur even during quiet, collective meditation. Notably, these moments often involve human sounds, "bundles of noise":

> Movements cluster and form bundles of noise: the movement of one woman would lead to a reaction of a few others. One person's cough would trigger others to join. It was clear that the movement of one person tends to lead to the movement of another. (Pagis 2010, 318)

Sensations of the group deliver confirmation and reassurance, as if conveying, "We are here together, in agreement that this is a good thing to do." Collective focus can be felt and observed in quiet rituals. The *heights* of intersubjectivity, though, are more elusive when things are quiet. Consistent with this, Matt and Steve and their focus group at the meditation center I studied (quoted earlier) emphasized that their collective chants, performed in small spaces with voices reverberating loudly in unison, are more invigorating than their collective meditations (Draper 2019).

Ritual Chains of Sound

Religious organizations build dynamic tension of loud and quiet sounds into their rituals, for example reserving quiet periods between hymns for confessional prayer. This tension is also extended *across* rituals, as in religious calendars, where times of somber reflection are scheduled ahead of festive celebrations, or vice versa, as in Ramadan fasting/communal iftar, Good Friday/Easter, and Rosh Hashana/Yom Kippur. A tradition's rituals, chained over time, can draw upon quiet rituals to intensify louder ones.

- Cultural expectations of scheduled noise/quietude will influence traditions' "emotional rhythms" over time, with louder periods positively correlating with emotional intensity. (Mariko Grant 2018; Summers-Effler 2010)

Durkheim's discussion of negative rites and negative cults (1912 [1995], 309–310) suggests how ascetic practices are placed within ritual chains to help accomplish this. "Negative rites" involve restraint or abstention, such as a fast or vow of silence, as a way to make a person or object sacred. "Positive rites" involve activity, such as a holy meal or chant, to induce the sacred. Regarding negative rites, Durkheim writes:

> Man can enter into close relations with sacred things only if he strips himself of what is profane in him. He cannot live a religious life of any intensity unless he first withdraws more or less completely from secular life. The negative cult in a sense is a means to an end; it is the precondition of access to the positive cult. (1912 [1995], 313)

Negative rites are scheduled as temporal frames that intensify, through their refusal of earthly pleasures and all the EE they provide, the effervescence of super-sacred positive rites. Restraint heightens subsequent action, together forging the sacred. Across traditions, periods of sound deprivation enhance the emotional invigoration of louder effervescent occasions that follow.

We can observe this pattern among some Catholic ascetic orders whose members practice extreme silence in order to prepare themselves as purer vessels for worshipping God during Mass. As is broadly true across Christianity, this worship centrally involves *making music*, a "joyful noise" to the Lord (Psalm 95:1, 98:4, 100:1, King James). But some monastic traditions do understand themselves as having a more extreme and disciplined calling, which may involve very little human contact or speaking. It is not the goal of ascetic silence, or of the ensuing Mass for that matter, to boost EE; the practitioner's attention is to be directed to God, and their vocation of giving God glory (Lawrence 2001; Wittberg 2019). That it is conceived by some as a duty, though, does not rule out CE (Durkheim 1974). The chain reaction can but does not have to be the point.

Monastic life is often scheduled around alternating rituals of silence and sound over the course of a day or year (Benedict 1998; Sbardella 2014). In Catholic asceticism, wordless IRs throughout the day accentuate the sounds of vocal praise during Mass. The most intense rituals are collective and with God. Long-term planning of ritual chains intensifies collective rituals by framing them before and after with quiet and/or solitude.

- Monastic communities who normally practice quietude but occasionally hold louder collective IRs will frequently experience intense CE during their louder IRs.

Negative rites intensify positive rites. In religions around the world, periods of quiet restraint are followed by bursts of communal sound-making—within songs and sermons, during worship services, and scheduled over time as ritual chains.

But the negative cult, Durkheim cautions, can become all-consuming, so that the most extreme ascetic lifestyles may offer very little CE:

> The negative cult usually serves as barely more than an introduction to, and a preparation for, the positive cult. But it sometimes escapes that subordination and becomes central, the system of prohibitions swelling and aggrandizing itself to the point of invading the whole of life. In this way, systematic asceticism is born; it is thus nothing more than a bloating of the negative cult. (1912 [1995], 316)

Long-term silence and solitude can be practiced for many reasons in asceticism and mysticism, but most religions presume such practices to be emotionally arduous. The sounds the negative ritualist shuts out or withholds may be worldly, sinful, jarring, illusory, etc., but the extreme practice of silence is still understood as the narrowest of paths.

Stated more forcefully: extreme, long-term suppression of speech and emotional expression is a social death. Consistent with this, initiation into the dead silent office of anchorite in the Middle Ages involved a requiem Mass and burial ceremony before being shut up alone within their tomb-like cells (Sauer 2016). We crave togetherness, and need to be jolted out of solipsistic modes. Making loud sounds at and with each other, when enjoined in rhythm, focus, and passion, is a reliable way to get there, as exhibited by noisy kids in congregations everywhere.

NOTES

1. Collins (2004) thinks of shared mood and shared focus as tightly linked in experience, and mutually generative, so I hyphenate them here. I'll also refer below to the closely related concept of "intersubjectivity"—a sensation of interpersonal unity that is mental, emotional, and embodied.

2. The observations occurred during field work for Draper (2019, 2021).

3. I've given pseudonyms to all individuals and organizations from my field notes.

4. EE is the individual-level residue of CE. When a person departs an effervescent occasion, the feeling remains for a time, often expressed as embodied interpersonal confidence. EE's charge is conducive to status and power in social situations. Collins (2004) presents it as the sensation humans seek most in life.

5. Over 1.5 billion people worldwide experience hearing loss (World Health Organization 2023). How does this shape their involvement in IRs? Hearing ability does not guarantee that a person is attuned to the sounds around them (Squires and Kay-Raining Bird 2022). Many with some hearing loss would readily agree that loudness is important for CE, and many who are completely deaf still enjoy feeling sound's vibrations, for example from percussion or bass at loud concerts (Glennie 1990). Certainly, people who are deaf do not require conventionally defined loudness to experience CE, providing a key early reason why this chapter's guiding question must be answered negatively: other sense modalities can promote CE when sounds are unavailable. Sign language facilitates a subtype of "quiet" CE we need to consider.

6. Solo effervescence, although an individual-level experience, is distinguishable from EE. Solo effervescence refers to ecstasy produced during third-order solitary practices, whereas EE is the individual-level, longer-term effect of effervescent rituals more generally.

REFERENCES

Bakhtin, Mikhail. 1986. *Speech Genres and Other Late Essays.* Translated by Vern W. McGee. University of Texas Press.

Baumann, Dorothea. 2015. "Music and Space in the Renaissance." In *Compositions for Audible Space,* edited by Martha Brech and Ralph Paland. Transcript.

Benedict, Saint. *The Rule of St. Benedict.* 1998. Edited by Timothy Fry. Vintage.

Benzecry, Claudio and Randall Collins. 2014. "The High of Cultural Experience: Toward a Microsociology of Cultural Consumption." *Sociological Theory* 32, no. 4: 307–326.

Brown, Brandon M. 2021. "Worshipping Vicariously: Religious Gatherings during the COVID-19 Pandemic." Presented at the *Annual Meeting for the Society for the Scientific Study of Religion,* October 22, Portland, Oregon.

Cage, John. 1966. *Silence.* MIT Press.

Cerulo, Karen. 2009. "Nonhumans in Social Interaction." *Annual Review of Sociology* 35: 531–552.

Clayman, Stephen E. 1993. "Booing: The Anatomy of a Disaffiliative Response." *American Sociological Review* 58: 110–130.

Collins, Randall. 1986. *Weberian Sociological Theory.* Cambridge University Press.

Collins, Randall. 2004. *Interaction Ritual Chains.* Princeton University Press.

Collins, Randall. 2020. *Charisma: Micro-Sociology of Power and Influence.* Routledge.

Damasio, Antonio. 1994. *Descartes' Error.* Avon.

Dauenhauer, Bernard P. 1980. *Silence, the Phenomenon and Its Ontological Significance.* Indiana University Press.

Draper, Scott. 2019. *Religious Interaction Ritual: The Microsociology of the Spirit.* Lexington.

Draper, Scott. 2021. "Effervescence Accelerators: Barriers to Outsiders in Christian Interaction Rituals." *Sociology of Religion* 82, no. 3: 357–379.

Durkheim, Émile. 1974. "The Determination of Moral Facts." In *Sociology and Philosophy,* translated by D. F. Pocock. Free Press.

Durkheim, Émile. 1995. *The Elementary Forms of Religious Life.* Translated by Karen E. Fields. Free Press. Originally published in 1912 by F. Alcan.

Egermann, Hauke, Marcus T. Pearce, Geraint A. Wiggins, and Stephen McAdams. 2013. "Probabilistic Models of Expectation Violation Predict Psychophysiological Emotional Responses to Live Concert Music." *Cognitive, Affective, and Behavioral Neuroscience* 13, no. 3: 533–553.

Ehrenreich, Barbara. 2006. *Dancing in the Streets.* Henry Holt.

Elias, Norbert. 1978. *The Development of Manners.* Vol. 1 of *The Civilizing Process.* Translated by Edmund Jephcott. Urizen.

Fowler, Megan. 2020. "Turning Up the Volume: Joyful Noise or Noise Ordinance Violation?" *Christianity Today,* March 2. https://christianitytoday.com/news/2020/march/church-worship-too-loud-noise-ordinance-violation.html.

Froese, Paul. 2016. *On Purpose: How We Create the Meaning of Life.* Oxford.

Froese, Paul, and Rory Jones. 2021. "The Sociology of Prayer: Dimensions and Mechanisms." *Social Sciences* 10, no. 1: 1–18.

Garfinkel, Harold. 1967. *Studies in Ethnomethodology.* Prentice-Hall.

Glennie, Evelyn. 1990. *Good Vibrations: My Autobiography.* Hutchinson.
Goffman, Erving. 1959. *The Presentation of Self in Everyday Life.* Doubleday.
Goffman, Erving. 1967. *Interaction Ritual.* Doubleday.
Goffman, Erving. 1986. *Frame Analysis.* Harper & Row.
Gregory, Stanford W. 1983. "A Quantitative Analysis of Temporal Symmetry in Microsocial Relations." *American Sociological Review* 48, no. 1: 129–135.
Heider, Anne and R. Stephen Warner. 2010. "Bodies in Sync: Interaction Ritual Theory Applied to Sacred Harp Singing." *Sociology of Religion* 71, no. 1: 76–97.
Heinskou, Marie Bruvik and Lasse Suonperä Liebst. 2016. "On the Elementary Neural Forms of Micro-Interactional Rituals: Integrating Autonomic Nervous System Functioning into Interaction Ritual Theory." *Sociological Forum* 31, no. 2: 354–376.
Inbody, Joel. 2015. "Sensing God: Bodily Manifestations and Their Interpretation in Pentecostal Rituals and Everyday Life." *Sociology of Religion* 76, no. 3: 337–355.
James, William. 1961. *Varieties of Religious Experience.* Collier Macmillan. Originally published in 1902 by Longmans, Green, and Co.
Lawrence, C. H. 2001. *Medieval Monasticism.* Pearson.
Loeb, Laura. 2014. "Call and Response: An Anatomy of Religious Practice." *Discourse Studies* 16, no. 4: 514–533.
Luhrmann, Tanya. 2012. *When God Talks Back.* Alfred A. Knopf.
Mannes, Elena. 2011. *The Power of Music.* Walker.
Mariko Grant, Andrea. 2018. "Noise and Silence in Rwanda's Postgenocide Religious Soundscape." *Journal of Religion in Africa* 48:35–64.
Mead, George Herbert. 1934. *Mind, Self, and Society.* University of Chicago Press.
Nārada, Mahāthera. 1993. *A Comprehensive Manual of Abhidhamma.* Translated by Bhikku Bodhi. Buddhist Publication Society.
Pagis, Michal. 2010. "Producing Intersubjectivity in Silence: An Ethnography of Meditation Practices." *Ethnography* 11:309–328.
Parker, John N. and Edward J. Hackett. 2012. "Hot Spots and Hot Moments in Scientific Collaborations and Social Movements." *American Sociological Review* 77, no. 1: 21–44.
Plancke, Carine. 2014. "Affect, Creativity, and Community-Making in a Congolese Song-Dance Performance." *The Journal of the Royal Anthropological Institute* 20, no. 4: 653–669.
Rawls, Anne Warfield. 2004. *Epistemology and Practice.* Cambridge University Press.
Sacks, Harvey, Emanuel A. Schegloff, and Gail Jefferson. 1974. "A Simplest Systematics for the Organization of Turn-Taking for Conversation." *Language* 50, no. 4: 696–735.
Sauer, Michelle M. 2016. "Introduction: Anchoritism, Liminality, and the Boundaries of Vocational Withdrawal." *Journal of Medieval Religious Cultures* 42, no. 1: v–xii.
Sbardella, Francesca. 2014. "Ethnography of Cloistered Life: Field Work into Silence." *Annual Review of the Sociology of Religion* 5: 55–70.
Schütz, Alfred. 1951. "Making Music Together." *Social Research* 18, no. 1: 76–97.
Sim, Stuart. 2007. *Manifesto for Silence.* Edinburgh University Press.
Smith, Philip. 2020. *Durkheim and After.* Polity.
Squires, Bonita, and Elizabeth Kay-Raining Bird. 2022. "Self-Reported Listening Abilities in Educational Settings of Typically Hearing Children and Those Who Are Deaf/Hard-of-Hearing." *Communication Disorders Quarterly* 44, no. 2: 107–116.
Stark, Rodney. 2001. *One True God.* Princeton University Press.
Stivers, Tanya, N. J. Enfield, Penelope Brown, Christina Englert, Makota Hayashi, Trine Heinemann, Gertie Hoymann, Federico Rossano, Jan Peter de Ruiter, Hkung-Eun Yoon, Stephen C. Levinson, and Paul Kay. 2009. "Universals and Cultural Variation in Turn-

Taking in Conversation." *Proceedings of the National Academy of Sciences of the United States of America* 106, no. 26: 10587–10592.

Summers-Effler, Erika. 2004. "A Theory of the Self, Emotion, and Culture." In *Theory and Research on Human Emotions*, edited by Jonathan H. Turner. Emerald Group.

Summers-Effler, Erika. 2010. *Laughing Saints and Righteous Heroes.* University of Chicago Press.

Tallon, Andrew. 2016. "Acoustics at the Intersection of Architecture and Music." *Journal of the Society of Architectural Historians* 75, no. 3: 263–280.

Trungpa, Chogyam. 1973. *Cutting Through Spiritual Materialism.* Shambhala.

Tutenges, Sébastien. 2013. "Stirring Up Effervescence: An Ethnographic Study of Youth at a Nightlife Resort." *Leisure Studies* 32, no. 3: 233–248.

Tutenges, Sébastien. 2023. *Intoxication.* Rutgers.

Weber, Max. (1904) 2001. *The Protestant Ethic and the Spirit of Capitalism.* Translated by Stephen Kalberg. Fitzroy Dearborn.

Weber, Max. 1968. *The Sociology of Religion.* Translated by Guenther Roth and Klaus Wittich. Bedminster Press. Originally published in 1922 by J. C. B. Mohr (Paul Siebeck).

Wellman, James K., Jr., Katie E. Corcoran, and Kate J. Stockly. 2020. *High on God.* Oxford.

Wittberg, Patricia. 2019. "Author Meets Critics: Religious Interaction Ritual." Presented at the *Annual Meeting for the Society for the Scientific Study of Religion*, October 26, St. Louis, Missouri.

Wollschleger, Jason. 2017. "The Rite Way: Integrating Emotion and Rationality in Religious Participation." *Rationality and Society* 29, no. 2: 179–202.

World Health Organization. 2023. "Deafness and Hearing Loss." Accessed September 29, 2023. https://www.who.int/health-topics/hearing-loss#tab=tab_2.

6

Transformative Work

Individual Pursuits of Self-Improvement in Collective Ayahuasca Ceremonies

Margit Anne Petersen

In a remote, rural area of Denmark, where corn fields, wild forest, and the sea meet, ayahuasca ceremonies are taking place. A small community of people have dedicated their everyday life to organizing and facilitating these ceremonies on a regular basis, serving the psychoactive brew that has its origin in the Amazonian region of South America. This chapter is based on ethnographic fieldwork in and around such a community and focuses on both those who have built it, and regularly facilitate retreats, as well as those who come to attend them. The chapter focuses specifically on the contested boundaries between the individual and the collective in these ceremonies. Using the concept "collective effervescence" (Durkheim [1912] 1995), I explore how the ceremonial setting and collective experience of drinking ayahuasca gives shape to individual trajectories of self-discovery and healing. While people come to the ceremonies with personal understandings of and motivations for attending them, these individual trajectories nevertheless become intertwined with or are transformed into collective sentiments at both the experiential and epistemological level. In other words, it is through collective experiences and connections that individual pursuits are given meaning, form, and content. Following the recent work of Tutenges (2023), this chapter is an attempt to elaborate on and empirically flesh out the concept of psychedelic effervescence. Psychedelic effervescence is a particular subtype of effervescence during which individuals experience themselves, the world, and others in new, surprising ways and influence each other for example, but not exclusively, during consumption of hallucinogenic substances (Tutenges 2023, 8). By focusing on the ceremonial setting and how it is organized and curated, as well as participants' intentions with and experiences of taking part in ceremonies, I suggest that psychedelic effervescence plays an important role in participants' and facilitators' lives by providing a way to look at themselves and their lives from the outside. Psychedelic effervescence forces people to realize that what they perceive as individual problems of the self are in fact deeply collective matters that cannot and should not be dealt with alone.

Drug Use for Self-Improvement Purposes and the Psychedelic Renaissance

As of the early 2000s, there has been an increasing interest within the social sciences to study the use of substances beyond recreational settings and purposes. Such "functional drug use" (Bancroft 2009) concerns, for example, the use of prescription pharmaceuticals to increase study skills and motivation (Petersen, M.A., Nørgaard, L. S., and Traulsen, J. M. 2015, Petersen, M.A., Lyngsø-Dahl, L., and Nørgaard L. S., 2019), enhance sexual abilities (Moyle et al. 2020), or improve moods, creativity, and well-being through psychedelics in small or large doses (Johnstad 2018; Lea et al. 2020; Petersen et al. 2022). What these studies have in common is a focus on the individual's quest for improving everyday life and personal abilities. Much of this work has pointed to the blurred boundaries between enhancement and treatment, and what constitutes a "drug" as opposed to a "medicine." The psychedelic renaissance—the renewed interest in psychedelics as a potential medicine—is an example of how such categories shift. With an increasing number of clinical studies showing promising results for treating alcohol and drug use disorders, depression, PTSD, and several other psychological and psychiatric conditions (Ducharme 2023; Belouin et al. 2022, Bird et al. 2021; Yaden et al. 2021; Nutt 2019; Carhart-Harris & Goodwin 2017), substances such as psilocybin, LSD, and MDMA (i.e., Ecstasy)[1] are slowly gaining a new position in some parts of the world (Petersen et al. 2024). In most countries, these substances are illegal, and underground practices including these and related substances are not commonly accepted. Psilocybin has recently been legalized in some U.S. states, and in Australia, MDMA and psilocybin has been approved as a form of psychiatric treatment (Siegel et al. 2023; Zagorski 2023). In many countries, however, the use of naturally occurring psychedelic substances (i.e., plants, mushrooms, plant brews such as ayahuasca) for medicinal and spiritual purposes has existed for years and is still today practiced legally, as they are recognized as part of Indigenous culture. In this chapter, the focus is exclusively on ayahuasca and the setting in which it is consumed. Ayahuasca is typically made from the bark and stems of the Banisteriopsis caapi, a vine from the Amazon jungle, soaked and boiled together with other plants, often with leaves from another Amazonian plant Psychotria viridis (McKenna 2004). These two plants are a necessary mix, as the Banisteriopsis caapi vine contains harmala alkaloids, also known as MAO inhibitors, while the Psychotria viridis leaves contain the hallucinogen DMT (Tupper 2008). Without MAO inhibitors, DMT, which is consumed orally, does not give any effect, as it is metabolized before reaching the brain (McKenna 2004; Tupper 2008; Callaway et al. 1999). Ayahuasca translates to "vine of the soul" and has a long history of medicinal, spiritual, and religious use among various Indigenous groups in Brazil, Peru, and several other countries in the Amazonian region (Labate et al. 2017). Researchers have documented a growing interest among people in the Global North for what is often termed "ayahuasca tourism" (Winkelman 2005; Prayag et al. 2015), referring to the steady stream of visitors to the Amazon to take part in ceremonies and retreats. Others describe the expanding notions and uses of ayahuasca around the world through concepts such as the "globalization of ayahuasca" (Tupper 2008; Fotiou 2016) and the "ayahuasca diaspora" (Labate et al. 2017).

Researching Ayahuasca Ceremonies and Collective Effervescence

How does one study phenomena such as ayahuasca ceremonies and collective effervescence? The methodological approach that I have used is inspired by phenomenologically informed fieldwork in nightlife settings (Tutenges 2022; O'Grady 2013). While there are substantial differences between nightclubs or music festivals and the ayahausca ceremonies and retreat center that make up this study's field, there are some important similarities concerning methodological and ethical considerations that make such an approach suitable. The ethnographic fieldwork was conducted in Denmark between 2018 and 2023 and consisted of a mixture of participant observation, interviews, and informal conversations. Gaining access to the field was an ongoing process of negotiation that required several steps. Since ayahuasca ceremonies are somewhat hidden from the general public, people and places were first located through online Danish communities where psychedelic substances are discussed (Petersen et al. 2024). With permission from group administrators, I used discussion forums to learn about the use of psychedelics by reading discussion threads. I eventually posted a request to meet and interview people who had been to at least one ayahuasca retreat in Denmark. While it can sometimes be difficult to reach populations who engage in illegal or morally contested activities such as drug use (Petersen et al. 2019), it was not the case with this study. Within the first hour, I already had more than ten people interested in making an appointment. In total, I conducted twenty semistructured interviews with individuals who had participated in ayahuasca retreats in Denmark. Most of them had participated in multiple ceremonies but there were some who had only little experience. Some of the more experienced participants had also been to ceremonies at other retreat centers in Denmark, and some even had international experience with ayahuasca. Additionally, I conducted ten interviews with facilitators and helpers and observed participants during retreats, informal gatherings, and integration circles (i.e., monthly meetings where individuals meet to share and discuss their psychedelic experiences). Whereas participants were generally eager to tell me about their experiences without having met me before, being allowed to observe participants at retreats and other gatherings and setting up interviews with facilitators, took time and was only established through several informal meetings as well as recommendations from those who had trusted relations with Adam,[2] the founder of the retreat center. Besides wanting to know about my motives for studying ayahuasca, Adam and his cofacilitators' concerns were also related to my presence and its influence, especially during ceremonies. We agreed that I should explicitly say that I was there to study ayahuasca ceremonies. But he also asked me to have an intention with being there, an intention that was personal and not related to my academic interest. He also asked me to participate in and help during some of the activities at the retreats and to share some personal thoughts and experiences with others when I felt it was appropriate. Taking such an embodied approach seemed the only way to study these retreats without interrupting or altering the ceremonies and other activities related to them (O'Grady 2013; Tutenges 2022). This sympathetic position can be understood as a middle ground between full immersion and observational distance, using the classic ethnographic "double gaze" that allows for the engagement and flow of emotions of others and oneself (Tutenges 2022; Bøhling 2014; O'Grady 2013) while still having an explicit purpose and role as ethnographer. Taking part in emotional flows and connections can also be considered an example of relational ethics in which the interpersonal ties and responsibilities between researchers and the people they study become less asymmetrical and more cocreative (Denshire 2014). In this way, the ethnographic process of studying and coming to understand ayahuasca drinking and collective effervescence mirrors what participants in ceremonies do and experience with each other.

The Ceremonial Setting

The ceremony is about to begin. Twelve participants have entered the spacious tepee and are asked to take a seat on each of the mattresses surrounding the fireplace in the middle. The two facilitators are organizing their props and tools near the entrance of the tepee—placing a small carpet with a wooden bowl and some ornaments, a few papers, musical instruments, and two bottles containing the plant medicine about to be consumed. Five assistants are also present. One is setting up with a guitar and a blanket. Another is adding wood to the fire in the middle, pushing the logs into the flames with a long stick. The participants are quietly getting comfortable, taking off shoes and tucking them away behind the their mattress, pulling the blanket over their legs, and placing the distributed buckets, toilet paper rolls, and water bottles on the side, easily accessible for later. A young guy signals to an assistant to come over and whispers a quick question but otherwise there is more or less silence, except for the crackling sounds of burning wood and the quiet flickering of flames as they dance between the logs in the center of the tepee. One of the assistants pulls the entrance closed and participants direct their attention toward the facilitator team as they anticipate the awaited ceremony.

As scholars have long pointed out, the setting in which drug use takes place plays an important role beyond the pharmacological effects of the substance. Norman Zinberg's famous concepts "drug," "set," and "setting" have been applied to psychedelics, both as an analytical tool to understand such drug practices but also by users themselves as well as facilitators of underground psychedelic ceremonies and by researchers in clinical studies as a way of ensuring safety and best possible effects (Kozak and Miller 2024; Noorani 2021). "Set" refers to the state of mind and sometimes intention with which one engages in the drug use, and "setting" describes the contextual aspects such as the physical surroundings, the people, the time, and location (Zinberg 1984). The ceremonial setting described here is created to be as traditional as possible, according to Adam. He says that of the places that he knows of that offer such ceremonies in Denmark, his is closer to how it is practiced in the jungle, where he has received his training and where he learned the Ikaros songs that form an important frame around the ceremonies. He describes other ceremonies in a Danish context as more "general psychedelic" involving large screens with visuals and lights and various psychedelic substances, or ceremonies based more on "tantric traditions" and body therapy. Adam used to facilitate ceremonies in a small, urban apartment. But as the interest grew beyond his circle of friends and he experienced a need to be in a more secluded place, closer to nature and away from people who did not sympathize with his practices and lifestyle, he and his cofacilitators moved to the countryside. He says:

> We got tired of it. Our neighbors got tired of it. The apartment was constantly trashed. For a little while we got a space in an office building, but we couldn't stand the concrete surroundings. And then, after

> some time, we realized that we needed to quit our jobs and move out of the city.

Moving the ceremonies away from the gaze of "outsiders" made it possible for Adam and his group of cofacilitators and assistants to build a small community where people can stay for extended periods of time and contribute with various kinds of work. Several participants talk about how coming to the retreat center feels particularly safe and comfortable because it is far away from their everyday life and because there is a community feeling, a tendency that has also been noted in other research (Dunell 2024). But as Merika, a participant and sometimes a helper at the retreat center, suggests, it also creates a contrast in her life:

> It is so nice for me to go there and be with like-minded people. There is always someone who knows how to listen and understand. But I also feel that the gap is widening because there is my soul family at the retreat center, and then there are normal people . . . so it sometimes makes it more difficult.

The ornaments, the tepee in the forest, the musical instruments, and particularly the Ikaros songs, are all powerful symbols that Adam and his group have built their ceremonies around. They learned to sing the Ikaros songs in the Amazon, and some of the ornaments and the little wooden cup from which everyone drinks the ayahuasca from were brought back from the jungle. The plants that the brew is made from are sent from the jungle, where Adam learned to cook it. In many ways, these symbols and the wider drug setting represent a traditional view of ayahuasca as a medicine, *la medicina*, exactly as it is sung in many of the songs. The setting thereby contributes to presenting ayahausca ceremonies as legitimate and connected to Indigenous cultures and practices rather than as illicit drug consumption, which some people, and certainly the law, would in a Danish or European context (Dunell 2024; Fotiou 2020). Merika describes how she, at first, was scared because she thought of it as a drug, but that she has since learned to think differently about it:

> At first, I also thought that it was a drug, you know, but now, if people talk about it being illegal, and question why I do it, I actually don't understand them. Because . . . it's just medicine.

The understanding of ayahuasca thus changes through involvement in the community of ayahuasca users. The community has its preferred definitions and narratives about the substance, and these significantly influence the community members' understandings of it and possibly also the way it makes them feel and behave (Tutenges and Sandberg 2013). Besides conveying the emphasis on Indigenous medicinal and spiritual practices through the setting, the gathering of participants together for a weekend or longer and getting people out of their everyday routines "*away from the rat race*" as Adam puts it, is a central feature of the ceremonial setting. The shortest retreats are over the weekend, with two ayahausca ceremonies in the evenings, and walks, yoga, sharing circles, and relaxing time during the day. But Adam often talks about how the longer retreats give people more time and depth, that many people are too busy to spend time helping themselves, and that is why the short weekend retreats appeal to so many. But the most important thing to him is that people come. And they seem to do so. His retreats are booked long in advance, and he has facilitated events for thousands of people already.

> The most beautiful thing about this is that twelve people who don't know each other, really are there for each other. They are open, they dare to show their vulnerability, and they don't judge each other the way people normally do. I think of it a little like going to a sauna. People don't ask each other what they do for work. I really notice this. In a way everyone is naked.

The emphasis on how people are in this ceremonial setting together is of particular interest in this chapter. In his work on intoxication and collective effervescence, Tutenges (2023) investigates the altered state of heightened intersubjectivity that takes place among people when gathered in the same place. For collective effervescence to unfold, Tutenges suggests that certain conditions need to be in place: being part of a community, intense emotions and transgressive urges that carry people away from everyday life, the use or identification of symbols, and a sense of purpose and solidarity (Tutenges 2023, 6). All of these components are present in the observed ayahausca ceremonies. But while collective effervescence is primarily conceptualized through communal and emotional bonds along with transgressive activities, Adam describes the necessity of a physical structure that contains the collective energy that arises during ceremonies:

> There has to be a roof. And some sort of construction, because otherwise . . . the energy kind of disappears, if there isn't something to contain it. I have tried to do ceremonies outdoors, and it doesn't really work.

In the tepee, Terese, Adam's cofacilitator, asks everyone to think strongly of their intention for being there. Her voice is calm but serious as she goes on to say, "*Today we are going to go deep, do deep work, each one of us.*" Adam pours a serving of the brew into the wooden cup and nods to the first participant on his left. He gets up from the mattress and kneels in front of Adam. The cup is handed to him, and he drinks it all in one go as the rest of the participants watch. Adam says a few ritual words and then signals to the guy to go back to his mattress. The cup is washed, and a new serving is poured. The next participant is asked to come forth. When all participants have been served a cup, the assistant with the guitar begins to play as Adam and Terese sing the first Ikaros song of the ceremony.

Seeking Personal Change

"Transformative work" is an emic and very present term in and around the community. The initial contact between facilitator and participant is very much focused on the purpose of drinking ayahuasca, and retreats are framed as "transformative work" in both their written and oral descriptions. Ayahuasca is represented as a medicine this helps facilitate the transformative work. This points to the importance of understanding not only what goes on during the ceremonies per se; one must also consider the preexisting cultural codes, symbols, and narratives that shape the way ayahuasca is experienced and made sense of (Fotiou 2020; Smith 2019). Before each ceremony, people sit in a circle and are asked to say something about their intentions to the group. Not surprisingly, most people come to such retreats because there is something they want to work on in relation to themselves and their lives. Some are grappling with depression, anxiety, grief, addiction, and other conditions that make their everyday lives difficult in various ways. Some talk about coming to work on their egos; that their egos are too big and get in the way of them being good people. Others are confused and unsure of themselves and seek clarity and guidance. A few are there to explore the hidden potential in their selves and lives—and talk about ayahuasca less as a plant medicine and more as a spiritual guide or event. No matter the motivation, participants describe their engagement as some sort of quest for personal change. Alice, a young woman in her twenties, describes her intentions with ayahausca as a way to deal with depressive moods and anxiety in everyday life:

> When I first went there it was because I felt it was such a tough life. I felt so much resistance and I just wanted to feel better. So, I think my main intention has been to be happier and find the courage to live life. Not be so afraid of the future and new things.

Alice has never sought help from health-care practitioners, as is the case with many other participants, also in psychedelic communities more generally (Petersen et al. 2024). Many have a basic mistrust in the official health-care system and believe that psychedelics offer a more holistic and in-depth approach to solving their difficult feelings and mental challenges (Petersen et al. 2024; Petersen et al. 2022).

Jacob, a man in his forties describes his intentions with ayahuasca as a way to get out of his heavy alcohol consumption:

> I kind of was aware that I had an addiction. With my alcohol. And I was kind of ready to give up drinking, you know, if I wanted to live many more years, it was kind of that bad. I have managed though, kept my job, did my things and so on. But one day my brother showed up—and he was really into yoga and such things—and in my opinion yoga is the slow way—ayahuasca is the shortcut—but they are related. Definitely. And he had heard someone in the changing room at his yoga studio talk about these ceremonies, and he got their contact details, and then we went.

After the ceremony, Jacob lost all interest in alcohol and went from drinking a bottle of liquor a day to not drinking at all, even six months after the first ceremony, when I met him again. Jacob was far from the only one coming to ayahuasca retreats with intentions to resolve addictive or problematic alcohol and drug consumption. It is also a field of interest in clinical studies, in Denmark and in the United States, where psychedelic substances are tested on people with alcohol consumption disorder (Pagni and Bogenschutz 2024). Several members of the online Danish psychedelic communities follow such studies and sometimes experiment on their own (Holm et al. 2023).

Some participants have a more open and curious intention such as whether life could be different or whether they could unlock new sides of themselves. Mette, a woman in her thirties, explains:

> I have never really used drugs or been troubled in my youth. So, it is actually not until I was quite settled, after finishing my education, and having full-time work and settling down with my boyfriend, that it started to appear in my thoughts and awaken a sort of curiosity.

Wanting to explore other aspects of the self and everyday life is a common theme among users of psychedelics in general (Holm et al. 2023; Amada et al. 2020), and although most of the participants at Adam's retreat center have intentions of treating mental health conditions, a few do have less specific or health-oriented intentions. Regardless of what their intentions are about, at a first glance they seem mainly individually focused in the sense that they are about improving some aspect of their own abilities or feelings.

Ceremony participants are working on different issues in their individual lives and often don't know or see each other outside a retreat. But as Jonathan, a participant in his thirties, explains, even though everyone works on "*their own thing*," they are doing it together.

> I think when you "travel" together, you reach a point where you start to communicate beyond language and bodies, you meet at a different level, and you support each other's journeys. Sometimes this happens by someone taking over someone else's pain. And I also think it makes us see that at some level, we are all the same, it is a way of practicing compassion, simply just being in pain together because that is part of being human.

These processes of working on the self might be understood as efforts to overcome vulnerability (Petersen et al. 2024, 2022). The Dutch philosopher Mark Coeckelbergh has in his book *Human Being @risk* described vulnerability as a basic human condition, not only when something is wrong, but as an always present aspect of human life (2013). Using Coeckelbergh's focus on "technologies of vulnerability," strategies and actions directed toward reducing or changing feelings of vulnerability makes it possible to understand enhancement and treatment not only as similar efforts instead of opposites (Petersen et al. 2022) but also as efforts that are not only self-focused but also contain a more collective and unifying aspect. Adam reflects on how important the presence of other people is for the process of self-change:

> Most people think about what they themselves are going to get out of drinking this, but they often don't think about how the other people matter. Everyone is in their little bubble. But it may very well be that what happens in the ceremony is influenced by others. Everyone comes here because they want to change something. Rarely just because they are curious. Most people have tried other things that didn't work. Some have just heard about it. But they all want a change in life. And it is very intense. Many describe this strong bond with each other afterward, even if they don't see each other outside the retreat.

Perhaps it is precisely because participants are in a structurally similar position that they develop strong bonds with each other. They have all left their everyday lives for a few days. They are gathered to participate in something most people don't understand or know about. And they all hear about and acknowledge each other's deeply felt intentions with being there. All of this opens up for mutual attunement and the experience of collective effervescence (Collins 2004; Tutenges 2023).

Individual Pursuits through Collective Sentiments

Jonathan came to the ayahuasca ceremony with the intention of figuring out what to do with his long-term relationship, which, according to him, was in such a difficult state, that he was in doubt about whether to terminate it or not. He was hoping that drinking ayahuasca would bring him clarity and guidance on which decision to make. At some point in the ceremony, he feels ill and very uncomfortable. He doesn't say anything, but he is physically struggling on his mattress. One of the assistants in the tepee notices, and goes to sit beside him as a silent way to offer her help. He reaches out for her and says he is not feeling well. She tells him he will feel better if he pukes and hands him the bucket next to his mattress. He tries but is unable to. Nothing comes out. But he is nauseous, and his stomach is turning. He is sweating and in pain. Some time goes by, and his nausea is still strong. It seems he is unable to move on or resolve the situation. The assistant finally gets up, whispers that she thinks she knows what to do, and slowly moves toward the exit of the tepee. She goes outside and starts to puke. As she is puking outside the tepee, his stomach slowly eases inside the tepee. His nausea is gone and after a few minutes of relief, he lies down again on the mattress, continuing onward with his ceremonial journey. The assistant comes back in and sits next to Jonathan again. She watches him relaxed and out of pain, and asks, *Did that help?*

Such interactions suggest an emotional connection as Collins describes in rituals where high levels of collective effervescence are generated (2004). The ceremonial setting, the ayahuasca drinking, and the shared space and experience live up to the components for a successful ritual (Collins 2004; Tutenges 2023, 2022). However, the interaction and effervescence between Jonathan and the assistant was not something everyone in the tepee noticed or was part of. There were multiple interactions, connections, and experiences going on at the same time, and even though all those present in the ceremony shared the same experience at some level, there were many variations in the particular interactions and emotional connections, echoing Tutenges's focus on collective effervescence as a processual, multifaceted, and ambiguous condition that affects participants differently (Tutenges 2023, 13) For example, while Jonathan was unable to puke, Alice was struggling with the "*heavy atmosphere*" in the tepee and needed to move her mattress outside. She was crying, sometimes loudly, sometimes more quietly, and had two assistants lie next to her, comforting her much of the time. In a conversation the day after the ceremony, she describes why she had to move outside, and how much people and the surroundings in general influence her, even in everyday life, but especially emphasized during an ayahuasca ceremony:

> I was in a mental space where I almost saw all the worries of the world and how some people take in all these worries. You know, take in the energies . . . I do that often. And then I can't get rid of them again. That's one of the reasons I drink ayahuacsa because that is how I get out of this again. When I was lying on the mattress under the trees, I felt that all these energies were swarming around me. The trees were healing me, but they were also showing me all their worries.

Alice often talks about connecting with nature and especially animals, and that ayahuasca helps her reach this goal, not just during ceremonies but also sometimes afterward in everyday life, as if the abilities and sensitivities stay with her for a prolonged period.

> I think we are very closed off. Closed in our brains and closed in our hearts and other places so that we are not using the full potential. When I drink ayahuasca I always have the intention of speaking with animals, and after a ceremony I feel that my abilities to do this are stronger. When an animal looks at me, I feel a thirst, or a hunger or some need. As if it is their need I feel. And I am able to communicate with them. I once had an experience with an ant on my mattress. I tell it that I feel like killing it because it is on my mattress. And then suddenly it turns around and walks off the mattress. The mattress next to mine has several ants on it, but mine has none. And then I start to have a conversation with the grass next to me, and I remember thinking that this grass is so brainy, so intelligent, it knows so many things.

During ceremonies there are often a couple of dogs present in the tepee, and several participants talk about how the dogs provide comfort and seem to know when their close physical presence is needed. From that perspective, the dogs move around just like the assistants and sometimes sit or lie next to people in the tepee. Connecting with animals is a common topic among participants, but it doesn't always happen in the ways they intended or imagined it, as Jonathan explains:

> I became a cow that was going to be slaughtered. And I was watching this happen and at the same time felt the meat that I was or had, and what it felt like . . . the fear and anxiety of running through the corridors before it happened. And then I felt what it was like to eat such meat, how my body would spend so much energy and time digesting it. I was then told that I had a choice. In a way it showed me that my soul is not worth more than an animal's soul.

After this experience, Jonathan became a vegetarian. And he is not the only one. Many participants talk about changes they have made to their lifestyle and eating habits. But sometimes bigger changes also occur. For example, Mark, a lumberjack described how he met the souls of the trees during a ceremony, and afterward he was unable to cut down trees, changed his career, and became a nature guide. Several of these examples suggest that the psychedelic effervescence lasts or has effects beyond the duration of the ceremony. Collins (2004) has pointed out that high levels of collective effervescence may in several ways influence participants for a long time even though the actual heightened intersubjectivity only takes place while participants are together in the ritual. In ayahuasca retreats, the collective effervescence may shift from higher to lower levels, depending on whether it is during a ceremony or between ceremonies as well as how much ayahuasca has been consumed. And because participants are together for a whole weekend or longer, and not just during a single ceremony, the different periods of collective effervescence may build upon or influence each other across time. Thus, it can be difficult to separate between collective effervescence and its effects.

When I ask participants how they make sense of the inexplicable or mystical interactions and connections that take place during ayahuasca ceremonies, they tell me about the spirit of Aya—the spirit that they believe is connected to or part of the ayahuasca brew. It is a common point of view to say that ayahuasca is intelligent and knows what people need. Adam thinks back to his first ayahuasca experience, where he believes the spirit gave him what he had no idea he needed, and made him promise to spend his life facilitating ceremonies and helping others:

> At first, I see all kinds of patterns and images. And I start to laugh. My friend gets nervous because he thinks maybe it doesn't work for me. But then suddenly it explodes. I ruin the entire ceremony. The others have to leave because I am walking around and they cannot hold me down. I walk around and throw up all over the place. I don't use the bucket. I see snakes and demons coming out of my body. Evil stuff is coming out of me. I am shown all the pain I have caused other people, especially my mom, and several girlfriends. At some point I leave my body, and I am given a choice: Do you want to go back to your body, or do you want to stop breathing and stay here? And then my experience is that I stop breathing. And the shamans experience is the same. He sees a change in me and moves very close, singing his Ikaros right in my face. He sings and sings and communicates with me through the song, suggesting that I come back. He doesn't want me to do this, that he will get in trouble, and I remember thinking that

> normally I don't care about other people's problems but this time I do. I enter my body again and wake up. The ceremony is over, and I tell him that I am really, really sorry that I have been such an idiot in life.

It seems that what the examples in this study have in common is the way in which the heightened intersubjectivity plays a role in giving ceremony participants insights at a collective rather than only at an individual level. It is through the emotional connections in and between the ceremonies that participants become aware and learn about themselves. Adam realizes that he has made all the wrong choices and hurt a lot of people and indirectly himself. Alice becomes aware that she carries all the worries and heavy energies of people and surroundings on her shoulders and that it wears her down. Jonathan wants to solve his relationship problems but is unable to deal with his uncomfortable feelings and situation and realizes that he cannot decide what to do until he is able to see how he is influencing the relationship. None of these people were able to feel it or realize it on their own.

Psychedelic Effervescence and Embodied Knowledge

The collective effervescence that arises in relation to ayahuasca retreats is strongest during the actual ceremonies where ritualistic elements and consumption of the ayahuasca brew take place. This is where everyone is in the same space and focused on the overall same thing, namely, participating in the ceremony and engaging with their individual situations through collective experiences. The ceremonies are what most resemble other arenas in which collective effervescence plays out such as festivals and nightlife (Tutenges 2023), religious rituals (see Draper's chapter in this book), political uprisings and revolutions (see Wagoner and Awad in this book), or sports activities (Corte 2022). But there are some notable differences that are worth taking a closer look at. It has been suggested that psychedelic effervescence is a qualitatively different form of effervescence than, for example, drunken effervescence (Tutenges 2023). Both involve intoxication typically from a substance, as well as strong emotional connections between people who are gathered in close proximity. But it seems that psychedelic effervescence also brings into play the crafting of relationships between human and nonhuman actors in ways that drunken or other forms of effervescence do not. Humans and animals, plants, substances, or spirits meet and connect during these effervescent moments, however short-lived or prolonged they may be. Many of the encounters and interactions that take place during psychedelic effervescence go beyond what is normally expected of emotional bonds and connections, even when they take place between only human beings. They are difficult to conceptualize or understand, even describe. But they manifest themselves in a very corporeal and intense way that transform the person's understanding and view of him or herself and aspects of the world. Transformative experiences are, according to the philosopher L. A. Paul (2014), radically new experiences that significantly change our personal preferences by teaching us things that we can only know from the experience itself and not from any other source. In a way it seems that the psychedelic effervescence that is produced during ayahausca ceremonies functions as an embodied learning process in which insights and understandings about the self and others become clear. Part of what makes these insights and understandings so strong and lasting might have to do with their embodied character, where boundaries between self and other or mind and body become blurred or impossible to uphold (Csordas 1994). Even the ethnographic process of learning about what goes on during an ayahuasca ceremony follows this logic, as an excerpt of my field notes bear witness to, written the morning after the second ceremony in a weekend retreat:

> My bones were in pain. I was hurting and I had no idea why. It felt like growing pains but in all the bones in my body at once. I was lying on the mattress restlessly and couldn't get comfortable. And I felt clueless about what was going on. But then suddenly I knew. From one moment to the next clarity arose. I was told, not by a voice or a person, but I was somehow told that I wanted to know what people worked on, when they drank ayahuasca. That the pain in my bones was the total sum of all the pain in the tepee, the pain that everyone was working through in this particular ceremony.

Through psychedelic effervescence, we as humans come to experience that our individuality at some level is an illusion and that while our bodies are held individually accountable for the situations we find ourselves in and the lives we live, we need to connect with others, humans and other types of beings, in order to understand and improve who we are and how we are in the world. Christopher, a participant and therapist in the ayahuasca community explains it like this:

> It is very beautiful. It is not that you always understand what goes on in there, but you feel it in your body and can use your body as a tuning fork to understand and cocreate these processes. It is all about understanding how to tune into the place where everyone connects and vibrate together. That way we can raise collective energy. And that way the sum of everyone present is larger than each individual

altogether. We are each other's medicine. And when we dare tune into the bigger community, something happens.

I think Christopher's words sum up quite precisely how and why psychedelic effervescence works and how it contributes to not only creating meaning in individual lives, but also providing an alternative to the, sometimes, alienating experience of contemporary living.

NOTES

1. MDMA is not a psychedelic drug but often figures in research related to the psychedelic renaissance as it is often used in similar ways
2. Adam, and all other names or places in this chapter, are fictional for anonymity purposes.

REFERENCES

Amada, N., Lea, T., Letheby, C., and Shane, J. (2020). "Psychedelic Experience and the Narrative Self: An Exploratory Qualitative Study." *Journal of Consciousness Studies* 27, nos. 9–10: 6–33.

Bancroft, A. (2009) *Drugs, Intoxication and Society.* Polity.

Belouin, S. J., Averill, L. A., Henningfield, J. E., Xenakis, S. N., Donato, I., Grob, C. S., Berger, A., Magar, V., Danforth, A. L., and Anderson, B. T. (2022). "Policy Considerations That Support Equitable Access to Responsible, Accountable, Safe, and Ethical Uses of Psychedelic Medicines." *Neuropharmacology* 219:109214. https://doi.org/10.1016/j.neuropharm.2022.109214.

Bird, C. I. V., Modlin, N. L., and Rucker, J. H. (2021). "Psilocybin and MDMA for the Treatment of Trauma-Related Psychopathology." *International Review of Psychiatry* 33, no. 3: 229–249. https://doi.org/10.1080/09540261.2021.1919062.

Bøhling, F. (2014) "Crowded Contexts: On the Affective Dynamics of Alcohol and Other Drug Use in Nightlife Spaces." *Contemporary Drug Problems* 41, no. 3: 361–392.

Callaway, J. C., McKenna, D. J.,. Grob, C. S., Brito, G. W., Raymon, L. P., Poland, R. E., Andrade, E. N., Andrade, E. O., and Mash, D. C. (1999). "Pharmacokinetics of Hoasca Alkaloids in Healthy Humans." *Journal of Ethnopharmacology* 65, no. 3.

Carhart-Harris, R. L., and Goodwin, G. M. (2017). "The Therapeutic Potential of Psychedelics Drugs: Past, Present and Future." *Neuropsychopharmacology* 42, no. 11: 2105–2113. https://doi.org/10.1038/npp.2017.84.

Coeckelbergh, M. (2013). *Human Being @ Risk. Enhancement, Technology and the Evaluation of Vulnerability Transformations.* Springer Netherlands.

Collins, R. (2004). *Interaction Ritual Chains.* Princeton University Press.

Corte, U. (2022). *Dangerous Fun: The Social Lives of Big Wave Surfers.* University of Chicago Press.

Csordas, T. J. (1994). *Embodiment and Experience: The existential Ground of Culture and Self.* Cambridge University Press.

Denshire, S. (2014). On Auto-Ethnography. *Current Sociology* 62, no. 6: 831–850. https://doi.org/10.1177/0011392114533339.

Ducharme, J. (2023). "Psychedelics May Be Part of U.S. Medicine Sooner Than You Think." *Time Magazine*, February 8, https://time.com/6253702/psychedelics-psilocybin-mdma-legalization/.

Dunell, J. (2024). "A Psilocybin Haven: The Use of Comparison to Legitimate Transgression at a Psychedelic Retreat." *Drugs: Education, Prevention and Policy*, 1–9. https://doi.org/10.1080/09687637.2024.2412636.

Durkheim, E. (1995). *The Elementary Forms of Religious Life.* Free Press. Originally published in 1912 by F. Alcan.

Fotiou, E. (2016). "The Globalization of Ayahuasca Shamanism and the Erasure of Indigenous Shamanism." *Anthropology of Consciousness* 27, no. 2: 151–179.

Fotiou, E. (2020). "The Importance of Ritual Discourse in Framing Ayahuasca Experiences in the Context of Shamanic Tourism." *Anthropology of Consciousness* 31, no. 2: 223–244.

Holm, S., Petersen, M.A., Enghoff, O., and Hesse, M. (2023). "Psychedelic Discourses: A Qualitative Study of Discussions in a Danish Online Forum." *International Journal of Drug Policy* 112 (103945): ISSN 0955-3959.

Johnstad P. G. (2018). "Powerful Substances in Tiny Amounts: An Interview Study of Psychedelic Microdosing." *Nordic Studies on Alcohol and Drugs* 35, no. 1: 39–51. https://doi.org/10.1177/1455072517753339.

Kozak, Z., and Miller, C. W. T. (2024). "Beyond Psychedelics: Set and Setting in General Psychiatric Practice." *International Review of Psychiatry* 36, no. 8: 833–840. https://doi.org/10.1080/09540261.2024.2419662.

Labate, B. C., Cavnar, C., and Gearin, A. (2017). "Introduction: The Shifting Journey of Ayahuasca in Diaspora." In *The World Ayahuasca Diaspora: Reinventions and Controversies*, edited by B. C. Labate, C. C. Cavnar, and A. Gearin. Routledge.

Lea, T., Amada, N., Jungaberle, H., Schecke, H., and Klein, M. (2020). "Microdosing Psychedelics: Motivations, Subjective Effects and Harm Reduction." *International Journal of Drug Policy* 75:102600. https://doi.org/10.1016/j.drugpo.2019.11.008.

McKenna, D. J. (2004). "Clinical Investigations of the Therapeutic Potential of Ayahuasca: Rationale and Regulatory Challenges." *Pharmacology & Therapeutics* 102, no. 2: 111–129.

Moyle, L., Dymock, A., Aldridge, A., and Mechen, B. (2020). "Pharmacosex: Reimagining Sex, Drugs and Enhancement." *International Journal of Drug Policy* 86 (102943): 102943. https://doi.org/10.1016/j.drugpo.2020.102943.

Noorani, T. (2021). "Containment Matters: Set and Setting in Contemporary Psychedelic Psychiatry." *Philosophy, Psychiatry, & Psychology* 28, no. 3: 201–216. https://dx.doi.org/10.1353/ppp.2021.0032.

Nutt, D. (2019). "Psychedelic Drugs—A New Era in Psychiatry?" *Dialogues in Clinical Neuroscience* 21, no. 2: 139–147. https://doi.org/10.31887/DCNS.2019.21.2/dnutt.

O'Grady, A. (2013). "Interrupting Flow: Researching Play, Performance and Immersion in Festival Scenes." *Dancecult: Journal of Electronic Dance Music Culture* 5, no. 1: 18–38.

Pagni, B. A., Wong, J., and Bogenschutz, M. P. (2024). "The Therapeutic Effects of Classic Psychedelics in Alcohol Use Disorder." *Current Addiction Reports* 11: 916–927. https://doi.org/10.1007/s40429-024-00581-z.

Paul, L. A. (2014). *Transformative Experience.* Oxford University Press.

Petersen, M. A., Enghoff, O., and Demant, J. (2019). "The Uncertainties of Enhancement: A Mixed-Methods Study on the Use of Substances for Cognitive Enhancement and it's Unintended Consequences." *Performance Enhancement & Health* 6 nos. 3–4: 111–120. https://doi.org/10.1016/j.peh.2018.09.001.

Petersen, M. A., Enghoff, O., Hesse, M., and Holm, S. (2024). "Psykedeliske Stoffer i Arbejdet med Sårbarhed." In *Psykisk Sårbarhed & Rusmidler: Sammenhænge og Perspekti-*

ver, edited by Birgitte Thylstrup, Morten Hesse, Margit Anne Petersen & Sidsel Karsberg. Aarhus Universitetsforlag.

Petersen M. A., Lyngsø-Dahl, L., and Nørgaard L. S. (2019). "Contextualizing Study Drugs—An Exploratory Study of Perceptions and Practices Among Study Counsellors, General Practitioners, Psychiatrists and Student Polls." *Research in Social and Administrative Pharmacy* 15 (10):1204–1211. https://doi.org/10.1016/j.sapharm.2018.10.005.

Petersen, M. A., Nørgaard, L. S., and Traulsen, J. M. (2015). "Pursuing Pleasures of Productivity: University Students' Use of Prescription Stimulants for Enhancement and the Moral Uncertainty of Making Work Fun." *Culture, Medicine & Psychiatry* 39, no. 4: 665–679. https://doi.org/10.1007/s11013-015-9457-4.

Petersen, M. A., Smith, A., Kristensen, D. B., and Høyer, K. (2022). *Subjects in the Making: Technologies of the Self and Pursuits of a Good Life in Contemporary Denmark.* Taylor & Francis.

Prayag, G., Mura, P., Hall, M., and Fontaine, J. (2015). "Drug or Spirituality Seekers? Consuming Ayahuasca." *Annals of Tourism Research* 52 (C): 175–177.

Siegel, J. S., Daily, J. E., Perry, D. A., and Nicol, G. E. (2023). "Psychedelic Drug Legislative Reform and Legalization in the US." *JAMA Psychiatry* 80, no. 1:77–83. https://doi.org/10.1001/jamapsychiatry.2022.4101.

Smith, P. (2019). *Why War? The Cultural Logic of Iraq, the Gulf War, and Suez.* University of Chicago Press.

Tupper, K. W. (2008). "The Globalization of Ayahuasca: Harm Reduction or Benefit Maximization?" *International Journal of Drug Policy* 19, no 4: 297–303.

Tutenges, S. (2022). "Nightlife Ethnography: A Phenomenological Approach." In *Oxford University Handbook of Ethnographies of Crime and Criminal Justice*, edited by Sandra M. Bucerius, Kevin D. Haggerty, and Luca Berardi. Oxford University Press.

Tutenges, S. (2023). *Intoxication: An Ethnography of Effervescent Revelry.* Rutgers University Press.

Tutenges, S., and Sandberg, S. (2013). "Intoxicating Stories: The Characteristics, Contexts and Implications of Drinking Stories Among Danish Youth." *International Journal of Drug Policy* 24, no. 6: 538–544.

Winkelman, M. (2005). "Drug Tourism or Spiritual Healing? Ayahuasca Seekers in Amazonia." *Journal of Psychoactive Drugs* 37, no. 2: 209–218.

Yaden, D. B., Berghella, A. P., Reiger, P. S., Garcia-Romeu, A., Johnson, M. W., and Hendricks, P. S. (2021). "Classic Psychedelics in the Treatment of Substance Use Disorder: Potential Synergies with Twelve-Step Programs." *International Journal of Drug Policy* 98:103380. https://doi.org/10.1016/j.drugpo.2021.103380.

Zagorski, N. (2023). "Australia Legalizes Psychedelics for Use in Depression, PTSD Therapy." *Psychiatry News* 58, no. 9.

Zinberg, N. E. (1984). *Drug, Set, and Setting: The Basis for Controlled Intoxicant Use.* Yale University Press.

7

Producing Esprit de Corps

On the Effervescent and Ritual Genesis of "Police Culture"

David Sausdal

> It's a rush, a rush that stays with you. It builds up as you're approaching. It's the expectation—you know from prior experiences what might happen, but you also know that this is something new, something you can't be sure of. You sit there in the car with the others, your colleagues, waiting, and we get quieter and quieter as we get closer and closer. We're ready. We have to be. We get the green light. We go in, hard and fast. It's chaos—shouting and movements everywhere. But there is also control. Control is a must. . . . So, yeah, you make the arrest. You leave. You breathe. But the tingling sensation stays with you for a long time after the arrest is done. It really does.
>
> —Danish Police Officer Sørensen

All police officers know this. And anyone who works in situations where similar incidents and intensities occur probably recognizes it as well. For me, at least, as an ethnographer who has spent many years studying law enforcement and detective work across Europe, it is clear that policing is a peculiar vocation—a job with its own emotiveness, its own Stimmung, as Simmel (2023) might have put it. Unlike the habitual flatline of much academic work (or my work, at least), and many other professions, the work of police officers oscillates between utter boredom and peaking passions (Phillips, 2015; Fassin, 2017; Sausdal, 2018). There is a rhythm to it. An officer might be sitting at her desk at 8:30 a.m., slowly sorting out yesterday's paperwork, only to find herself fully immersed in a potentially forceful arrest of a supposed criminal half an hour later.

True, policing is mostly tedious, monotonous work, even though HBO and true crime podcasts may tell us otherwise. But it does have its sparks of drama and excitement, which inevitably absorbs the undivided body and mind of police officers, if only for a moment. These moments, or "tingling sensations," as Danish police officer Sørensen puts it, bleed into and shape the entire police profession.

In essence, these are the moments or rituals of everyday policing that this chapter aims to focus on. More specifically, the focus is on how the "drama of policing" (Manning, 2012) shapes the police's self-image and "work culture." In (ethnographic) policing research, one of the most studied themes is precisely "work(ing) culture" (cf. Herbert, 1998; Waddington, 1999; Westmarland, 2008; Loftus, 2009; Martin, 2018; Cockcroft, 2020; Rowe, 2023), that is, the police's occupational culture and the norms and values that underpin it. Many articles and books have been written discussing its causes and consequences, and many public and political debates are still being had—debates often focusing on the negatives of a too cynical, conservative, macho, violent, and insular work culture.

Indeed, it is certainly relevant for researchers (and society) to continue studying and debating the risks of a problematic vocational culture (e.g., the risks of police xenophobia, discrimination, brutality, misconduct, inefficiency, etc.). In this chapter, however, the focus is not on the risks of police work culture as such but rather on the question of its origin. Contributing to the debate, this chapter applies the Durkheimian concept of collective effervescence (CE) (Durkheim, 1915; Tiryakian, 1995; Collins, 2014; Olaveson, 2001; Throop and Laughlin, 2002; Liebst, 2019; Tutenges, 2022) to explore a central yet under-researched way in which police culture comes into being: through the existence and importance of an esprit de corps.

Though several scholars have noticed that the police possess a "common bond" or "team spirit," few, if any, have thoroughly analyzed how such feelings of in-group devotion are produced, or what they mean in terms of police in-group identifications and vocational ideals. This is a missed opportunity. Contrasting Émile Durkheim's and others' work on effervescence with empirical examples from my own and others' ethnographies of day-to-day police work, this chapter argues for a more ritualistic understanding of policing. As it ultimately concludes, the (work) culture spirit of policing does not just reside in and get reproduced through legal statutes, academies, offices, or the minds of the police, as most research suggests (cf. Bittner, 1970; Van Maanen, 1973; Oberfield, 2014). As Rowe (2023) hints at, police culture-cum-spirit is also cooperatively and continuously produced—not only through the pressures of rules and regulations but also through the collective and community-generating effervescence of "policing rituals"—that is, especially meaningful rituals such as preparing for and carrying out an arrest, as described by Officer Sørensen in this chapter's introductory quote.

The Study

Before the police's esprit de corps is further explored and theorized, a few words on the study from which it draws its lessons are in order. In sum, the empirical material and examples used in this chapter stem from more than one thousand hours of observations of day-to-day police work (primarily detective work), as well as more than sixty semistructured interviews conducted between 2013 and 2023. More specifically, the majority of the empirical material originates from a 2015 ethnographic study of Danish detectives (based in the wider Copenhagen metropolitan area) and their investigations and stakeouts of transnational crimes and criminals. The empirical material also includes several observations and interviews with Portuguese, Spanish, and Romanian officers and policing officials all involved in the policing of transnational crime. In this way, the study represents a more multisited and less "methodologically nationalist" dataset compared to what is usually seen in most policing research (and criminology more broadly; for similar methodological reflections see Vigh and Sausdal, 2021).

In addition, compared to other studies of CE, which define key concepts and use statistical modeling to (dis)prove the existence and etiology of CE (cf. Liebst, 2019), this chapter is not focused on evidencing its size or substance. On the contrary, the chapter and the study it builds on are arguably more in line with the original spirit of Durkheim (1915; [1893] 2014), as the aim is, first and foremost, to observe and theorize the communal flows and formations that may result from effervescence—in this case, the potential formative aspects of everyday policing rituals. In this way, the study is more of a qualitative endeavor. The purpose isn't to test whether effervescence generates profound feelings of community (we assume it does) nor to measure its size or strength. Instead, the point of the chapter is to illustrate and contemplate how such effervescent sentiments come to life in given circumstances, later materializing into what is known as "police culture"—from ritual feeling to organizational fact.

The Spirit of Rituals and Socializing

> The very act of congregating is an exceptionally powerful stimulant. Once the individuals are gathered together, a sort of electricity is generated from their closeness and quickly launches them to an extraordinary height of exaltation. . . . *The effervescence* often becomes so intense that it leads to outlandish behaviour. . . . People are so far outside the ordinary conditions of life, and so conscious of the fact, that they feel a certain need to set themselves above and beyond ordinary morality. (Durkheim, 1915: 91–92, emphasis added)

This is how Durkheim described the core of what he understood as collective effervescence (see also Olaveson, 2001), that is, a kind of socioelectrical outcome of ritualized gatherings and processes, which he saw as elemental to the formation of religious life as well as society itself. In his discovery of what he thus believed to be the central worth of ritual practice, Durkheim did what most armchair anthropologists of his time had done: he intellectually (but not physically) relocated himself to a distant place where the possibility of freeing himself from what his contemporary and active fieldworker Bronislaw Malinowski (2002) famously called "the imponderabilia" of one's own everyday life and culture was greater. By browsing a variety of ethnographic and archival accounts of Australian natives, Durkheim hence admitted how it is "very strange that one must turn back, and be transported to the very beginnings of history, in order to arrive at an understanding of humanity as it is at present" (1915: 2). Nevertheless, that is what he did. In his own mind, at least, he found a piece of universal humanity in the life of Australia's Indigenous peoples. Moreover, Durkheim believed he had discovered one of the fundamental ingredients of religiosity in the peoples' ritual conduct—namely, a ritual's ability to reaffirm ruling metaphysics, that is, for human society to confirm and celebrate its own order, as Durkheim argued, but also to emotionally strengthen these communal bonds and beliefs.

In this process, CE plays a central role. Yet contrary to the standard critique of Durkheim's admittedly unsystematic discussion of the specific role and elements of effervescence, this is not just a matter of "run amok" crowd psychology (cf. Torres, 2014), as seen in overly excited or enraged mobs, for example, as discussed in research on charismatic demagogues (Lindholm, 1992) or riot research (Hörnqvist, 2016; Newburn, 2021). Although Durkheim acknowledged both the potentially damaging as well as the creative forces involved, he didn't envision effervescence as a haphazard exaltation. As Durkheim clearly argued:

> Every communion of conscience does not produce what is religious. It must moreover fulfil certain specific conditions. Notably, it must possess a degree of unity, of intimacy, and the forces which it releases must be sufficiently intense to take the individual outside himself and to raise him to a superior life. (1915: 84)

In other words, not all impassioned gatherings are directed at a greater purpose, nor do they produce such a sense. They may stir up emotions, but for it to amount to CE, as Olaveson and others have explained, "it must be characterized by intimacy, intensity, and immediacy [as well as involving] will and intention, and symbolic focus" (Olaveson 2001: 101). Effervescence is not a mere melting pot of random forces and passions. There is a recognizable formula to it—key ingredients that must be added.

A more plainly put interpretation of this can be found in Tutenges's (2022) work on intoxication. Agreeing with Pickering (2009) that Durkheim's work on CE needs further clarification and categorization to become a more understandable and useful concept, Tutenges not only rehashes Pickering's noted distinction between "creative" and "re-creative" effervescence but also lays out six distinct subtypes of effervescence. In Tutenges's perspective, CE should not only be understood as strictly a religious ritual sediment but as something that exists and occurs in various, more or less everyday interactions where people come together in ways that generate strong feelings of togetherness beyond the individual herself.

Furthermore, drawing on Collins's (2014) microsociology (which one might cheekily term "recipe sociology" at times), Tutenges (2022: 11) points to Collins's proposed "four main ingredients" of CE, included in his famous discussion of "interactional ritual chains." In Collins's view, the first CE ingredient is physical closeness. Bodies must be in the same room, close enough to easily sense the signals (and hormones) we all transmit, especially in intense situations. Secondly, there must be an "us and them," an in-group and out-group differentiation that clarifies who is part of the ritual and who is not. Without this, the ritual's power may fizzle out if there is nothing to keep it grounded. In short, CE depends on demarcation. Relatedly, the third ingredient is the need for direction. The bubbling sensation of a higher-order ceremony dissolves if people are too far removed from one another, or if there is no mirror opposite to reflect the sensation (e.g., a humdrum everyday life to mirror and make sense of a wildly drunken night). The sensation also fades if attention is not directed at the same thing. A soccer match becomes a crowd pleaser, generating fanatic fans who adorn themselves and their living rooms with Manchester United memorabilia, only if we all focus on the pitch and the players. Lastly, for CE to occur, and not just random individual sparks, there must be a collective feeling. What we sense and experience should be, more or less, the same as what the next person feels. If we cannot share the experience, the ritual's socioculturally (re)creative force falters. It becomes neither religion nor a shared conviction. It becomes a fluke, rather than something foundational.

Three Policing Examples

With these descriptions of effective rituals and CE fresh in mind, we may again turn to the empirical. For anyone with even a vague notion of police work, it should already be clear how the concept applies. In many ways, this may be an example of how the wisdom of emic and popular notions outweighs that of academic abstractions. In my experience, it is rare to have a conversation with a police officer without them mentioning the defining draws of the action-based events that policing involves. As much research has pointed out, police officers frequently speak of "real police work" as close encounter crime fighting rather than paperwork and bureaucratic dealings (cf. Manning and Van Maanen, 1978; Sausdal, 2021a). It is almost impossible to watch a movie, TV series, or listen to a true crime podcast about policing without these fiery events being central to the plot and the profession.

Nevertheless, in academic policing literature, the drama remains strangely peripheral (but see Manning, 1982; 2010; O'Neill, 2017; Terpstra and Salet, 2020; Sausdal and Lohne, 2021). Sure, the drama, and the esprit de corps it may produce, is frequently mentioned (Karp and Stenmark, 2011; de Maillard and Skogan, 2020; Graeff and Kleinewiese, 2020), but not often in a profound theoretical sense. Instead, it is more frequently a line of criticism, with scholars and commentators pointing out how the police often overvalue these eventful yet relatively rare parts of their profession, how they may become a source of corruption, or how the police fetishize action and antagonism as indicative of what real policing is all about—essentially a "fighting fetish" (cf. Sausdal, 2021a).

I must admit that I often tend to agree with this critique. The police's (over) valuing of a specific dramatic part of their job often stands in the way of other, less dramatic and confrontational approaches to policing (Sausdal, 2021b). Still, what happens if we were to, for a moment, set aside these critical viewpoints? What would happen if we were to take more seriously, in theoretical terms, the fact that police officers truly feel that the eventful, action-packed aspects of their job are emblematic and thus generative of what policing really is? What if their yearning for raids and clashes is not merely a matter of wrongful fixations, machismo, or deep-rooted habits but something more organizationally and culturally profound?

With these questions in mind, I want to provide a few examples of what may be termed "policing rituals" that generate a sense of CE and thus a broader esprit de corps within the police. These rituals include "the bust," "the confrontation," and "the war story"—day-to-day policing rituals that not only form a significant part of my field notes but also appear in many policing ethnographies. To allow the reader to better sense the emotional draws of the situations described, the examples are largely stripped of analytical commentary. Instead, the analysis comes afterward, as I contrast and further explore the empirical examples through the concept of CE.

The Bust

It's 1 P.M., in the middle of May, and a group of Copenhagen police detectives and I are taking a break, enjoying a bite. Everything is nice and calm. Suddenly, the chief inspector comes barging in with a determined stare and a note in his hand. "Guys, this just came in from one of our stakeout teams. The suspect in several violent robberies is believed to be at his mom's house now, and we need to go pick him up. Get your gear and get ready, guys. We leave in five. And remember," the chief inspector reminds us calmly, "this guy could be dangerous. He may fight us and try to escape." Leaving everything behind—food and all—the detectives rush to grab their phones, earpieces, weapons, handcuffs, and bulletproof vests. They suit up. Three minutes later, they all run and jump into their unmarked patrol cars parked outside. The detectives are armed and ready, and so am I, pen and paper in hand. The shift from rest and relaxation to being in the car, armed and alert, happened swiftly and quietly—but with a palpable sense of importance and tension.

The drive is a bit of a blur, to say the least. I recall seeing houses speed by outside the window, and a bit of conversation, but not much. At some point, the leader of the operation's voice comes over the radio. In a few clear words he instructs his colleagues on what to do upon arrival. A few more minutes pass. "Get ready, fellows, we're almost there," says the officer driving our car, as we arrive at the suspect's flat—a stereotypical dismal council estate on the outskirts of town. We wait. The detectives in the car, consisting of two seasoned detectives and two cadets, repeat each person's role. One of the older detectives tells the younger colleagues to reconfirm what they've been instructed to do. "Paulsen won't enter the flat with you but will guard the door so no one escapes that way. I'll stay behind outside in the hallway with the researcher [me] until everything is in order and we can come in," he says. "Sounds about right," the older colleague confirms. "But even you two must stay alert," he says, pointing at us. "Listen, it all starts now and ends with this asshole in cuffs and sitting in a holding cell, right?" We both nod. Everyone's ready—or as ready as can be.

"Go," comes the order, and everyone jumps out of the car, except for two detectives in another car who remain seated. I remember thinking they must be ready to follow and chase down the suspect if he somehow manages to escape—an assumption later confirmed by one of the detectives leading "the attack." Three other groups of police detectives have now formed, with two groups silently going up the main entrance staircase to the second floor where the suspect is supposed to be. "No need to mind the elevator," the group leader says. "We'd see if he was coming down that way, and no one is using it at the moment." The third group is stationed at the back entrance.

We reach the suspect's door. The detectives look at each other for a moment, all of them with their hands on their service weapons, just in case. "Ready," one of them whispers. "Ok, now!" He knocks hard on the door—three times. Then three more times, all while announcing that they are the police and that the door needs to be opened. Nothing happens. "I hear voices," one detective says, pressing his ear against the door. "We hear you," he now shouts through the mail slot, trying to get a better view of who's inside the flat. "Open this door right now, or we will knock it down. You have ten seconds." Another detective stands ready, holding a ram. "Say the word," he says. The atmosphere is thick with anticipation.

Just before the iron ram can hit the door, the suspect's mother opens it. She only manages to open it a crack before the detectives push her back and enters. As promised, the cadet and I wait in the hallway. Through the open door we catch a glimpse of detectives searching the different rooms. Seconds later, a couple more detectives rush up the stairs and barge in, taking me and their younger colleague with them. As we turn left and enter the living room, two detectives have already cuffed a young man, with his sister and mother sitting on a nearby couch. "What the hell are you doing?!" the sister demands. "What has he done?" The detectives don't respond. I can't tell why—maybe they had already explained or read the suspect his Miranda rights.

With the suspect cuffed and escorted by one of the detectives, we head back down the stairs to the cars. Some detectives stay behind to search the flat for stolen goods or other evidence. The suspect is placed in the back seat of a vehicle. I sense how the detectives are starting to relax a bit—quite the contrast to the restrained young man, who, after a bit of initial complaining, now stares angrily into space. Smiles start to show on the detectives' faces. One tells me to get in the front seat so he and a colleague can sit in the back with the suspect. "What do you think?" a detective asks out loud. "I think this went kinda well, no?" It seems like both a reassurance to his colleagues and a way to provoke the suspect. "In and out, like 'bang!'" another detective replies. They all agree. The initial apprehension and focus before and during the arrest gradually fade, giving way to high spirits and congratulations. I feel it too—exhausted from the experience (as I am also a novice) but with a lingering sense of thrill and excitement that stays with me throughout the day. The same goes for the detectives. Even the following day, they're still talking about "the fine bust yesterday." "Yes, that's what it's all about," another says as he prepares coffee for his tired but still animated colleagues. The following day turns out to be a quiet one filled with deskwork and tedious meetings. But the drama of yesterday—and many other raids and arrests before and after—always lingers.

Confrontations

Raids, busts, arrests, and seizures—whatever terms are used to describe these intense events—are obviously exemplary of police work and of what this chapter seeks to convey. In many ways, "the bust" remains the dramaturgical pinnacle of the profession—something that plays out in the minds of individual officers as well as on the big screen. That said, there are other events (or rites) of importance. One of these is "the confrontation." Confrontations come in different shapes and sizes. It might be a small street encounter between patrolling officers and some disorderly citizens, or it might be a larger event where the police seek to control football hooligans or a heated mob of activists. The latter is described in studies of protest policing (Atak and Bayram, 2017; Mutsaers and van Nuenen, 2018), but here I want to offer an example of regular street-level confrontations that police officers often engage in—confrontations that may be slightly serendipitous, but which nevertheless follow a recognizable and rousing pattern.

I'm on foot patrol with the local police in Lisbon. We are walking up and down the streets of Mouraria, a neighborhood known for prostitution, drugs, drinking, and all the other vices that many similar neighborhoods around the world also bear witness to. Crime is here, and so are the police. As part of the patrol work, the two Portuguese officers, whom I have been allowed to follow, occasionally strike up conversations with different local shop owners as well as groups of sketchy people hanging around on the corners—people whom I'm told are involved in local gangs. Though things are slow and friendly, there's a constant feeling that something may happen.

We walk up one of the neighborhood's main roads to one of its many bars. "This is probably the most famous one," Officer Silva tells me. "Or infamous, to be more exact," he adds. His colleague, Officer Almeida, nods. Apparently, before the municipality decided to clean up the neighborhood and gentrification reduced street crime, this bar was notorious for being a drug hub as well as a place where even the police couldn't easily enter "without the risk of an ass-kicking," Officer Almeida explains.

"Seems about right," I think to myself, as the place still looks pretty grim to me. People are entering the bar with stern faces. Outside, a man has been staring at us ever since we arrived. Apparently, his patience has run out. "What the fuck are you doing here? What are you looking at?!" he shouts at us. At first, both officers are unfazed by his aggression. They've seen and heard worse. They continue talking to me and each other, gently reminding the angry man to calm down. But he doesn't. Instead, he starts walking toward us. Immediately, the officers switch from friendly to fierce. "Police! Step back!" Officer Silva orders. No luck. The man continues to advance. "Last warning," both officers tell him, but the man doesn't listen. My heart starts pounding. Two seconds ago, I was strolling around, nice and easy, but now adrenaline is kicking in. "This isn't good," I remember thinking.

Two more seconds pass. The officers act quickly, throwing the man to the ground, with Officer Almeida sitting on top of him. "Will you listen to us now?" he asks the man. But the man resists. He keeps complaining and threatening the officer. Officer Almeida retaliates by becoming more commanding, tightening his grip, and pushing his knee further into the man's back. Though it's not pleasant to watch, it works. Slowly, the man starts to calm down, likely encouraged by the growing pain. "Okay, okay, I'm sorry," he says. "I didn't know you were police. I thought you were somebody else," he stammers. "I'm sorry. I'm good now, I promise," he pleads.

The officers accept his apology. After a few more reprimands and threats of fines or prison, the officers release him and tell him to leave the bar. "You've had your last drink today, my friend. And if we see you again or if you do anything stupid, we'll get you. That's a promise." The man leaves, and the crowd that had gathered disperses. After a quick dusting off and a look around, the officers and I continue on. "Shit," Officer Silva says as we walk a couple of hundred feet away from the bar. "Here we were having a nice time, and then suddenly this shit happens . . . you see what we mean. This is patrolling. You have to stay on your toes. You never know when the next asshole will come your way." His colleague smiles. "Yeah, right. . . . It really gets you going, though. It's a jumpstart—a real-life reminder not to get too complacent; that we are the police, and there are idiots out there who need a talking-to—or worse."

That day in Lisbon, nothing else happened. We continued walking around the neighborhood, and the officers only had to raise their voices a couple more times. In other countries and contexts, I've had many similar experiences with the ebbs and flows of everyday policing and patrol work. Often, you're cruising in your car or on foot, only to be suddenly engrossed in a verbal or physical confrontation. Quantitatively speaking, uneventful cruising far outweighs the occasional drama, but qualitatively—psychologically and physically—the confrontation takes the prize.

War Stories

One thing is the actual incidents where police officers go out to arrest or confront people. Another, and an even more frequent example of day-to-day police drama, are the stories they tell about these events—their "war stories." Such storytelling often takes place during downtime, either while off duty or between tasks. Officers may share stories in the canteen, while sitting in their cars on the way to or from a specific task, or during uneventful stakeouts. Spirited conversations are even more common when sharing a drink after a long day's work or during other casual get-togethers. As several scholars (Fielding, 1994; Waddington, 1999; van Hulst, 2013; Sausdal, 2020) have pointed out, this is not only where police officers tell each other stories; it's where they share stories about what policing is, thus reaffirming their professional identities and what Halbwachs (2020) may speak of as the police's "collective memory."

As an ethnographer observing everyday police work, one cannot avoid hearing this "canteen talk," as it is often called in policing research. In numerical terms, this might be one of the kinds of police "work" that takes up the most time—certainly more than confrontations or arrests. Yet to dismiss police banter as mere pastime chatter would be a mistake. Theoretically, there is much to be said about how police officers talk to each other when no outsiders (besides the occasional ethnographer) are listening. Various scholars have discussed how the police's "canteen talk" may reveal their worldview and practices as well as serve as a way to cope with the often-harsh realities of their job. I agree. But through the lens of policing rituals and effervescence, there may be more to their stories than simply venting frustrations or communicating cynical perspectives on society. As I've discussed elsewhere (Sausdal, 2020), the stories police officers tell themselves are not just pragmatic but also emotional and entertaining. Police officers talk a lot of "bullshit" (Sausdal, 2020), and often the most important thing isn't just what's being said but that crazy and stirring words are being thrown around—content and form. Here's an example.

It's one of those days again when police work seems far removed from what I had initially imagined, first from reading crime fiction, later from watching cop shows. On this particular morning, I arrived at the station when the Danish police officers also showed up for work, but so far, this has been a day spent sitting in the lunchroom waiting for things to happen. "We could drive around a bit," Officer Nicolaisen suggests to his patrol partner. "Nah," the partner says, "I have a few things to take care of. Also, I'd rather hang out here today. I'm okay with it being slow." And slow it is. Nothing much happens. Some officers go out and drive around the streets of Copenhagen, just to pass the time. Some have been given a few tasks that have come in. Others, like me, sit in the lunchroom or in their offices, taking care of paperwork or drinking yet another cup of coffee. This is the everyday life of policing: mundane, monotonous, and requiring patience.

As I flick through my moleskin notebook, revisiting some of my notes, I hear a bit of chuckling. It seems to be coming from the kitchen. The chuckling grows louder. More laughter, some commotion, and now massive laughter. Like a hunter tracking his prey, not just me but most of the others sitting in the lunchroom get up and follow the sound of glee. In the kitchen we find Officer Holm—fully engaged, body and all—telling a story about an arrest he and a couple of colleagues made last week. "I know this story," I think to myself, also remembering that this isn't unusual. Like any good bar chatter, joking and storytelling aren't necessarily about telling something new but about revisiting the classics, perhaps even perfecting them. The story Officer Holm tells, while swinging his fists illustratively in the air, is about how he "almost" caught a well-known pickpocket at Østerport Station, north of downtown Copenhagen.

> The fucking Polak made a run for it—sprinting onto the tracks, from one platform to another. He had me thinking, that's for sure. Running on the tracks is super dangerous, and I didn't really know what to do. Problem was, the others [his colleagues] weren't around but were on the other side of the station—so I called them on the radio and shouted that I was in pursuit, making my way over the tracks with the suspect galloping away. Let me tell you, he was a goddamn Kipketer [a famous Danish athlete], that one. But I was in luck. I'm getting fat, as you can all see, but the suspect was too quick for his own good and fell as he made his way up on the last platform. He had almost escaped. But now he was lying there, screaming, holding his ankle.
>
> Now, I remember that I started to laugh as I eventually climbed up onto the platform as well, thinking to myself, "I got you, you fucking asshole." The trouble was, I, too, was an idiot. Just like the Polish pickpocket, I also messed up and tripped. Don't know how. It just happened. Haha! It was a goddamn tragedy, a farce! Fortunately, I didn't wreck my ankle as badly as he did. So, I eventually reached him. But before cuffing him, I made sure to give him a good slap and a bit of pepper spray. I made him pay for being such a dick—and for forcing me to hurt myself. I made him pay!!

Officer Holm almost screamed, ending the story as dramatically as possible, with his colleagues and the rest of us saluting him. Then others quickly joined in, telling their stories. And suddenly, an hour or so had passed with the officers sharing what they believed to be iconic stories from their work as police—stories that most often involved intense, forceful, and/or satirical encounters with perpetrators or the public.

In this way, their workday had been punctuated by something fun—something to lift the spirits. As always, I scribbled it all down. I also had to give it to Officer Holm—the story was getting better and better with each retelling. However, it was also getting further and further away from what had really happened. According to his colleagues who were there with him at Østerport Station, Officer Holm had added a bit of extra violence and action to the plot. "Truth be told, the arrest wasn't that crazy. But hey," his colleague Officer Christensen went on to remind me, "a war story can't be about something boring and uneventful, can it? I mean, what's the point in that?"

The Spirit of Policing?

What is the point, indeed? What is "the spirit" that springs from a story told in a police station's kitchen, from a successful arrest, or from a street corner confrontation? And how does this all relate to, as this chapter explores, the police's esprit de corps?

Current policing literature is often focused on more conventional organizational arguments when deciphering how police principles and practices are shaped. Here, the concept of the police's occupational culture, or simply "police culture," stands out. As policing scholar Mike Rowe accurately outlines it:

> Police culture is a concept widely used, often critically, to characterise the working attitudes and behaviours of (usually uniformed) police officers. It is shorthand for a workplace imbued with machismo, racism, sexism, a thirst for danger and excitement, cynicism and conservatism. (2023)

Moreover, in searching for the genesis of such "police culture," most research has settled on ideas about on-the-job socialization and the notion that the greenhorn cadet learns from their police elders. Alternatively, the argument has been that the potential cadet already possesses police-like attitudes, that is, the police attract individuals who more or less adhere to the above-described norms and values of "police culture." While such arguments are not wrong, they appear rather culturalist and even essentialist: the police officer has cultural views, the police have a work culture, and then it all just reproduces itself.

In my view, a more practice-oriented approach is more convincing. One such approach is promoted by Loftus (2009) and Reiner (2010), who argue in their studies on police norms and values that the police's occupational culture (and its consistency across time and space) is formed not just by the police but by society's notion of what policing is about. As long as the police are seen as law enforcers (rather than, for example, "peacemakers" [Banton, 1964]), "real" policing will be about enforcing the law, about action and confrontation, more than appeasement and conversation (see also Sausdal, 2021b). I agree. Hierarchies of prestige and practice generate their own cultural arguments—or "police fetish," as Reiner (2010) puts it. However, this reading of police culture (or the spirit of policing) still overlooks the concrete psychosocial draws of different practices themselves, treating them less as meaningful rituals and more as "mere" residual aspects of organizational or societal biases and decisions.

Following Rowe's (2023) Latour-inspired analysis, and in a more anthropological spirit (as this is how Latour [2005] essentially framed his critique of sociology), there is room for a more processual analysis of "police culture" that understands culture as something that (also) comes into being through the practices of everyday life. As Rowe puts it in his Actor-Network (ANT) theory-inspired critique of the concept:

> Rather than looking for culture or identifying how culture affects behaviours, [we may instead] [i]dentif[y] factors that influence the decisions and actions, including technology, targets, training, timing, intelligence, geography and supervision, thus reassembling police culture much as Bruno Latour sought to reassemble the social. (2023)

Turning the tables—not just looking for "culture" and what culture does but searching for that which becomes culture—Rowe's book is an important contribution to the discussion and understanding of police culture, which, frankly, often appears somewhat outdated and essentialist. While Rowe's ANT inspiration focuses more on the materiality and technologies of police work, this chapter seeks to draw attention to the ritualistic properties and effects of certain police tasks, namely the empirical examples of "a bust," "a confrontation," and "a war story."

In this way, I believe we have finally arrived at the spirit of policing, the esprit de corps—what draws the police's attention to certain dramatic aspects of their job and, simultaneously, generates feelings of collectivity and significance that spread beyond the event itself and thus form broader police thinking and custom—from police incidents to police ideology. This is true, at least, if we accept the Durkheimian understanding of discrete rituals and their function in shaping the worldview of groups. Even more so, it is true if we return to his concept of CE as a key component in a useful ritual. In many ways, it should be intuitively obvious that this concept works to explain what happens in the aforementioned examples, as well as in other instances of intense and fervent police practices—and the broader metaphysical aspects surrounding them.

To drive the point home, we can "test" the empirical examples against Collins's earlier mentioned "four main ingredients" of ritual practice and CE: 1) physical proximity, 2) in-group and out-group differentiation, 3) a united direction/focus point, and 4) a collective feeling, that is, that the emotions evoked by the ritual are comparable. Obviously, all of the examples I have provided emphasize physical closeness. When carrying out an arrest, you prepare and execute it together. You sit crammed together in the car, waiting. You jump out together. You kick in the door and make the arrest in unison, coordinating and carrying out the arrest just as you have trained and rehearsed many times before. Arresting someone is all about teamwork—with the added tension that comes from not knowing exactly what will happen when you enter the door or how the suspects will react. A similar sensation occurs when the police engage in smaller or larger confrontations. In the Lisbon case, we saw how two officers suddenly had to handle a local, aggressive drunkard by physically throwing themselves at him. In this way, confrontations are all about bodies being close to one another, with the police synchronizing their movements to control or overpower an opponent. War stories told in a police station's kitchen don't involve the same physicality, or violence, but they do feed on physical proximity. As I aimed to demonstrate with the example of the Danish police "war story," we were all drawn to the story. It felt like something special was happening in the police station's kitchen, and we all wanted to be part of it. More importantly, the story and storyteller needed us to take part for it to become a significant, effervescence-producing ritual. As we all know, good stories demand a crowd—they feed off the energy the crowd gives, repaid through jubilation. None of us (or most of us) had been there when Officer Holm caught and chastised a runaway suspect, but in that police station kitchen, we were all sharing in the sensation.

"Us and them"—police and "everyone who isn't police," as officers often put it—is a binary that defines, if not haunts, police organizations. It is central to "police culture." This binary is also emblematic of the examples of effervescent police rituals provided in this chapter. One thing is the uniform, the badge, the weaponry, the title, and the legal statutes that make the police who they are. Another thing is the insider/outsider demarcation that defines these situations. A bust is about the police "being police," arresting a suspect. No one in that room, in that flat, had any doubts about who the police were and who their adversaries were. The same clarity was present when the police confronted the rowdy man on a Lisbon street. And the whole narrative of the described war story, and many other stories the police tell, is exactly about signaling who belongs to the in-group (the police) and who belongs to the out-group (the suspect, the criminal, the "asshole," the public, etc.).

A united focus—that is, something or someone that holds the crowd's sole attention—is Collins's third ingredient of CE, and it is part and parcel of police rituals. You are arresting someone. You are opposing a person or a problem. You are telling a story. In all the cases, the police officers didn't just enter into a ceremonial setting or situation with a multitude of focuses and purposes. They knew what they were there for. To put it more precisely: to do good and effective police work, the police need to have a united focus. If they are undecided, a bust or confrontation is likely to turn bad. Obviously, this is also true of a good (war) story. No story is worth listening to if it doesn't have focus and meaning. It becomes senseless and unappealing. Lastly, Collins's fourth ingredient—that the ritual should produce a similar feeling among all participants—is also clearly recognizable. While scholars of symbols and rituals may argue that symbols and rituals don't need to produce the exact same thoughts (Cohen, 1976), it is safe to say that the strong and animated emotions produced when the police go on "a raid," control a mob, or deal with disorderly conduct are familiar to all police officers. Clearly, as I witnessed that day in the police station's kitchen, and as I and many other police ethnographers have experienced on multiple occasions, what fuels the evocative stories the police tell each other (about themselves and what policing is) is exactly the shared feelings they all have—a feeling that stems from having participated in often-dramatic policing rituals, which they now passionately relive and revive through "canteen talk" and other telltale spoils of war. Where the former (the bust and the confrontation) more clearly resembles Durkheim's and Collins's aforementioned electro-analogies about how rituals "charge" people and fill them with high voltage energy that, even though it is socially episodic, may detonate into societal chronicity (as in religion or, in this case, police culture), the latter (the war story) serves as an important aide-memoire of how CE may also come into being not through radical rituals as such but through less costly yet more recurring repetitions and remembrances. Indeed, as Halbwachs (2020) also argues in relation to his somewhat similar concept of "collective memory," both our mutual memories and the mutual emotions springing therefrom (CE) may very well need the singular to erupt, but it needs more daily and minute rituals to stay alive—reminders as well as the more revelatory.

Conclusion

> Esprit de corps is a feeling of loyalty and pride that is shared by the members of a group who consider themselves to be different from other people in some special way.
>
> —Collins Dictionary

The *Collins Dictionary* puts it well. When we discuss the police's esprit de corps, it has much to do with a sense of higher meaning and collegial allegiance, as well as the idea that being a police officer makes you different from others—people who, from a police perspective, are often naïve, with little understanding of how the world really works (and how dark it is!). But where does such a "team spirit" (or police culture) come from?

Essentially, this chapter was written with a simple purpose: to argue that the many writings and discussions about the existence of police occupational culture have paradoxically avoided one of the most obvious answers—namely, that "police culture" is shaped by the collective spirit that arises from the various workaday rituals in which police officers are involved. Of course, the norms and values that underpin police organizations are also a matter of the juridical and societal frameworks and ideals that surround and support the police. And yes, there is much to support the argument that "police culture" is (re)produced both by passing it on from older to younger generations and by the recruitment of certain types of individuals. Very few people from an upper-class academic, activist, or minority background pursue a police career. These are simply facts. However, it is also well-known to any police officer, as well as to any consumer of popular depictions of policing, that "real policing" is often thought to involve the more action-based and dramatic aspects of their work. Why? Some say it's habit. Some argue it's a fetish or perhaps an outdated patriarchal, macho ideal.

They're not entirely wrong. But they're not completely right either. As I have aimed to illustrate through a Durkheimian-inspired focus on the CE properties of (policing) rituals, the police's strong focus on certain aspects of their job as vocationally emblematic tells a story not just about police preferences but about the generative capacities of these rituals. If you know, you know. If you have ever been involved in similar ritualistic situations, you will know how much sentiment and purpose you can draw from them—even if the situation itself may have been a minuscule part of your overall efforts. The qualitative often outweighs the quantitative. To be sure, this won't be a surprising finding for many other scholars and disciplines outside policing research. In anthropology and social psychology, for example, it has long been noted how individual dramatic (wonderful or woeful) life occurrences regularly form people's outlooks and actions much more than the quotidian (cf. Maslow, 1961; Jackson, 2002). And although champions of the importance of everyday life are right in pointing to how routinized and habituated living is a form of subtle and unrecognized power (cf. Foucault, 2012), narrative scholars (see Jackson, 2002; Sandberg, 2016) have repeatedly shown how people's stories and self-conceptions often revolve around believed existential events and "turning points" (cf. Laub and Sampson, 1993). People, as it is, rarely define themselves through the mundane—even though they perhaps should.

And, of course, this is also true for the police. Police officers are frequently involved in events and occasions that are so intense, emotional, and symbolic that they—from their vantage point—come to define the wider whole. The few percentages of policing defining the many. This is where their esprit de corps springs from. In Pickering's (2009) more conceptual language, these policing rituals produce what may be termed "re-creative" CE. A good bust or confrontation reminds and strengthens the police officer's idea about the overall value and meaning of their profession.

Additionally, as Durkheim was well aware, and as other scholars of effervescence and ritual have reminded us (cf. Pickering, 2009; Tutenges, 2022), the sparks and emotions that come from dramatic collective occurrences carry both the possibility of change and chaos—that is, an instance of "creative" effervescence. Spirits are set in motion. A well-coordinated and well-structured ritual keeps emotions in their place, so they don't run amok. However, as we unfortunately see from time to time, police violence and brutality often occur in situations where clashes with the public get out of control.

Although this chapter must end here, there is much more to say regarding a more ritual and emotional analysis of police misconduct. In my (Danish/European) experiences, at least, few officers plan to be overly violent against the public when they leave their offices and head out into the streets. Some do, of course. Yet in most of the instances where I have witnessed acts of police brutality, it has come about as smaller groups of officers or individuals fail to control their emotions. Violence comes into the equation less as a rigid plan and more as ritual effect. Effervescence takes over. And the spirit of policing takes the wrong shape. This is not an excuse, of course not. And it is also a banal point. Indeed, all police officers and professionals with similar control-oriented jobs are taught how to keep cool. Contrary to Collins's (2008) argument that violence is a difficult task, it is often an easy and even tempting thing for a law enforcer (as well as many others whose lives and professions are filled with confrontation and conflict). Violence calls on them. And we better hope they have learned not to answer—or, more accurately, to answer it correctly.

REFERENCES

Atak, K., and I. E. Bayram. 2017. "Protest Policing Alla Turca: Threat, Insurgency, and the Repression of Pro-Kurdish Protests in Turkey." *Social Forces* 95, no. 4: 1667–1694.

Banton, M. 1964. *The Policeman in the Community.* Basic Books.

Bittner, E. 1970. *The Functions of the Police in Modern Society: A Review of Background Factors, Current Practices, and Possible Role Models.* Center for Studies of Crime and Delinquency, National Institute of Mental Health.

Cockcroft, T. 2020. *Police Culture: Research and Practice.* Policy Press.

Cohen, A. 1976. *Two-Dimensional Man: An Essay on the Anthropology of Power and Symbolism in Complex Society.* University of California Press.

Collins, R. 2008. *Violence: A Micro-Sociological Theory.* Princeton University Press.

Collins, R. 2014. "Interaction Ritual Chains and Collective Effervescence." In *Collective Emotions: Perspectives from Psychology, Philosophy, and Sociology*, edited by C. von Scheve and M. Salmella.. Oxford University Press.

de Maillard, J., and W. G. Skogan. 2020. *Policing in France.* Routledge.

Durkheim, É. 1915. *The Elementary Forms of the Religious Life.* Translated by Joseph Ward Swain. George Allen & Unwin, Ltd.

Durkheim, É. 2014 *The Division of Labor in Society.* New York: Simon and Schuster. Originally published in 1893 by Alcan.

Fassin, D. 2017. "Boredom: Accounting for the Ordinary in the Work of Policing (France)." In *Writing the World of Policing: The Difference Ethnography Makes*, edited by D. Fassin. University of Chicago Press.

Fielding, N. 1994. "Cop Canteen Culture." In *Just Boys Doing Business*, edited by T. Newburn and E. Stanko. Routledge.

Foucault, M. 2012. *Discipline and Punish: The Birth of the Prison.* Vintage.

Graeff, P., and J. Kleinewiese. 2020. "Esprit de Corps as a Source of Deviant Behavior in Organizations: Applying an Old Concept with a New Livery." In *Bribery, Fraud, Cheating: How to Explain and to Avoid Organizational Wrongdoing.*

Halbwachs, M. 2020. *On Collective Memory.* University of Chicago Press.

Herbert, S. 1998. "Police Subculture Reconsidered." *Criminology* 36, no. 2: 343–370.
Hörnqvist, M. 2016. "Riots in the Welfare State: The Contours of a Modern-Day Moral Economy." *European Journal of Criminology* 13, no. 5: 573–589.
Jackson, M. 2002. *The Politics of Storytelling: Violence, Transgression, and Intersubjectivity.* Vol. 3. Museum Tusculanum Press.
Karp, S., and H. Stenmark. 2011. "Learning to Be a Police Officer: Tradition and Change in the Training and Professional Lives of Police Officers." *Police Practice and Research: An International Journal* 12, no. 1: 4–15.
Latour, B. 2005. *Reassembling the Social: An Introduction to Actor-Network-Theory.* Oxford University Press.
Laub, J. H., and R. J. Sampson. 1993. "Turning Points in the Life Course: Why Change Matters to the Study of Crime." *Criminology* 31, no. 3: 301–325.
Liebst, L. S. 2019. "Exploring the Sources of Collective Effervescence: A Multilevel Study." *Sociological Science* 6:27–42.
Lindholm, C. 1992. "Charisma, Crowd Psychology and Altered States of Consciousness." *Culture, Medicine and Psychiatry* 16, no. 3: 287–310.
Loftus, B. 2009. *Police Culture in a Changing World.* Oxford University Press.
Malinowski, B. 2002. *Argonauts of the Western Pacific: An Account of Native Enterprise and Adventure in the Archipelagoes of Melanesian New Guinea.* Routledge.
Manning, P. K. 1982. "Producing Drama: Symbolic Communication and the Police." *Symbolic Interaction* 5, no. 2: 223–242.
Manning, P. K. 2010. *Policing Contingencies.* University of Chicago Press.
Manning, P. K. 2012. "Drama, the Police and the Sacred." In *Policing: Politics, Culture and Control: Essays in Honour of Robert Reiner*, edited by T. Newburn and J. Peay. Hart Publishing.
Manning, P. K., and J. Van Maanen. 1978. *Policing: A View from the Street.* Goodyear Publishing.
Martin, J. T. 2018. "Police Culture: What It Is, What It Does, and What We Should Do with It." In *The Anthropology of Police*, edited by K. G. Karpiakand and W. Garriott. Taylor and Francis.
Maslow, A. H. 1961. "Peak Experiences as Acute Identity Experiences." *The American Journal of Psychoanalysis* 21, no. 3: 254–262.
Mutsaers, P., and T. van Nuenen. 2018. "Protesting Police." In *The Anthropology of Police*, edited by K. G. Karpiak and W. Garriott, 153–172. Routledge.
Newburn, T. 2021. "The Causes and Consequences of Urban Riot and Unrest." *Annual Review of Criminology* 4, no. 1: 53–73.
Oberfield, Z. W. 2014. *Becoming Bureaucrats: Socialization at the Front Lines of Government Service.* University of Pennsylvania Press.
Olaveson, T. 2001. "Collective Effervescence and Communitas: Processual Models of Ritual and Society in Emile Durkheim and Victor Turner." *Dialectical Anthropology* 26, no. 2: 89–124.
O'Neill, M. 2017. "Police Community Support Officers in England: A Dramaturgical Analysis." *Policing and Society* 27, no. 1: 21–39.
Phillips, S. W. 2016. "Police Discretion and Boredom: What Officers Do When There Is Nothing to Do." *Journal of Contemporary Ethnography* 45, no. 5: 580–601.
Pickering, W. S. F. 2009. *Durkheim's Sociology of Religion: Themes and Theories.* James Clarke & Co.
Reiner, R. 2010. *The Politics of the Police.* Oxford University Press.
Rowe, M. 2023. *Disassembling Police Culture.* Routledge.

Sandberg, S. 2016. "The Importance of Stories Untold: Life-Story, Event-Story and Trope." *Crime, Media, Culture* 12, no. 2: 153–171.

Sausdal, D. 2018. "Pleasures of Policing: An Additional Analysis of Xenophobia." *Theoretical Criminology* 22, no. 2: 226–242.

Sausdal, D. 2020. "Police Bullshit." *Journal of Extreme Anthropology* 4, no. 1: 94–115.

Sausdal, D. 2021a. "A Fighting Fetish: On Transnational Police and Their Warlike Presentation of Self." *Theoretical Criminology* 25, no. 3: 400–418.

Sausdal, D. 2021b. *Looking Beyond the Police-as-Control Narrative.* Policy Press.

Sausdal, D., and K. Lohne. 2021. "Theatrics of Transnational Criminal Justice: Ethnographies of Penality in a Global Age." Sage.

Simmel, G. 2023. "Soziologie der Sinne." In *Soziologische Ästhetik*, edited by Klaus Lichtblau. Springer.

Terpstra, J., and R. Salet. 2020. "The Social Construction of Police Heroes." *International Journal of Police Science & Management* 22, no. 1: 16–25.

Throop, C. J., and C. D. Laughlin. 2002. "Ritual, Collective Effervescence, and the Categories: Toward a Neo-Durkheimian Model of the Nature of Human Consciousness, Feeling and Understanding." *Journal of Ritual Studies.*

Tiryakian, E. A. 1995. "Collective Effervescence, Social Change, and Charisma: Durkheim, Weber, and 1989." *International Sociology* 10, no. 3: 269–281.

Torres, E. C. 2014. "Durkheim's Concealed Sociology of the Crowd." *Durkheimian Studies* 20, no. 1: 89–114.

Tutenges, S. 2022. *Intoxication: An Ethnography of Effervescent Revelry.* Rutgers University Press.

van Hulst, M. 2013. "Storytelling at the Police Station: The Canteen Culture Revisited." *British Journal of Criminology* 53, no. 4: 624–642.

Van Maanen, J. 1973. "Observations on the Making of Policemen." *Human Organization* 32, no. 4: 407–418.

Vigh, H., and D. Sausdal. 2021. "Global Crime Ethnographies: Three Suggestions for a Criminology That Truly Travels." In *The Oxford Handbook of Ethnographies of Crime and Criminal Justice.* Oxford University Press.

Waddington, P. A. 1999. "Police (Canteen) Sub-Culture: An Appreciation." *British Journal of Criminology* 39, no. 2: 287–309.

Westmarland, L. 2008. "Police Cultures." In *Handbook of Policing.*

8

Subversive Effervescence

The Case of Detention Homes

David Wästerfors

As Collins puts it, collective effervescence "is the exciting place to be" (2022: 17). It is the shared enthusiasm that a group of individuals develops when engaged in a joint ritual. When they assemble face-to-face (sometimes also digitally), focus on the same object, and fall into a shared rhythm of some sort, they "magnify whatever emotion participants are feeling" (Collins: 2022:17). A sense of we-ness is felt, a sense of group solidarity, as if the participants were taken out of their individual selves and "into something larger and more important" (Collins 2022: 17). It is matter of heightened subjectivity through shared action and awareness (Collins 2004: 35).

But what if this heightened subjectivity, this magnified emotion and this "larger and more important" entity, involves countering authority, and turning some kind of social power on its head? What if the activities are forbidden in the context at issue, or at least defined as slightly wrong?

In this chapter I will use examples from my ethnographic studies of youth detention homes in Sweden (Wästerfors 2019; Wästerfors 2023) to illuminate and discuss these questions. The purpose is to advance the theory of collective effervescence concerning practices associated with obvious or subtle wrongdoing in relation to normative structures.

My chapter is intended as a contribution to the conceptualization of what could be called *subversive effervescence*—effervescence that revolves around dissidence, rebellion, destabilizing actions, joint acts of noncompliance, or subtle disobedience. When something "wrong" is done and cherished, something "right" is profaned. Social control inevitably plays a part in this type of effervescence, which I think has become somewhat forgotten. Collins, for instance, mainly emphasizes synchronization and solidarity in *Interaction Ritual Chains* (2004) rather than subversion (see also the chapter by Paéz and colleagues in this book), whereas the original formulations of Émile Durkheim do include offenses and transgressions (Tutenges 2023: 5–6, Durkheim 1912 [2001]: 157–158).

My chapter, therefore, serves as a reminder that the original sociological interest in effervescence encompassed and even presumed that transgressing social control served to energize participants, and that not all ritual performance is devoted to the conventionally edifying aspects of society.

Tutenges (2023: 6) points out that Durkheim's examples included the French Revolution, the St. Bartholomew's Day Massacre, and the Dreyfus affair—events that were violent, unsettling, or otherwise shocking (see also Tutenges 2023: 79)—and he concludes with a definition that specifically includes "transgressive urges," namely urges "that make people do what they would not normally do, ranging from innocent breaches of etiquette to lawbreaking" (Tutenges 2023: 6). Durkheim wrote:

> The effervescence often becomes so intense it leads to unpredictable behaviour. The ordinary set of conditions of life are set aside so definitely and so consciously that people feel the need to put themselves above and beyond customary morality. (1912 [2001]: 163)

This makes it logical to attend to drunken and violent effervescence, two of Tutenges's (2023) types, that definitely cannot be reduced to the construction of conventional social order or the reproduction of "customary morality." Collins's observations are still valid—shared enthusiasm, a face-to-face gathering, a shared rhythm, and a sense of we-ness, etc.—but a subversive keying must be underlined. That is how I would like to define the focus for this chapter, which in many respects builds on Tutenges's (2023) work on transgressive revelry. An attack on order and morality stands in the center—this can define "the exciting place to be." And a sense of play is evident, to which I will return in my concluding discussion with the help of the work of Huzinga (1938 [1971]) and Caillois (1958 [2001]).

Institutional Background

Now, a short note on the context at issue: so-called special approved homes in Sweden (in Swedish: *särskilda ungdomshem*), here called youth detention homes.

There are twenty-one special approved homes in Sweden, and they accommodate approximately 1,100 young people per year (Vogel Andersson and Enell 2018: 191). These young people are placed by Sweden's various municipalities, which have chosen the residential homes "from the range of services available to social services regarding young people with extensive psychosocial issues" (Enell, Gruber, and Vogel Andersson 2018: 30). The young people are among "the most difficult to educate," to use a historical formulation (Enell, Gruber, and Andersson Vogel 2018: 31). Most of them are between fifteen and seventeen years old, but some are younger or older, and almost all are placed involuntarily. The reasons for placement are substance abuse, criminality, or other so-called socially destructive behavior, a rather vivid term that can be used for a variety of life circumstances (Enell, Gruber, and Andersson Vogel 2018: 32). Most are placed in accordance with the LVU Act (the Swedish Care of Young Persons Act), but the special approved homes also receive young people sentenced for crimes under the Secure Youth Care Act LSU.

Living quarters are often located in rural areas and in the same buildings as former reformatory institutions and child protective services homes (Enell, Gruber, and Andersson Vogel 2018: 30). Visitors are greeted with fences; locked gates, doors, and barriers; enclosed playgrounds; cameras; and alarms. The staff are primarily comprised of treatment assistants spread across different departments in different houses, cottages, wings, etc. Teachers, administrators, psychologists, and nurses also work at these locations, but they meet with the young people infrequently or in limited ways.

As an outsider, it is easy to get lost in the legal barriers and red tape of these detention homes. In what follows, I will instead stick to an ethnographic frame built on my fieldwork in six of these homes, because as Tutenges points out, "This style of writing can bring us close to embodied, emotional, and sensory facets of existence" (2023: 14). I draw on data that I gathered via observations and interviews to present the setting and its events as vividly and accurately as possible. I employ ethnography as a communicative strategy to bring readers closer to the core of the phenomenon at issue and its sited specificity (see also Wästerfors 2023).

I first show how subversive effervescence occurs among the young people at these institutions when they engage in locally destabilizing projects. The aspect of "fun" stands at the center, as well as that of collectivity in these arrangements. Then I discuss the sacred element of this kind of effervescence, arguing that normative destruction comes close to being worshipped by the excited actors. This is similar to Katz's (1988) analysis of the emotional attraction of crime and "doing evil," although his links to Durkheim and the effervescence tradition are rather implicit. Katz has illuminated the appeal of reverting or knocking down social order, an appeal that can find nurture and strength in settings that are neatly ordered and controlled.

I complete my analysis with some examples that complicate my argument by showing that staff also may participate in subversive effervescence, albeit in a much milder, more contained, and bounded way.

Chaos Can Be Fun

News reports on uprisings or unrest in youth detention homes seldom communicate "fun." For several years these specially approved homes in Sweden have been reported on in the Swedish media in connection with a series of scandals relating to care, threats against the staff, and other anomalies. In response, the government proposed to move young criminals from these institutions to a set of new, though not yet materialized, youth departments within prisons.

A 2023 news article reported on the Health and Social Care Inspectorate (IVO), a governmental body in Sweden that has criticized these homes for mismanagement:

> The Health and Social Care Inspectorate (IVO) warns that criminals affiliated with gangs exert control through threats and violence at the SIS facility Tysslinge in Södertälje, as reported by Ekot on Swedish Radio.
>
> According to IVO's report, based on two inspections during the fall, the staff have lost control.
>
> "Employees testify that it's only a matter of time before someone living there or a staff member is killed inside the institution," says Pia Karlsson, unit manager at IVO, to the radio.
>
> "The youths are in control, and the staff are concerned about reprisals outside the facility if they intervene."
>
> Tysslinge is one of two facilities with the highest security classification. Almost all youths living there have links to criminal gangs, reports Ekot. . . . The authority is issuing a warning. If the deficiencies are not addressed, the next step could be to close the facility.[1]

"Threats and violence," "the staff have lost control"—the situation does not seem fun at all. The staff are supposed to be in control, but the young people appear to have turned this detention home upside down. I have not examined the situation reported here, but my data includes similar situations, although less grave. And if we turn to the young people's narratives and depictions of their efforts to challenge staff and defy institutional order, there are indeed elements of fun. One might say that to portray revolts and unrest within institutions of this type, without an analytical capacity to include the fun aspect, is to tell the adults' story. Media reports are dressed up in adult discourse: "inspections," "concerned," "intervene," "security classification," "threats and violence," etc.

I am certainly not saying that all young people would find it entertaining to break the rules and confront their masters; many, of course, stay away from any trouble and employ what Goffman has called a playing-it-cool approach (1961 [1990]: 64). Most of the time they keep a low profile, adapt to the rules and regulations, and accept what staff tell them. But it is still fair to say that finding something thrilling, compelling, and enjoyable in a revolt—at least sometimes, in certain situations—constitutes part of the young inmates' recurring practices and perspectives. The enjoyment felt when things go wrong for the staff or when the institutional order is smashed or damaged is quite tangible.

One example of this dynamic can be found in the stories of Tess, a sixteen-year-old girl whom I met on a ward in a detention home.[2] She was very occupied with creating "chaos," as she said, and which the staff also testified to, and she used several expressions to describe the appeal of causing trouble and being violent. I will linger a bit on her accounts to illustrate how rebellious acts can be defined from the point of view of the rebel.

First, the fun aspect was clearly noticeable. Tess found it fun to annoy the staff and she enjoyed the fact that it's "allowed" (as she sees it) to hit the staff and then be subdued by them. She talked about just "going for it" and provided several examples of wild and exhilarating situations in which things had spiraled out of control. She gets "worked up," "runs around," and "just like, aah, seriously. . . . Sometimes it's actually quite fun to create chaos," she said, smiling.

Tess recounted an escape attempt in which the police and rescue services were eventually involved, and she was chased deep into the forest and across a heath without having any real goal for her escape. She described an incident in which she once jumped on a treatment assistant and started "kind of hitting him a lot," even though she actually liked him. Eventually, she let go and calmed down (she "goes to the window and counts to ten"), but a little later, she jumped on him again. Tess kicked him between his legs "so that he flies into this window," she said showing me how, "and into the computer" too. She was kind of proud over the fact that it took "not just two but like ten" staff to wrestle her down and force her to the isolation cell. She obviously liked the kicks and thrills of violent effervescence (Tutenges 2023: 8).

Tess talked about several occasions on which she had been beaten up and had also beaten up others. She easily gets "excited," she said, "in the mood for mischief," and also angry. She laughed when she told her stories and gave the impression that it is fun when the order of the ward collapses. As we talked, I tried to make a distinction between violence as an expression of anger and anger-as-entertainment, but did not quite succeed in this respect. Tess found something fun in *both* variants. There is something refreshing about being a rebel, she believed, regardless of whether it unfolds in a painful or easygoing way. Seeking action seemed to the common denominator, creating chaos.

Second, the collective aspect was also conspicuous. It did not take long before Tess mentioned Jolanda, her friend and "accomplice" in the chaos. Jolanda was also involved in the event that I am about to relate, which seemed to be one in a series of very similar and closely related episodes. But when I met Tess, Jolanda was not present; she had run away. "Otherwise, she would have helped tell the story," said Tess.

With amusement, and admiration, Tess recounted Jolanda's antics. She stated that she, too, had been involved in these antics to some extent. Once, Jolanda had smuggled a hair straightener onto the institution's school premises, plugged it in, and placed it in a laptop where it caught fire. Tess described Jolanda's approach in detail. Just as a teacher was about to discover the sabotage, another girl helped by loosening a bookshelf, thus distracting the teacher. The teacher—according to Tess's account—still complained that whoever wants to "create chaos" can do so on the ward and therefore "leave this place." Tess and Jolanda took him at his word. On the way from the school premises to the ward, they escaped. "Then we ran like hell once we were out," said Tess.

The staff sounded the alarm. Colleagues rushed out and tried to catch up. Jolanda took off her shoes and jacket to run faster and managed to climb over a fence at the edge of the institution's grounds. Tess was unable to, being dressed too heavily, she said. "Then the staff came, and I was just like 'damn.'" She tried to run away from them, but they "kick so hard that you just fly." Eventually, Jolanda was also caught (she later escaped again and with more success). In the evening, the staff discovered that the laptop had been burned. Tess laughed and said that Jolanda then pretended as if nothing had happened, "Jolanda just 'lalala,' can we go now. . . . It was so much fun."

For Tess, causing chaos was the same as disturbing order and "messing around all the time": setting fire to a shirt with a lighter that had been smuggled in, teasing someone "a lot," kicking a staff member, causing a flood, running away and resisting when caught, and so on. Sometimes she calms down on her own, other times she continues to mess around until the staff stop her. The expressions "messing around" and "creating chaos" were used by the staff when describing Tess's behavior. Tess used the same expression when she described the staff's replies. For example, she added this line when describing the staff's reaction in her story: "Tess, that's enough now, you've been messing around all day." In this way, she let the adults narratively confirm and underline her chaotic behavior. The staff both named and expressed opposition to the dangerous and crazy energy involved when Tess "messes around."

It was quite clear that both Jolanda (and occasionally other girls) and the staff contributed to Tess's enjoyment and excitement. Without Jolanda, Tess would have had no teammate to orchestrate their adventures, and without the staff, there would be no audience or normative contrast. The excitement that mesmerized Tess was deeply collaborative, involving both a partner in crime and a collective counterpart.

The opposite was boredom. What is there to do in a youth detention home? Tess didn't get any proper treatment, she said. She went to school, ate, slept, and watched TV. "Sometimes we get to go to the gym, but do you know how small it is?"

The aspects I have highlighted so far in Tess's stories coincide with features in the interpretations of effervescence made by Collins (2004), Tutenges (2023), and Durkheim (1912 [2001]). The feeling of being uplifted and having fun is evident, as is the longing for adventure and action. The companionship between Tess and Jolanda is clearly visible, that is, a small community strengthened by their crazy antics and the resistance they encounter. To these two aspects—the fun and the collective—can be added the striving to break rules and challenging institutional order.

This particular contrast to the formal and orderly is somewhat downplayed in Collins's (2004) default version of effervescence, even though he does identify aggressive and stirred-up emotional energy in his subsequent studies of violence and conflict, such as in events during the French Revolution in 1789 and the assault on the capitol in 2021 (Collins 2022). The contrast is more central to Tutenges's interpretation of Durkheim, and it is clearly evident in Katz's work.

I will continue on this path.

"We Were Totally Crazy"

At one point, Tess recounted, "there was a lot of chaos." She and Jolanda were listening to punk music in the common room and turned up the volume so it was blaring. Tess then pulled off parts of the venetian window blinds and they climbed up on the coffee table engaging in a mock sword fight with them. They destroyed the sofa, ripped out the stuffing, and threw it at a unit manager who tried to talk sense into them. "So, she was completely pale," said Tess laughing (I laughed too).

Around the same time, the police arrived at the institution but for a different reason. Someone had hidden a weapon on another ward, "so the cops came," said Tess. Then she and Jolanda became even more excited. "I mean, we were totally crazy." They peeked at the police through the window, and soon Jolanda started kicking it. Tess and I were talking in the kitchen next to the common room, and Tess pointed out where everything happened. She showed me the window as well:

> Yeah, so she kicked here, cracks appeared everywhere, and then she kicked here and broke the lock, so everything just flew open [oh, wow], and then, like, so many staff came—I mean, there's a button on them [alarm phones], if they press it, a lot of staff comes [yes, I know, yes], and then a lot—there is a lot of staff, and they just tackled us—I mean, damn.

Tess told her story in a meandering way. She quickly brought up other times when the staff had been "so damn hard" during shutdowns that she had felt "really bad pain in her body." She seemed to be suggesting that she had also received rough treatment at that time. On another occasion, although she was only held by the hand, the staff had held it so tightly that her fingers "almost broke." But the points Tess made were not about abuse or misuse of power, they revolved around the wild and energetic: the fun of creating chaos and the excitement of her and Jolanda's projects.

When she was held firmly, for example, it was because she had darted away from her ward to a staff member she hadn't seen in a while, Pelle, whom she "loves." She wanted to hug Pelle at any cost. She was caught and dragged back to where she was supposed to be. She then started breaking a window—a different window. Jolanda was nearby, heard the noise, and shouted "what are you doing?" Tess replied, "'Yeah, but what the hell, I saw Pelle' and she just 'well of course (you should run to him).'"

Tess's stories contain a kind of recurrent, boundless enthusiasm for the in-the-moment impulses and the adventurous companionship she shared with Jolanda. Before the incident with the window blinds, the sofa, and the other forms of chaos on the day that the police arrived, she and Jolanda had torn the lid off a trash bin and caused flooding in a shower. Tess laughed again. "But I mean, we want attention. . . . I can actually admit that. . . . It's fun getting attention." Both she and Jolanda liked it, she said.

When I asked if there were other forms of attention that she might like—without destruction, fights, and shutdowns—she returned to the boredom of being at the institution. Nothing happened. But there were actually staff members who managed to distract her; sitting and drawing or discussing can attract and entertain her, for example. Tess said, "When I do something, I am completely focused. . . . Then I forget about the other chaos." A certain staff member, for example, could "grab" Tess and "take [her] away" to some interesting activity, and she accepted that. A therapist at a previous institution had managed to engage her in exciting conversations in the evenings.

The staff had tried to keep Tess and Jolanda separated, but then, as I have mentioned, Jolanda had run away. "I really miss Jolanda," said Tess, "because she was the best. I mean, it was so much fun." Tess enjoyed all the things they did, like causing chaos with the window, but also their various escape attempts. That Tess "keeps going" until she encounters resistance was evident in her descriptions. The institution's shaken, but eventually restored, formal monopoly on violence constitutes part of her adventures.

This is what I mean by social control being an integral part of subversive effervescence. To some extent it is present in all its forms, at least as long as we include transgression in the definition of the phenomenon. Effervescence, Tutenges underlines, "can push its members to do what they would not have been able, willing, or bold enough to do on their own, such as going beyond boundaries set by the law" (2023: 79). What makes some effervescence subversive, I would say, is that this aspect of it is put at the forefront. Established norms are not just a background issue or "ground floor," but something to attack, upend, ridicule, and laugh at. In subversive effervescence, the element of fun would not appear if it were not for social control.

Worshipping What?

Feelings of excitement; transcendence and solidarity; a shared activity; a sense of being transported beyond the here-and-now; unity and empowerment—quite a lot of the characteristics that Philip Smith and Sébastien Tutenges point to in this book's introduction can be found in stories like Tess's.

And it is worth quoting Durkheim again and the way he writes about the two phases of Australian societies, the second being characterized by "passions so strong and uncontrolled" that they are "bound to seek outward expressions," with violent gestures, shouts, and noises of all sorts. "The effervescence often becomes so intense it leads to unpredictable behaviour" (1912 [2001]: 163). When Tess and Jolanda mess around on their ward, much of their engagement can be described using Durkheim's terminology. They, too, feel a need to put themselves "above and beyond customary morality." There is a ritualistic aspect of revolt and improvised uprising within an institution of this type, and many young people find it attractive to become immersed in subversive projects to separate themselves from the institution and carve out and seize an alternative identity to the one they are formally given.

In short, subversive effervescence is appealing in institutional settings. Stirring up violent opposition is a very effective way of countering boredom. It makes people forget about the past and the future for a while, focusing on the here and now, on passions and adventures, and tantalizing risk-taking disobedience.

As Katz (1988: 142) has noted, what threatens criminally involved youths (such as those in gangs) is not primarily the police (or competing gangs) but boredom. It has to be fun to be part of the group, and therefore one needs to engage in adrenaline-kick activities, directed against social order and conventionality. Adventures and aggressions, violent posing and unpredictable outbreaks, vandalism, "crazy" behavior, etc.—such lines of action may keep the group together, even if it only consists of two individuals (as with Tess and Jolanda for the most part).

Katz (1988: 147) describes the attractiveness of transcendent projects, that is, projects that overthrow authority relations. School, for instance, can be desecrated, lessons can be sabotaged, teachers humiliated. In Tess's case, treatment assistants and the unit manager figure as the target, along with the detention home as a whole. The fact that these homes are carefully regulated—with detailed schedules for treatment and schooling, leisure and meals, morning rituals and bedtime rituals, etc.—provide the young people with a splendid opportunity. It is not difficult to defile the institutional order. It is enough to pull some blinds from a window and climb onto a coffee table to start fighting with them as if they were swords. Even within such a tiny instance of action there are plenty of norm deviations: one should not damage the blinds, one should not stand on tables, one should be having a quiet period in front of the TV, one should wait for the next scheduled activity. When young people on a ward are able to easily identify those points in the institutional order that can be pressed to make everything shake, the temptation resembles that of tipping the first domino in a long and—by others—carefully arranged row of dominoes, whereupon everything naturally collapses. Katz (1988) has pinpointed this very allure: the allure of destruction, sabotage, and the sometimes surprisingly easy gestures that can tip everything over.

Another characteristic is powerful escalation. Things can start in a small way and quickly intensify. Durkheim again: "The passions unleashed are so impetuous they cannot be contained" (1912 [2001]: 163). Tess's descriptions communicated a spiraling of events and an accelerating tempo, which both Tess and Jolanda seemed to find fun in themselves. This contradicts the institution's slow and predictable routines, grey and empty, and more similar to the first phase in Durkheim's (1912 [2001]: 162) Australian analysis, characterized by a "monotonous, lazy and dull" social life. The stillness of an ideal residential treatment facility—from the staff's point of view—can be seen as the very opposite of effervescence (even though I will soon complicate this argument), and consequently not "the exciting place to be" (Collins 2022: 17). When actions acquire the quality of "more and more," "crazier and crazier," transcending the adults' social order in ever more blatant ways, they can turn very interesting from the perspective of those who do not want to be inside the adults' social order in the first place.

Let me now briefly diverge to another type of data. "Crazy escalation" was a theme I used many years ago in a task I gave students in criminology classes. The students were asked to—anonymously—write a short story of their own experiences of crime or deviant behavior of some kind. One example revolved around a night at a golf driving range that had involved a kind of spontaneous and escalating vandalism:

> One evening, when my friends and I were celebrating one of our friends' birthdays, something happened. We decided to start at a golf course's driving range. We arrived quite late and began hitting balls while chatting with each other. This golf course had its driving range open 24/7, so after a while, everyone else, including the golf course owners, had gone home, and darkness had fallen. That's when we started fooling around. We hit various objects on the driving range, such as cans and sticks. We even set up the ball machine with cans. We also pulled up various signs that were positioned here and there. These signs ended up coming with us when we left. In those moments, we didn't think much about what we were doing or what would happen afterward. I mostly felt that it was fun and a bit thrilling to behave that way.

"That's when we start fooling around," "fun," "a bit thrilling"—a sort of tantalizing effervescence emerges in a story such as this, not unlike the tone in Tess's version, with various objects being hit with the golf clubs, things being stolen, and the whole local order of the facility being temporarily desecrated. The moment was narrated as a memorable one, a moment of group reinforcement and liberating disrespect.

How, then, can the sacred be defined? In this context, effervescence does not define or generate anything holy—unless, of course, the community among the villains can in itself be seen as sacred. Subversive effervescence keeps the subverting group intact and meaningful. However, what is more central when it comes to the emotionally mobilizing, power-up ritual is the temporary normative destruction.

This, I suggest, is the actual sacred entity in subversive effervescence: the provisional wiping out of conventional order and morality, the short-lived annihilation of "the good" and "right." Conventionality and law-abiding behavior thus serve as the material—a very necessary resource. In practice, it is the playfully framed and successful attack on a normative reality that stands out as being unquestionably idolized.

The Careful Contribution of the Staff

My field notes from detention homes contain quite a lot of instances in which young people defy the rules, try to circumvent the adults' order, or playfully mock the morality of the institution. Most are much more subtle than Tess's story: secretly having a smoke in the toilet, hiding a cell phone in one's room, stealing some towels and keeping them under one's bed, killing the fish in an aquarium, falling asleep during a lesson or joking the lesson away, etc.

What I want to emphasize in rounding up my analysis is the discreet participation of staff members. Of course, the staff do not steal towels or kill fish in aquariums, let alone help out in revolts or escape attempts, but they do engage in other things, such as collective jokes with the young people, teasing arguments, pranks, and pretend fights. One example that I have reported in an article on play fights at these institutions (Wästerfors 2016: 183–185) revolved around the teasing relationship between Ahmed (a young inmate) and Mia (a staff member). One day when Ahmed and Mia left the room on their ward after my interview with Ahmed, he struck a play fighting pose.

> He walks next to Mia, and she responds by doing the same. They exchange some blows in the air, and Mia says, "You!" in a sort of fictive warning-and-threatening manner. Ahmed, nineteen, is not that big but looks strong and has a tough style, and Mia (in her thirties) is not far from the same: she also has tattoos and a sort of "gym look," embodying a masculine attitude but still feminine (similar to "Kelly" in Messerschmidt [2004]). We are heading toward the kitchen, and when Mia unlocks the kitchen door, Ahmed is tickling her in her side quite hard so that she has to tense herself in order to not lose her grip on the key. There are hot sandwiches to be made in the kitchen, by staff and pupils together.
>
> A little later, Mia realized that Ahmed had not put his headphones back, and since the young people were not supposed to keep these in the shared living rooms (they should be kept in their private rooms) Mia firmly said, "What's this?" Not following the rules around headphones and similar things had been discussed before on this ward. Ahmed just responded, "Then confiscate them," but another staff member replied, "You know the rules." When Mia and Ahmed returned to his room with the headphones, the atmosphere was far from playful.
>
> But just a moment later, I can see that Mia gives Ahmed a punch on his back, a sort of slap. Now they are back in the kitchen, and I'm sitting in the living room with a direct view of what happens between

> them. Mia sees that I see, and I smile. She says that they have "an internal reckoning" going on, and she smiles, too, taking some steps out of the kitchen at the same time. "He is always doing that," she says, referring to Ahmed slapping her. "So now you got your chance [to strike back]?" I say. She nods with a happy face. Ahmed says, "That's how we communicate," pronouncing the last word quite distinctly and with an ironic smirk, as if trying to say that this description was both true and a little silly. He is making a sandwich.

Exchanging a few blows in the air, addressing one another in a fictively threatening manner, tickling one another or giving a slap on the back—we are now quite far from blatant revolts or violent attacks in a youth detention home. Still, we are not so far away from standing on a coffee table with pieces of a blind in one's hands pretending they are swords. What I mean is that the starting points of stories like Tess's do contain instances that staff—under certain circumstances, within certain relations—can tolerate and even participate in themselves, like the situation involving Mia and Ahmed. This situation certainly did not evolve into a "wild" and "crazy" performance intended to temporarily overthrow the institutional order, but it nonetheless offered some leeway for the members of the institution—both young people and staff—to unite in a warm and elevating emotion of transcendence. What can be observed is a very subtle instance of subversive effervescence, a scent of it.

Thus, the analysis has to become a bit more complicated. Staff can sometimes join in with subversive effervescence as long as the interactions underpinning it do not escalate, and as long as they can be ascribed a treatment-related meaning. In the last example involving Mia and Ahmed, "communicating" is the key ("that's how we communicate"). They both viewed their playful—and yet formally quite rule-breaking behavior (with slaps, touches, blows, and threats, etc.)—as part of their relationship, and they both found it fun to interact in an ambivalent is-this-serious-or-not manner. The institutional order is bracketed and downplayed, and Mia and Ahmed as people stand in the forefront, more salient and solid than the detention home.

The rituals of locally accepted play fighting come with subversive effervescence in this respect, in a sort of bounded version—bounded, that is, by the adults' local and institutional practices and accountability.

Discussion

In this chapter, I have demonstrated how subversive effervescence can manifest in situations in which joint acts of blatant or subtle disobedience and other normative attacks are accomplished. An aspect of fun and relative disorder or chaos is significant, together with the collective aspect, and what paradoxically seems sacred is the normative destruction itself, albeit in a temporary form. In my data from youth detention homes, young people most often carry out the bulk of such interactions, but staff also initiate and participate, as long as the normative destruction is mild, contained, and locally accountable. When staff do this, they seem to come socially closer to the young people, imitating some of their ways and styles.

Subversive effervescence is closely aligned with Tutenges's (2023) violent and drunken variants from which we can recognize transgressive and chaotic qualities. It can easily fit within Durkheim's (1912 [2001]) original perspective, which includes violent gestures, shouting, noise, vandalism etc. while also encompassing a typically playful and fun side. Normative destruction, which I see as indispensable in subversive effervescence, is defined as "entertaining" and "liberating" by those who engage in it, at least temporarily. Tess's stories are indicative in this regard. She emphasizes in various ways that the chaos on the ward feels like fun and makes her feel good, even though it results in violent responses and punishments from the institution. As Tutenges (2023: 113–123) points out, collective effervescence is revitalizing.

Theoretically, we need to both combine and trim existing conceptual frameworks. From Collins (2004), we need to complicate the typical constructive and consensus-oriented aspect of the effervescence in interaction rituals and instead focus on how it can just as easily tear down, attack, and mobilize conflict. It does not seem reasonable to understand effervescence solely in terms of the charging of common symbols and membership against the backdrop of violent and rebellious variants, where the commonality is rather the target of contempt, ridicule, destabilization, or at least irony. Subversive effervescence appears highly ephemeral and does not need to result in anything lasting. On the contrary, its fleeting nature is essential, and part of its pleasure lies in ignoring any long-term and enduring aspects.

In regard to the Durkheimian (1912 [2001]) tradition, with Tutenges (2023) at the forefront, we probably need to add two things: (a) a heightened interest in transgressions in the form of normative destruction and (b) an equally heightened interest in play and playfulness. I have already dwelled on the former, which examines the importance of a normative structure against which subversive effervescence can push and from which it can draw energy as evidenced by examples from institutional life. Tess and Jolanda's adventures would not be particularly attractive or narratively captivating if they did not take place in a strictly controlled environment where even the smallest movements and remarks can be subject to regulations and control measures. A normative framework or embedding is central to both understanding and being attracted to this type of negating engagement.

Huizinga (1938 [1971]: 2–4) argues that intensity and absorption are essential for play. People can throw themselves into and become absorbed by playful interactions precisely because they cannot be reduced to serious abstractions. Play is irrational or at least something beyond rationality, and it is voluntary; it cannot be commanded (Huizinga 1938 [1971]: 8). Play is also not real or ordinary; there is a transgression in play that means participants go beyond the ordinary in a confined way, creating a temporary sphere of activity. It takes place within certain boundaries in time and space and holds its own direction and meaning; it is autotelic. Play is about a temporary suspension of the world, with its own rules and assumptions (Huizinga 1938 [1971]: 10–11, 18), which makes it "dense" and very similar to rituals.

In fact, Huizinga claims that ritual has all the characteristics that define play, especially the ability to transport participants to another world. Huizinga also emphasizes the tension and uncertainty of play, which is particularly evident in agonistic games, that is, games characterized by struggle or competition. A game can be about outshining or outdoing the other and proving one's superiority. However, as civilizations develop and become more complex, the connection with their playful elements is often lost; civilization becomes increasingly serious, and play is given only a secondary and marginal place (Huizinga 1938 [1971]: 75). Another characteristic of play is exaggeration, even a megalomaniac tendency (Huizinga 1938 [1971]: 143). Grandiose gestures belong to the world of play, as do the magnificent and the dazzling.

In short, Huizinga presents a view of play that far exceeds what we usually associate with children's play, for example, the innocent and the pedagogical. And much of what he describes can be found in the cases of subversive effervescence that I have illustrated in this chapter. The intense, absorbing, irrational, and voluntary; the transgressive and confined; the autotelic but simultaneously uncertain, tension-filled, and exaggerated. A "civilized" entity like a ward in a treatment institution certainly does not put play at the center. If the young people (and staff) are attracted to it, they better do it in the periphery, exemplifying troubles or respite (Wästerfors 2016).

When Caillois (1958 [2001]: 23) develops Huizinga's approach, he distinguishes "ilinx" as a form of play, that is, a pursuit of vertigo and the destabilization of reality. This can involve fast, rotating, and accelerating movements that evoke a dizzying and sucking sensation—and Caillois (1958 [2001]: 24) argues that we can simultaneously speak of vertigo in relation to the moral order. *Ilinx*, Greek for "whirlpool," is Caillois's name for these games or plays, which move the actor morally toward disorder and destruction.

> In adults, nothing is more revealing of vertigo than the strange excitement that is felt in cutting down the tall prairie flowers with a switch, or in creating an avalanche of the snow on a rooftop, or, better, in the intoxication that is experienced in military barracks—for example, in noisily banging garbage cans. (Caillois 1958 [2001]: 24)

In the example of Tess and Jolanda, it is clear that they drive events until they come to a halt, until the staff intervene and put an end to their whirlpool. Their effervescence is clearly anchored in agonistic relationships and in pushing boundaries, demonstrating superiority, and temporarily suspending the ward's regime.

We can say that *they are playing with the institution and its moral order.*

The entire sequence is framed by an as-if feeling: the youths behave as if they could do anything, as if they could escape and vandalize, fight and threaten, break rules and create chaos, as if these things were socially and morally possible—and they are, for the moment. But the limitations in time and space are also clear. They cannot continue indefinitely, and the play cannot expand to just any place. Sooner or later there are limits: the play ends, seriousness steps in, the narratives conclude, and stillness and boredom return. The institution wins, and the youths have to comply with its order, but the effervescence was still subversive in the sense of being undermining, destabilizing, and disturbing. The "strange excitement" that Callois (1958 [2001]: 24) speaks of derives its strength and appeal from Tess and Jolanda's destabilization or ilinx on the ward, their fast and chaotic destruction filling them with a sense of action and energy.

But since the institution is formal and "civilized," play elements are hidden or placed at the margins. In my introductory excerpt from the news report on a violent uprising, no fun or "whirling" elements were seen.

Opposite of this type of effervescence is—as I have pointed out—boredom. To have nothing to do, to experience stillness and predictability, to long for "where the action is," to use Goffman's (1967) terminology, functions as a narrative contrast. Seeking and engaging in subversive effervescence seems to be more accountable in terms of seeking excitement and enjoyment rather than in terms of the normative attack as such, which speaks for the play element. One does not have to unite rhetorically in an ideological reason or theory of oppression to be subversive and seek effervescence with other rebels, one just has to unite in being rebellious. Still, a normative structure of some sort—a "what ought to be" in a socially defined way—is a must. There will be no subversive effervescence without an objectification of social control.

It is for this reason, I suggest, that we see quite clear formulations of socially ordered entities or representatives of control in stories of subversive effervescence: the unit manager at a detention home turning "completely pale" trying in vain to talk sense into the makers of chaos; of furniture being destroyed or used unexpectedly and disrespectfully; of a setting normally associated with neat style and etiquette; the use of a golf club; becoming the target of senseless vandalism, etc. The fun part turns even funnier when agents or symbols of social control are demonstratively desecrated and disrespected. The control is being outshone or outdone; megalomaniac gestures defile the place.

It is also for this reason that we find so many of these experiences and narratives among young people in today's society (teenagers, or people in their twenties), since being young is still culturally associated with being—at least at times—a bit rebellious, freedom-seeking, wanting to dodge or tear down the adult world, to play with it. To hesitate about growing up and becoming mature is to subvert adults' social control for a while and extend one's playful time in life.

Shilling and Mellor (1998: 203) point out that for Durkheim, social life is moral life. In the vitalism of collective effervescence, there is an achievement of communion taking place stimulating solidarity. The "rush of energy" that we feel when participating in a successful interaction ritual—to lean on Collins (2004)—is the societal forms being re-created: membership and shared symbols, sacred notions, and recognizable patterns of behavior. However, as Shilling and Mellor (1998: 205) also point out, nothing is gained if the analyst has a predetermined view of the exact consequences of effervescence. Durkheim associated the sacred with the development of social and moral solidarity and the productive side of social cohesion—a sort of socially beneficent solidarity—but he also identified something else. Without changing its essential nature, effervescence can also attack conventional society and produce dissolution, leading to unpredictable behavior "beyond customary morality" (Durkheim 1912 [2001]: 163). In revolutions, for instance, people are stirred by passion so intense that they can be satisfied only by violence and extreme acts (Shilling and Mellor 1998: 196). In less dramatic day-to-day interactions, people can experience a certain "rush of energy" even when they disagree with conventions, circumvent rules, and defy expectations, especially if they do so jointly, in a team constellation.[3]

Thus, I think we have to keep an eye on the multidimensional aspects of collective effervescence. It comes in various forms and has a varying scope, can be subtle or blatant and anything in between, and may as well destroy conventional social order as well as reproduce it.

So it would be a mistake to only focus on the educational or edifying aspects of Durkheim's theory. We need to look upon rituals and their associated variants of effervescence from a playful angle—and *that* is an exciting place to be.

NOTES

1. See the Swedish tabloid *Aftonbladet* December 12, 2023, https://www.aftonbladet.se/nyheter/a/Kn50xe/ivo-gangkriminella-styr-sis-hemmet, my translation.

2. The stories told by Tess have previously been analyzed in a Swedish book (Wästerfors 2019).

3. But I do not mean to say that the egoistic side of Durkheim's anthropology—his homo duplex—necessarily would be active when people behave subversively. The idea that individuals would be internally divided between egoistic impulses on the one hand and conceptual thought and morality on the other does not help us here. It would simplify matters to associate subversive effervescence with the opposite of "asocial passions" and "moral activity," since what is moral is "everything that is a source of solidarity" (Shilling and Mellor 1998: 196). There is morality being acted out in subversive effervescence, too, although not the kind of morality that adults or conventional agents of social control would prefer—and there is solidarity among the rebels.

REFERENCES

Caillois, Roger. (2001). *Man, Play and Games.* The University of Illinois Press.

Collins, Randall. (2004). *Interaction Ritual Chains.* Princeton University Press.

Collins, Randall. (2022). *Explosive Conflict. Time-Dynamics of Violence.* Routledge.

Durkheim, Émile. (2001). *The Elementary Forms of Religious Life.* Oxford University Press.

Enell, Sofia, Gruber, Sabine, and Vogel, Maria Andersson. (2018). "Tvångspraktiker på institution. En teoretisk och historisk inramning." In *Kontrollerade unga. Tvångspraktiker på institution* edited by S. Enell, S. Gruber, and Maria A. Vogel, Maria. Studentlitteratur.

Goffman, Erving. (1967). "Where the Action Is." In *Interaction Ritual. Essays on Face-to-face Behavior.* Anchor Books.

Goffman, Erving. (1990). *Asylums. Essays on the Social Situation of Mental Patients and Other Inmates.* Anchor Books.

Huizinga, Johan. (1971). *Homo Ludens. A Study of the Play-Element in Culture.* Boston: The Beacon Press. Originally published in 1938 by Tjeenk Willink.

Katz, Jack (1988). *Seductions of Crime. Moral and Sensual Attractions in Doing Evil.* Basic Books.

Messerschmidt, James A. (2004). *Flesh and Blood. Adolescent Gender Diversity and Violence.* Rowan & Littlefield.

Shilling, Chris, and Mellor, Philip A. (1998). "Durkheim, Morality and Modernity: Collective Effervescence, Homo Duplex and the Sources of Moral Action." *The British Journal of Sociology* 49 (2): 193–209.

Tutenges, Sébastien. (2023). *Intoxication. An ethnography of Effervescent Revelry.* Rutgers University Press.

Vogel Andersson, Maria, and Enell, Sofia. (2018). "Staten och kapitalet. Om statens institutionsstyrelses roll på barnavårdsmarknaden." In *Socialtjänstmarknaden. Om marknadsorientering och konkurrensutsättning av individ- och familjeomsorgen*, edited by M. Sallnäs, and S. Wiklund. Liber.

Wästerfors, David. (2016). "Playfights as Trouble and Respite." *Journal of Contemporary Ethnography* 45 (2): 168–197.

Wästerfors, David. (2019). *Vanskligt och kort. Om våldshändelser bland unga på institution.* Studentlitteratur.

Wästerfors, David. (2023). "Getting at the Experience of Confinement in Detention." In *Crafting Ethnographic Fieldwork: Sites, Selves, and Social Worlds*, first edition, edited by A. B. Marvasti and J. F. Gubrium, J. F. Routledge. https://doi.org/10.4324/9781003275121.

9

The Solitary Reader

The Anxieties of High-Culture Readers in the Time of Culture Wars

Daniel Smith

This chapter discusses participation in the life of an independent bookshop in a provincial English town. Cultlike in their devotion, my readers are passionate about what they read, and regard this bookshop, and bookshops in general, as special (of existential value for a vision of Englishness and English literature, even [D Smith 2023]). In Émile Durkheim's terms, the sacred is set apart from the world of the profane, that is, the routine, every day. And critical to making something sacred for a group, in Durkheim's theory, is the process of collective effervescence. While a fluid concept, many Durkheimians would follow Tutenges's definition of collective effervescence as "an altered state of heightened intersubjectivity marked by intense, transgressive, and yet mutually attuned actions and emotions among individuals who are gathered in the same place" (2023, 6). Given this definition, my fieldwork may appear as an anomaly: my empirical material is characterized by little to none of this collective experience. Instead of transgression and intense intersubjectivity, what you'll find is intrasubjective angst: intellectuals worried what the books they value say about them to others; how their fears about the profane realities of politics are inseparable from their anxious reading habits. Emotions do not run high, but angst does.

Nevertheless, I am contributing to Durkheimian sociology, albeit not in a traditionalist way. Let this chapter act as a limit case for the concept of effervescence. My suggestion is that the traditional definition of "effervescence" does not, in fact, serve the goal of effervescence in contemporary life, that is, social solidarity outright. Pointing to the Dreyfus affair or Bastille Day, in his own time, Durkheim thought there could be heightened moments of collective effervescence in mass societies, but when one observes contemporary life it seems Durkheim's hopes have been dashed: George Floyd and Black Lives Matter in the United States, Edward Colston's statue in the United Kingdom; the proliferation of populism, protest, and mass gathering witnessed in recent years are defined as much by effervescence as it is intense dread and uncertainty about social solidarity. My line of thought, in this chapter, is that something of this experience of dread in collective life finds its way into both individual and smaller group dynamics. Strange as it may appear, I offer the effect of anxiety as a signal not of some individual, psychological state but, in true Durkheim fashion, as a sui generis effect of collective life: angst signals a society compromised on what it values and how it values it. Angst is a signal of our fears about what collective effervescence entails: belonging together.

One ritual that I attended during my fieldwork brought this out: what appeared to be effervescence concealed something else. The Bookshop runs a silent reading group every Wednesday evening after business hours—a time set apart, sacred time—for those who sign up to its mailing list. One gives over their cell phone to the booksellers in exchange for a small glass of wine (transgression?), and then reads, in silence, a book they have brought themselves (perhaps heightened intersubjectivity?).

The Bookshop advertises this evening as follows:

> Considering the pace of modern life and the anxiety-inducing news we're all experiencing on a day-to-day basis, taking a quiet moment to stop, slow down, and focus on one thing isn't just good for well being—it's actually quite a rebellious act.

Reading is an antidote: it quells the anxiety of social and political tumult. Reading is a provocation: it rebels against the normative demands of a digital, platform economy. Reading is analog: the digital is sacrificed (in the form of the cell phone that one gives up), and the analog is sacralized. While it may appear that this solitary reading ritual is establishing clear boundaries between sacred-profane, pure-impure, it would be more appropriate to say these oppositions are being staged. These oppositions are not about keeping boundaries separate but more about outlining their fault lines, and dependency upon one another. The threat of digital technology is not the obsolescence of analog. Rather the analog is assumed to guarantee a vestige of individuality that digitalization eclipses. The problem of anxiety-inducing political and economic crisis is not fear of the future, it is fear of the uncertainty of the present: reading seems to fall somewhere in-between as it calms anxiety in one direction while it provokes in another. As such, the effervescence solitary reading "stages" (if not produced at the level of subjectivity) is a projection of collective anxieties: it is not about intense, intersubjective bonds in action and meaning, but instead a figuring of the angst-ridden ideals and counter-ideals that haunt much of what we are most passionate about in contemporary life.

This chapter examines these claims through interviews with booksellers and readers from The Bookshop, all circling around three anxieties that pervade our time: the relationship between aesthetic preferences and political values; the relationship between individual autonomy and the automated organization of art under digital algorithms; and between individual uniqueness and the uniqueness of others.

Aesthetic Autonomy and Its Anxieties

Our solitary reading evening harbors a set of anxieties that are by no means local or particular to reading. Extratextual meanings attached to our cultural pursuits have become a preeminent site of social anxiety: liking someone "canceled" (Can I watch *Annie Hall* today?); our complicity in racist histories and genealogies (Should I show my children Disney's *Peter Pan?*); and many more. How we inhabit aesthetic practices rank among some of our most abiding fears. Ironically, however, it is by engaging with these transgressive elements of our taste preferences that what is important and sacred about them comes to the fore, a process that Kurakin calls the "impure sacred" (2015, 377). Such a suggestion is in keeping with a long-standing sociological critique of Kantian philosophy: not only is taste socially determined (Bourdieu 1984), but one cannot separate moral desire from aesthetic judgments (Smith and Stoll 2022; Kuipers et al. 2019). As Smith and Stoll point out, separating a pleasing or displeasing aesthetic feeling from our moral desires of right or wrong is "empirically false" as "virtue or sin can augment and diminish pleasure" (2022, 2). In this context, the solitary reading evening described here can be interpreted as not only staging our collective anxieties about our relationship to aesthetics and morality, but how the experience of collective effervescence is contained or channeled into aesthetic objects.

Here we can extend the sociological critique of Kantian aesthetics in a more Durkheimian way. The domain of life we call "aesthetic," which Kantian philosophy associated with judgments of disinterested pleasure, arose in European modernity alongside efforts to control bodily sensations, and tame individual conduct: what Terry Eagleton (1990) calls the ideology of the aesthetic as a way of policing aesthetic sensation in the name of bourgeois rationality and individual autonomy. Politeness, modesty, understatement, and aloofness became mannered responses to art as the European middle classes began to fear what aesthetic sensation also had the potential for: excessive, transgressive, intense feelings. As Friedrich Nietzsche wrote in *Twilight of the Idols*,

> For any sort of aesthetic activity . . . to exist, a certain physiological precondition is indispensable: intoxication [*Rausch*]. . . . The essence of intoxication is the feeling of plenitude and increased energy. From out of this feeling, one gives to things . . . this procedure called idealizing. (1889 [1968], 82–83)

To a Durkheimian, Nietzsche's hypothesis is that all aesthetic forms arise from collective effervescence. But to the sociologist of modernity, this raises a problem. First it suggests that aesthetic products are sources of effervescence without the group. Or second, better yet, it suggests that aesthetic sensations could be read as always already, haunted by the specter of collective effervescence, of intense feelings of togetherness. Managing the two is how effervescence is internalized as angst.

Mazzarella's *Mana of Mass Society* (2017) has captured this thought in his concept of "anxious autonomy." Given that the anxiety underlying aesthetic experience is that external purpose could never quite be banished, modern subjects must negotiate between two ways of relating to aesthetic objects that he calls object-anxiety and subject-anxiety. While separate, both forms of anxiety have as their underlying fear that our autonomy is far from autonomous and our individuality far from a fait accompli.

With object-anxiety the anxiety is that our cherished artworks could betray us. For instance, a considerable number of people may enjoy Bruce Springsteen's song "Dancing in the Dark," but *my* "favorite" Springsteen song is "Used Cars" (a deep cut from his 1982 *Nebraska*, and one not on Spotify's "most played" list). Yet while this may mark me as distinctive, I am never able to quite banish the anxiety that "Used Cars" "speaks" to me in the same way as it speaks to those who like only "Dancing in the Dark." How much of *me* is really being addressed in "Used Cars"? Mazzarella calls this anxiety the problem of "perfect addressability": an anxiety that marks how aesthetic products are pulled in two different directions—the inner life of the individual recipient and the mass market—purposeless purpose always coincides with purposeful purpose (2017, 102–104).

With subject-anxiety, the problem is that the artwork says more about us than we may wish or says something about us in a way that banishes any and every sense of our individuality. In the context of my own fieldwork, a *New Statesman* article attempted to distill the landscape of British political unease and crisis through the figure of the "Waterstones Dad": an (upper) middle-class political anomaly (could vote Tory or Labour; could have voted Leave, or Remain; etc.; earns £80k-plus, has a second home; distrusts capitalism, yet works in marketing) (Jacobson 2023). The "Waterstones Dad" is defined less by who he is—socially, politically, economically—and more by the books "he" reads. The inference being: *If you've read Sapiens, and are a middle aged, middle-class white guy, you're probably a Waterstones Dad* (P. Smith 2023).

With object-anxiety, the dread is that one's singular, unique status as an autonomous self is threatened when faced with the possibility that one could just as well be addressed by other artworks and feel much the same passion as one does about their favored artworks. With subject-anxiety, the angst is social and relational: Who am I to the other person? Could another better recognize me by way of misrecognition? Common to these anxieties is that the distinction between self and others, self and object, dissipate and become hard to untangle. As psychoanalyst Jacques Lacan observes,

> The instant when the subject is suspended between a moment at which he no longer knows where he is, and a shift towards a moment when he will become something in which he will never be able to find himself again: that's what anxiety is. (2022, 218)

After having surveyed the subject- and object-anxieties of my participants, my conclusion will be that what Lacan describes regarding anxiety can supplement Durkheim's (1912 [2001]) concept of collective effervescence. For now, however, let us note how angst and effervescence share some important analog features at the level of affect.

Lacan's loss of orientation is akin to what Durkheim describes as the "delirium" of effervescence when experienced at its apogee: "What other name can we give to the burst of emotion in which men [*sic*] find themselves when, as the result of collective effervescence, they believe they have been swept up into a world quite different from the one they see?" (1912 [2001], 171). Critical to this "delirium" was not, exclusively, the loss of individual orientation but what such a loss allowed: the moral force of one's opinions could draw their power from the vitality of the collective. "This unusual surplus of forces is quite real: it comes to him [*sic*] from the very group he is addressing. [. . .] He is no longer a simple individual speaking; he is a group incarnate and personified" (Durkheim 1912 [2001], 158). It is on this point that this chapter wants to argue that intrasubjective angst owes itself the thwarted experience of collective effervescence we inhabit: as much as we require the normative force of the collective in the making of our opinions, that very opinion is always tarnished with an object or subject-anxiety that produces less the ecstasy of belonging and more the anguish of what it means to be included. Collective effervescence reveals itself as the dread of what it means to be lost to collective life.

The Research

To properly attend to the "anxious autonomy" discerned in my fieldwork, an account of the ethnographic material and context is necessary.

The Bookshop is a high-culture institution. Alongside solitary reading events, it offers private member book club events; evening talks from literary critics, poets, and philosophers; public intellectuals; and other members of the British intelligentsia. It also puts on its own literary festivals; prominent novelists have used its writing rooms in its attic to finish their novels, and it houses writers and poets in residence. The Bookshop regularly features in "Best Bookshop" lists in UK broadsheet newspapers and culture supplements. This cultural prestige is reflected in my participants' identities and sensibilities. George, proprietor of The Bookshop, worked as a writer and actor in television and theater before becoming a bookseller. John, chief bookseller at The Bookshop, has a degree in English literature from Oxford University and used to worked in digital marketing at the BBC. All fifteen interviewees were university educated and five had postgraduate degrees. Their professions also reflected their association with The Bookshop: two novelists and writers; two PhD students; one sometime, retired academic; two English literature and one art history graduate, as well as a publisher and a literary translator. Other professions included a mental health nurse and a civil servant. These are privileged people. But contrary to the Bourdieuian tradition of taste and sensibility, the aim of inquiry is to examine less how taste preferences map out class boundaries and symbolic struggles and more about how tastes index the social milieu of angst and dread that characterize much of collective life at present.

Anxiety is an unlikely concept for the interpretative strategies employed by sociology. However, cultural sociology is in a unique position. As Alexander says, "Cultural sociology is a kind of social psychoanalysis. Its goal is to bring the social unconscious up for view" (2003, 4). We have seen a glimpse of this early in this chapter, but in what follows I will use the long-form interviews I conducted as the basis for an interpretation of the anxiety detected. I adopt for this an interpretive procedure taken from the psychoanalytic session. While I did not attempt to become my participant's shrink (thankfully), the interviews were completely unstructured much in the same way an analytic session is: I would merely ask each participant one opening question, "So tell me how you came to reading?" From there I would listen intently, and when participants signaled that they had nothing more to say, I would pick up what they'd been speaking about to encourage them to say more. I had no questions to ask other than the questions their own speech provoked. As Alexander puts it, "A meaning-centered sociologist must learn to speak with the listening voice of the psychoanalyst, to employ the same hermeneutic method of deep interpretation, and to read structures of social feelings as imaginatively as psychotherapists read individual-feeling texts" (2014, xi). Therefore, the accounts provided by my participants refer less to the practical, lived realities of The Bookshop, and more to the meaningful construction of both The Bookshop and reading in their imaginations.

Anxiety 1: George

A persistent ethical assertion made by many participants was that reading, in and of itself, is a virtue. The act of reading was a *good* act: What you read makes you good? Well, we'll see. My participants, implicitly, were consequentialists: the act of reading produces good things and whether it makes you a good person is not the issue. My participants advocated a vision of reading situated in the legacies of Romanticism and Modernism, first in the sense that reading was associated with the imaginative and inner depths to individual selfhood and second, in the sense that reading prioritizes reflective, intrapersonal experience as it dissolves boundaries, identities, and biographies and emphasizes an openness to alterity and otherness. However, it is within these visions of reading that the good consequences, ironically, remain situated in the character of the reader: a romantic-modernist philosophy of reading, ironically, produces a social character-type. It was the social character-type they could be perceived as which became the anxiety for my participants.

To George, an independent bookshop

> could be, and should be, almost places of sedition. Places of dissent. That sounds a bit ridiculous—but certainly places of conversation and debate. And drinking, whether it is coffee or wine. . . . I just think that if you are, sort of, a small pretty little bookshop, that's fine, you're still selling books . . . but there is an air of, I find, smugness that goes with it. I just despise it.

George is aware of the class baggage of high-brow literature and high-culture (D Smith 2023). But he is steadfast in his belief that the independent bookshop has aesthetic affordances that are unique to advocating such sedition or dissent:

> When looking at an array of books like this it is like you're looking at an array of portals, and you could go down any of them, and what's right for now? And what's right for now will be different depending on where you are and what you've experienced—so if it is not therapy, it is not escapism either. Particularly as we stock a lot of non-fiction, in fact it is like arming yourself to go back and experience things differently. Differently rather than in a better way.

To George, dissent or sedition is an intrapersonal concept: the aesthetic affordances of literature encourage one to experience the world "differently." George is outlining a modernist self of relentless transformation: when he asks, "What's right for now?" he envisions the self as different from moment to moment and from person to person (Smith 2022). This is the ethical "good" of reading: it allows one to inhabit difference and privileges a disposition open to Otherness and alternative points of view on the world. Moreover, George took this intrapersonal disposition to foreground a political value: "It is like arming yourself to go back and experience things differently." At once George is evoking the aesthetic virtue of a modernist philosophy toward literature, but he is also invoking the books in front of him. At the time of my ethnography, The Bookshop's bestsellers were Eagleton's (2011) *Why Marx Was Right* and Eddo-Lodge's (2017) *Why I'm No Longer Talking to White People About Race.* He would, personally, tell me that the city in which The Bookshop is located is "an oasis of Remain in a surrounding Brexit vote" and that shop reflects this, culturally and intellectually. At once there is the aesthetic virtue of an intrapersonal self open to difference, and the political values of Marxism and critical race theory.

An incident that occurred in the wake of Donald Trump's election in the United States, and the 2016 EU referendum in the United Kingdon, brought out the knotted relationship between political values and aesthetic virtues for The Bookshop. A prominent author canceled her appearance at a local literary event and later wrote an opinion piece in a conservative periodical claiming censorship from The Bookshop. The context being that The Bookshop had been contacted by a local book group in the wake of the Trump election with an idea. This book group would personally buy copies of books such as George Orwell's *1984* or Margaret Atwood's *Handmaid's Tale* that would be given away for free to members of the public. George liked the idea. But the prominent author did not, and a national debate began with George appearing on BBC Radio 4 and providing interviews in national newspapers. The accusation that George took umbrage with was the claim, by this author, that his shop will *only* stock left-liberal nonfiction; that there are explicit political ideologies being expressed in the curation of The Bookshop. This is, of course, untrue and George was asserting as much. However, he did draw a line: he stated that he would never stock, nor order in for a customer, Adolf Hitler's *Mein Kampf.*

What is at issue here is not so much the rights or wrongs of the claims of censorship or political values being asserted with the literature on sale in The Bookshop, but more the way aesthetic virtues and political values become blurred and conflated. On the one hand, George is anti-Trump and pro-Remain and so on; on the other, his vision of a seditious or dissenting bookshop, coupled with the modernist aesthetic of intrapersonal experience that privileges alterity, is being contradicted by the claim he will not stock certain books. While Hitler and *Mein Kampf* rank among our culture's most "evil of evils," this limited example betrays an anxiety on the part of George. If the very act of reading can support a liberal or leftist politics of difference and Otherness, this would include *Mein Kampf*. The anxiety of the subject is that their privileged aesthetic object could betray them, and with it their critics could be right. At its most abject and extreme, an imagined critic could say, "If they sell lots of left-wing books, and won't buy in *Mein Kampf* if a customer asks for it, they *must be* leftist snowflakes!" That is, the anxiety of the object gives way to a subject-anxiety: being mistaken for a social semblance, a "snowflake," etc.

Anxiety 2: John

John, head bookseller at The Bookshop, shared the anxieties of being mistaken for not so much what he is not, but what he appears to be:

> Every year there's stats [from the Booksellers Association] about how intimidated people feel in book shops. You know, there is a feel or a look to "The Book Seller," traditionally. I mean I pretty much fit the bill of, like, a middle-class white guy with spectacles.

While John wanted to mitigate against false first impressions, it would be a mistake to say this is merely an issue of appearances, of wanting to undo the "reverse snobbery" of thinking bookseller's are conceited intellectual snobs. As we spoke, I noticed that John's worry about being mistaken for his social semblance was inseparable from his philosophy toward literature, and his obligation to sell books. John would insist on a distinction that called the difference between "liking and knowing":

> Knowing feels like it is "I know something you don't know," and there's a finite resource of a thing that you can have, and I might give it to you, but I might not. Whereas liking is totally free: an infinite number of people could like something.

To John, such a distinction is not only a way to move beyond the cultural snobbery that is attached to his profession, but also one that better captures the aesthetic pleasure of literature and its virtues. He gave the example of a recommendation he gave to a customer that I had witnessed prior to our interview beginning:

> I was only able to recommend that book [to the customer] not because I know about it but because I've read it and I loved it, and I'm

> interested in it. . . . And that's the "hand sell," that's the thing that will sell the book. Actually, forget that, the selling bit, that sounds crude. I mean that's the thing that will get someone else interested; is you being interested. And being excited and generous about it: saying "You, I hope, will also have pleasure from this thing." If you veer into the realm of knowing, that is not generous; that's hoarding. That's being like "I know stuff and you don't know, I'm a smart arse, and you're pleb who doesn't know about books." That's not going to sell anything. Your bookshop will fail.

There is a conscious effort to quell the exclusionary perception, and cultural snobbery, accompanying the independent bookshop. There is also an emphasis upon the purposeless purpose of literary pleasures, and the obligation of the bookseller to facilitate that pleasure. But John's speech tangles up and finds it hard to fully separate both the sale of alienable commodities and the inalienable pleasures of literature.

I couldn't help but notice in John's discussion that the substitution of knowing (exclusionary) for liking (invitational) was not only a way to resist the anxiety of being mistaken for his social semblance, but that it is also hiding something else: "liking" was hiding an anxiety that, culturally, expert knowledge and "liking" (qua a term for aesthetic, disinterested pleasure) are at the service of an external purpose. One way I became attentive of this was by way of a mistaken interpretation. As John states in the previous extract, he feels that to speak of "selling books" is crude. So, I offered the interpretation that he is not really "selling books" but perhaps "gifting them"? No, John insisted, he is trying to sell books *and* savor their aesthetic pleasures in the same instance.

The contrast John wanted to emphasize with his liking-knowing distinction was less gift-commodity and more the social semblance of "The Bookseller" and John:

> One of the most successful bookshops in the UK is [X] in [Y]. . . . They, for example, have a thing where—they've been very, very smart from a business point of view. . . . They've essentially commodified book recommendations. . . . They've created a thing . . . where you can pay . . . to spend half an hour with a bookseller where you have a cup of tea and slice of cake, and "I'll have a one-on-one interaction with you, we'll chat about the books you like, I'll go away, I'll come back with a pile of books. . . . " In my opinion, that is what I do every single day with someone who walks through the door, if they like that. So I slightly admire the, slightly almost, audacity of "because you're buying the time of this expert to sit down with you one-on-

> one, we'll do it." I sort of admire that. I like, in a way, the elevation of the bookseller as being something more. . . . I've got nothing against that, and part of me admires it in a strange way.

John is uncomfortable with this practice, he tells me, because it reinforces snobbery, but he does admire the elevation of the bookseller's social status. Does he, secretly, want to be a snob? No. What John fears is that being able to recommend books is nothing short of being a living Amazon algorithm: just like the tailored choices on Amazon based upon previous likes, the bookseller can speak with you for half an hour and do the exact same. By knowing (or "liking") books you've liked before, they can know you now. John fears being an automaton: the admiration he has toward that "Most Successful Bookshop" is that if he worked there, being a snob is a small price to pay for his "liking" credentials to be understood as what they are: *his*.

One could consider John's angst as a facet of what Smith calls "near pollution." "Near pollution" is the uneasiness that arises as "nearness and similarity, not distance or Otherness" (Smith 2014, 333) put our cultural boundaries and their values in contention. The archetypal example of "near pollution" is the nonlinear operation of the "uncanny valley": the specific, perceptible moment the human morphs seemingly into the artificial produces profound unease. If John were simply uncomfortable with being mistaken for a snob, we could just say that this is his own neurosis. But because knowing (snobbery) and liking (algorithm) are so close on the uncanny scale, John's insistence on the distinction can be understood as a reparative, near pollution ritual. When Lacan connected the experience of anxiety with that of the uncanny, he said "anxiety is the sudden appearance of the *Heimliche* [homely] within the frame" (2016, 76). Anxiety is not the intrusion of a foreign, polluting phenomenon but the exposure, to ourselves, of the way we make sense of ourselves becoming unveiled, to ourselves. The uncanny feeling of "something too close to home" is the exposure of the "how" element in the practice of our self-making.

Let us turn to an interview with a customer of The Bookshop to explore this anxiety in more detail.

Anxiety 3: Sue

Sue was diffident. But it was a diffidence that hid fierce intelligence. A literature graduate of Oxford University (but she did not tell me this, John did), she had a modest upbringing but a solidly middle-class career as a civil servant. She was in her sixties. A chance encounter highlighted Sue's diffidence, her awkward class position, and her upbringing. Our interview happened directly after I had conducted another interview with an esteemed literary critic who was "very posh" (upper class), well-known to Sue. Before we began to record our conversation, she expressed the fear that I would be disappointed with her interview after speaking with him first.

I initially thought that Sue's diffidence to be a class phenomenon. People in England have a lot of consciousness of class, if not class consciousness. But Sue's diffidence was only superficially about social status. On the one hand she would use diffidence to deflect any perceived pretentiousness she felt creeping up upon her (when I asked her where she takes her book recommendations from, she told me she does not read the *London Review of Books* [*LRB*] as it is "very pretentious"). While, on the other hand, this diffidence was used for other purposes. It would cover a contradiction in how she would relate to reading and its cultural significance. She adored reading, and wanted to endorse the belief that reading, of any kind, was virtuous, but also, did not want to do that. But not for class-based reasons. Let us not be misled by the *LRB*'s pretentiousness!

During our interview I found myself seeking to find a rule Sue was, implicitly, applying when it came to books. She at once had a lot to say about what she had read, and at the same time felt that everything she could say about them was neither here nor there. Whenever I asked her about what she liked about the nonfiction she was reading, she'd reply matter-of-factly, "It is good to learn, you're always learning." Despite this, she was repeatedly telling me how "obsessive" she is when it comes to books, which I initially thought was the master key to her philosophy of reading: "If I really like a book, I try and lend it to as many people as possible. Fifty percent of my books I give away. Mostly to charity shops, except the local history books and trade directories that are going nowhere!" She laughed a nervous laugh at this statement, but I felt we might have a rule here that could explain her ambivalence. To Sue, what she reads becomes entered into a gift economy: she gives away half of what she reads. But the most prized books, the ones she keeps and will never give away, seemingly have the least cultural cache or literary value: local history books, trade directories; that is., not high art or "pretentious literature." Is this because these trade directories and local history books do not intimidate her, like our upper-class literary critic that she felt dwarfed by? Quite the opposite.

The origin of the rule "a loved book is given to loved people" comes from a story about her father:

> SUE: If you get a really good book, you get transported to wherever. The book that, I suppose, my dad kept saying to me "you must read this book, you must read this book." And I kept saying "Oh, God. Ok, go on then." He handed me a book, and he took me for a drive around North Wales, and I actually read the book the

entire way and didn't see anything of North Wales. . . . It was *The House of the Spirits* by Isabel Allende, which I now know is just a rehash of *One Hundred Years of Solitude*, but at the time I just thought it was magnificent! I was reading it, and I could see them! I could see the people, and I could see the places. And so I just went to the library and grabbed as many Latin American magical realism novels I could possibly read. And that's what I ended up doing my dissertation on, actually.

DANIEL: Did that enhance your love of those books?

SUE: It did, actually. But now my copy is covered in marker pens!

Allende's *House of the Spirits* being covered in marker pens is an issue because the book is now unable to be given away. Sue would tell me of those books that she gives to charity shops, none have been written on. The first rule is "If you love a book, give it away." The second rule is "If a book is of no literary worth, keep it." The problem is the first rule means that the *House of the Spirits* should be entered into a gift economy; the second rule means that the *House of the Spirits* is unable to be given away as a written upon book because it diminishes literary value. The implicit rule being that if you scribble on a book, you make it worthless.

The implicit rule is hiding Sue's anxiety. Allende's *House of the Spirits*, and Gabriel García Márquez's *One Hundred Years of Solitude* are the same as Sue's local history and trade directories that are, also, kept out of circulation:

SUE: Except the local history books and trade directories which are going nowhere!

DANIEL: Really, why is that?

SUE: Because I am mildly obsessed with the history of [her town].

DANIEL: Why?

SUE: Well, it's just really interesting, isn't it! I don't care about who built the castle. What interests me is "what did that building, that looks like a pub, was it a pub and when was it a pub, and what was it called?" And trade directories are fantastic for that.

DANIEL: So you're going from the histories to the trade directories to connect the two?

SUE: Yeah! Our house is 1883, so I started doing it because I wanted to know all the people who lived there. Then I started doing the neighbors. . . . Guess I'm a bit nosy, really.

Sue wants to know who lived in her house before, and who she is sharing her spaces with in her city. Not people in the present, but in the past. Not unlike Marquez's *One Hundred Years of Solitude*, a novel that occurs over multiple generations, where the characters are visited by ghosts from previous generations; a novel that concerns the repetitions and echoes of the past. Solitude arises from the fact that connections are unable to be found between past and present. Sue appears to be doing much the same in her gift economy: some books are unable to be connected to other people, while others are. Her trade directories and personal copy of a written upon *The House of the Spirit* are retained from circulation as they are completely solitary obsessions.

So, Sue's diffidence should not be reduced to her class or status. It is completely within the realm of the aesthetic, of purposeless purpose. Diffidence has more to do with what the aesthetic experience of reading holds for her. At home in her obsession, she is very happy: in Allende or trade directories, she solitarily connects past with present. There, her inner life does not trouble her. What does trouble her, however, is how books are not all about solitude, but sociability (Smith 2022).

And later in our interview I had good reason to understand why her gift economy came with so many, explicit and implicit, rules:

> SUE: I have given some books away without reading them, and this is only when I realize that the people who've written them are . . . a bit dubious [nervous laughter]. . . . I bought that, whatever it is, however many *Lessons for Life* [*sic*] by Jordan Peterson. And I read up about Jordan Peterson and I thought, "I don't want this in my library! I don't want a misogynist, racist. Jog on!"
>
> DANIEL: How did you find the Jordan Peterson book?
>
> SUE: I read an interview with him, and I didn't really read the rest of the interview with him, but in his book there is one chapter that says "say hello to every cat you meet on the street," which is what I am prone to doing anyway. So I thought, "Anyone who recommends greeting every cat on the street can't be all bad!" Not realizing the rest of it is all about telling young men how to be basically misogynists.
>
> DANIEL: He hooked you in with the cats!
>
> SUE: He lured me in with cats and turned out to be a complete git! . . . How dare he appropriate cats for his sexist regime!
>
> DANIEL: So there's books you give aways as gifts, books you give away to charity, and there's books you have to get rid of because they're dirty?
>
> SUE: They just offend me!

Sue's diffidence is driven by the aesthetic, and her anxiety is when purpose comes back into purposeless purpose. Petersons' *12 Rules of Life* "spoke to her" and her love of cats, but as an aesthetic-object it spoke more about gender and race, implicating Sue in a politics she finds unsavory. There is a further case of Smith's "near pollution" and that near pollution is unable to be fully banished or disposed of. Even if given away, or written on, Peterson's book is not destroyed, burned, buried, torn up, etc. Books are sacred, even if some are more scared than others in Sue's estimations.

Solitude, like our silent reading evening, marks our angst of being included and stages the ways we are unable to be subtracted from the whole.

Conclusion

On this point, we return to the suggestion that this small ethnography of English, high-culture readers can act as a limit case for how we can rethink collective effervescence via the index of intragroup angst. Durkheim is right to observe that effervescence witnesses a loss of orientation in terms of individual consciousness and collective representations, but too often Durkheimian sociology is seeking to reaffirm our oneness with collective experience in rituals reminiscent of the elementary forms of religious life.

Covered here is how far being at one with a collective way of life is closer to fear than it is the ebullient certainty that comes from knowing that our opinions are at one with collective sentiment. When Durkheim talked about opinion formation as "a pre-eminently social thing" (1912 [2001], 156), he deduced that the authority of opinions owed itself to an externalization of our individual powers of reasoning and judgment. It is because "social action works in circuitous and obscure ways, using psychic mechanisms that are too complex for the ordinary observer to perceive their source" (Durkheim [1912] 2001, 157), that we attribute the source of our beliefs to higher authorities (gods, deities, mana). Our society has no shortage of these higher powers, but it is pluralistic about them. And as our empirical case demonstrates, when it comes to our opinions, beliefs, or morals, we have a good intuition that any opinion we make is unable to "suppress representations that contradict it" as Durkheim ([1912] 2001, 156) claimed effervescence does. If anything, it is the attendant contradictions to our sacred beliefs that are doing the work of effervescence.

In this way, angst is instructive: in Lacan's thought, anxiety is where the pleasure principle breaks down while nevertheless trying to sustain a relation to objects of desire, "even if it is an unbearable mode" (2017, 365). And what we have been tracing is how far aesthetic pleasures remain far from purposeless or devoid of moralism (Smith and Stoll 2022; Mazzarella 2017), while nevertheless trying to retain a sense of their importance as ends in themselves. Georg Simmel appreciated something of the uneasy, impure mana of Kant's *Critique of Judgement* (2007). Simmel argued by defining aesthetic pleasure as purposeless purpose was "the first attempt . . . to reconcile, within the realm of aesthetics, the inalienable individual subjectivity of modern man [*sic*] with the—no less inalienable—supra-individual commonality of everyone" (2020, 120). We all make up our minds in the same way, and this provides us two things: one is a well of individual uniqueness, and two the realization that any authority upon which our judgments are based is always of equal authority with the differing judgments or opinions others. Moral consensus derived from aesthetic judgment can only be consensus cut through with discord and disharmony. What else could our aesthetic-moral judgments be but angst-ridden if all our inalienable opinions are born of the "supraindividual commonality of everyone" else? On this point, Simmel noted that aesthetic judgments circle around "one basic question" that plagues modernity: "How can there be freedom and diversity of individuals without lawlessness and isolation?" (2020, 120).

Angst is the law that registers one's inclusion in collective life by acting as a signal that one's judgments are always, in a very real sense, dependent upon the judgments of others. Anxiety is a signal not so much of the dangers of how we make up our minds being liable to failure, rather anxiety is a signal that the origin of moral desire inexorably belongs to the common, collective pool of everyone's capacity for judgment.

Anxiety ought to be understood as a positive and integrative collective phenomenon. Counterintuitive, certainly, and not the process Durkheim imagined for social solidarity. But nevertheless, an advance on a central problem in social theory: how we remain intelligible to one another, even if the status of our intelligibility is unsettling. Anxiety pervades all that we consider sacred not because collective life has broken down, but because anxiety is a signal of the form of our relatedness takes: there really is no getting away from each other—we're in this together, like it or not.

REFERENCES

Alexander, Jeffrey C. 2003. *The Meanings of Social Life.* Cambridge University Press.

Alexander, Jeffrey C. 2014. "Preface." In *The Unhappy Divorce between Sociology and Psychoanalysis,* edited by Lynn Chancer and John Andrews. Palgrave.

Bourdieu, Pierre. 1984. *Distinction: A Social Critique of Judgement and Taste.* Routledge.

Durkheim, Émile. 2001. *The Elementary Forms of Religious Life.* Oxford University Press. Originally published in 1912 by Librairie Félix Alcan.

Eagleton, Terry. 1990. *The Ideology of the Aesthetic.* Blackwell.

Eagleton, Terry. 2011. *Why Marx Was Right.* Yale University Press.

Eddo-Lodge, Reni. 2017. *Why I'm No Longer Talking to White People About Race.* Bloomsbury Publishing.

Jacobson, Gavin. 2023. "The Rise of Waterstones Dad." *The New Statesman,* June 21, 2023.

Kant, Immanuel. 2007. *Critique of Judgement.* Translated by James Creed Meredith. Oxford University Press. Originally published in 1790 by Friderich Nicolovius.

Kuipers, Giselinde, Franssen, Thomas, and Holla, Sylvia. 2019. "Clouded Judgements? Aesthetics, Morality and Everyday Life in early 21st Century Culture." *European Journal of Cultural Studies* 22 (4): 383–398.

Kurakin, Dmitry. 2015. "Reassembling the Ambiguity of the Sacred: A Neglected Inconsistency in Readings of Durkheim." *Journal of Classical Sociology* 15 (4): 377–395.

Lacan, Jacques. 2016. *Anxiety: The Seminar of Jacques Lacan, Book X, 1962–1963.* Translated by A. R. Price. Edited by Jacques-Alain Miller. Polity.

Lacan, Jacques. 2017. *Transference: The Seminar of Jacques Lacan, Book VIII, 1960–1961.* Translated by Bruce Fink. Edited by Jacques-Alain Miller. Polity.

Lacan, Jacques. 2022. *The Object Relation: The Seminar of Jacques Lacan, Book IV, 1956–1957.* Translated by A. R. Price. Edited by Jacques-Alain Miller. Polity.

Mazzarella, William. 2017. *The Mana of Mass Society.* University of Chicago Press.

Nietzsche, Friedrich. 1968. *Twilight of the Idols.* Translated by Reginald J. Hollingdale. Penguin. Originally published in 1889 by C. G. Naumann.

Simmel, Georg. 2020. "Kant and Modern Aesthetics." In *Georg Simmel: Essays in Art and Aesthetics*, edited by Austin Harrington. University of Chicago Press.

Smith, Daniel R. 2022. "Reading, Novels & The Ethics of Sociability: Taking Simmel to an Independent English Bookshop." In *The Cultural Sociology of Reading: The meanings of reading and books across the world*, edited by Angélica Thumala-Olave. Palgrave Macmillan.

Smith, Daniel R. 2023. *The Fall & Rise of the English Upper-Class: Houses, Kinship, and Capital Since 1945.* Manchester University Press.

Smith, Philip. 2014. "Of 'Near-Pollution' and Non-Linear Cultural Effects: Reflections on Masahiro Mori and the Uncanny Valley." *American Journal of Cultural Sociology* 2 (3): 329–347.

Smith, Philip. 2023. "Class as Collective Representation: Lessons from Wagner and Bayreuth on the Discrete Harms of the Bourgeoisie." *Theory, Culture & Society* 41 (2): 3–19.

Smith, Philip, and Stoll, Florian. 2022. "Why Fans of the Evil Genius Remain Fans: The Case of Richard Wagner and the Bayreuth Festival." *Cultural Sociology* 17 (3): 351–372.

Tutenges, Sébastien. 2022. *Intoxication: An Ethnography of Effervescent Revelry.* Rutgers University Press.

Zelinsky, Dominik, Smith, Philip, and Simonsen, Sandra. 2021. "From Artistic Consecration to Degradation: The Case of Sven Hassel." *Acta Sociologica* 65 (2): 207–222.

10

In the Wake of Collective Effervescence

Habitus and Identity Dysfunction in Military to Civilian Work Transition

Brad West, Sharon Mascall-Dare,
and Heather Margrison

The horrors of World War II had a fundamental influence on the nature of sociological theory, with one effect seeing Durkheimian sociology cast as politically conservative because of its central concern with social order and solidarity. The revival of Émile Durkheim's intellectual legacy since the late twentieth century has sought to address this misunderstanding, illustrating how Durkheimian thought can uniquely comprehend social conflict, injustice, and inequality (Alexander and Smith 2018). Durkheim's concept and idea of collective effervescence (CE) has been particularly significant in this regard. Whereas CE was traditionally understood in reference to the ways in which interactions that foster attachment to others are functional for social integration, CE and Durkheim's associated theories of ritual and charisma have become increasingly utilized to understand the way in which power is attained and enacted. This has included comprehending CE in the rise of authoritarian figures and social crises, such as the role of rallies and rites involved in propagating populist critiques and reimagining history (Alexander 2018; Morgan 2022; West 2022). An emerging tradition of research also has sought to study CE as it relates to political protest and resistance to authority, what David Wästerfors in this volume terms subversive effervescence (see Chapter 8), that which contributes to dissidence, rebellions, and acts of noncompliance. David Sausdal, in this volume (see Chapter 7), also highlights how CE can be used to comprehend organizational culture, illustrating how the search for heightened experiences by members of the police force contributes to deviance and discrimination within law enforcement.

However, CE can be associated with a different type of disruption and dysfunction that latently stems from the loss of its experience. This chapter will explore this dynamic in relation to contemporary military to civilian transition and the struggle of veterans in attaining meaningful employment. Through interviews with a sample of Australian Defence Force (ADF) veterans who had experienced underemployment and unemployment following discharge, the study details how the loss of ritual and emotional engagement directly contributes to their difficulties. Utilizing Weber's ([1921] 1978) writing on value spheres, it is argued that the value of everyday social interaction and the esprit de corps within the military also contributes to the link between under- and unemployment and well-being issues among this population. Conversely, the data also illustrates how veteran employability, and well-being can be enhanced through veterans being provided with a better understanding of how CE is a form of capital that can be exchanged between different value spheres. This enhances the well-being of veterans by them reattaining a symbolic connection to their CE experiences attained while in the military and perceiving a greater sense of civilian recognition for their service. This argument is contrasted with sociological explanations of the difficulties that veterans experience in military to civilian work transition because of institutionalization and traumatic organizational experiences within the armed forces.

Researching the Loss of Collective Effervescence Experiences by Veterans

Working within cultural sociological traditions stemming from Durkheim's ([1912] 1995) work on CE, sociologists have long pointed to the role of initiation rites, formal training, and close social interactions as being key enablers of modern military culture (Elias 1950; King 2006; Malešević 2022; Shils 1950). However, far less is known about consequences stemming from the loss of such ritual and emotional engagement following discharge. This gap in academic literature reflects a broader ambiguity in sociologically comprehending the relationship between CE and well-being. While sociological research will often discuss the way in which certain groups experience marginalization or a loss of meaning in life, with this anomie being both associated with poor health and subscription to extremist political ideologies, rarely do such studies specifically analyze the experience of CE nor see remedies directly in terms of CE experiences.

This ambiguity in assigning causal significance to CE is illustrated in the sociological research into veteran unemployment and associated social problems. While scholars often note the loss of comradeship bonds that had provided military lives with direction and meaning during service and allude to these as contributing factors to poor veteran well-being, this tends to be merely contextual with the study of the issue being focused on other factors, most commonly the traumatic elements of military experience. The primarily analytic focus in the sociology study of veteran well-being is on military personnel's experiences of abuse, belittlement, and being subject to instrumental forms of power. These factors are thought to inevitably leave veterans without a strong sense of self and agency for navigating the world (Bulmer and Eichler 2017; Wadham and Connor 2024).

In contrast, this chapter, through a study of contemporary veterans' difficulty in attaining meaningful civilian employment, attempts to comprehend how this and related difficulties around military to civilian transition may directly emerge from the loss of close group activity experienced in the military. As we will see in the data, the CE that is most significant for the interview sample is not the intense social moments experienced through training and combat, which involves risk and the enactment of real or simulated violence, but rather everyday organizational interactions that contribute to an esprit de corps. This analytic focus on CE and its loss is not to suggest that traumatic or abusive experiences are not a common part of military service, nor that these do not have profound consequences for veteran well-being. Rather we contend that effective policy and programs for veteran transition also need to be informed by evidence comprehending other dimensions of military culture. This includes those aspects of service that military personnel view positively and attain a nostalgia for as veterans (Smith 2008). In doing so we aim to avoid the pitfalls of the dominant critical sociological tradition of analyzing the military, which following Foucault comprehends the military only as a symbol of a disciplinary power in which increased subjection and domination results in military personnel and veterans overwhelmingly being seen as "docile . . . an inapt body" (1975, 135). As we will argue, this perspective denies the finding of our data that evidence the significant agency of veterans to overcome their employment challenges and draw on their military experience to successfully reimagine themselves in a civilian context.

The potential of CE to provide a broader and alternative view of the military and our understanding of military to civilian transition is significant as contemporary military veterans not only have much worse employment rates but also health and well-being than those in the general population and their peers who are still members of the armed forces. For example, male veterans aged eighteen to twenty-four years who have served in the ADF have a suicide rate twice that observed for Australian men the same age (Baker et al. 2022). The rate of suicide among those males still serving in the ADF though is about half that of their equivalents in the general national population. As suggested by Australia's National Mental Health Commission there is a general acknowledgment in the study of veterans that "psychological transition from being a 'warrior' to becoming a civilian is an essential aspect of successful transition to civilian life" (2017, 21). However, we argue that there also needs to be an acknowledgment that solutions to military to civilian transition difficulties can also be found in facilitating veterans retaining and translating, rather than necessarily leaving behind, their military experience and identity. To address this issue we will attempt to integrate Max Weber's writing into our study of CE. The chapter will then outline details of the interview sample.

Value Spheres and StoryRight

For the purposes of this study, we conceptualize military and civilian employment as two distinct value spheres, a concept we adopt from the classical sociologist Max Weber who usefully defined it as societal domains that have distinct ethical, aesthetic, and religious characteristics such as "associations, business corporations, foundations . . . a nation, . . . a family, or an army corps" (Weber 1978, 13). The concept of value sphere shares various characteristics with Bourdieu's (1994) concept of field that refers to different societal domains as they are characterized by a "distinct hierarchy, values, struggles, styles of improvising action, and forms of capital" (Calhoun 2013). However, Weber is chosen for our analysis as Bourdieu's field theory and his associated conceptualization of habitus are born out of concern with contests for domination (Friedland 2009), "a state of the power relations among the agents or institutions engaged in the struggle" (Bourdieu 1994, 73), and habitus being aligned with the reproduction of social order. In contrast, our concern with habitus is more with comprehending body pedagogics as a creative enterprise connected to social mobility, group solidarity, and societal meaning (Mellor and Shilling 2010). As such, our use of the term "habitus" is in its more general and longer established sociological sense (Elias 1939; Mauss 1934), refers to how persons embody social structures such as personal habits, skills, and dispositions.

The data for the study is drawn from life narrative interviews with military veterans who have served in the ADF and undertaken the StoryRight program. StoryRight was designed by the current serving veteran Sharon Mascall-Dare, a coauthor of this chapter, with the aim of helping the current generation of veterans attain meaningful employment by assisting them with translating their military service to civilian employers. This interview method and sample allows for an analysis of both firsthand accounts of military service and difficulties experienced when transitioning from military to civilian work. It also provides potential insights into the cultural factors that assist veterans to overcome the barriers they face in transitioning to civilian employment.

The StoryRight workshops undertaken by the participants in this study comprise four distinct elements within a one-day (seven-hour delivery) format: an introduction to target audience analysis and targeting; military skills translation into language a civilian target audience will easily understand; the drafting of a 150-word personal "bio" or profile for use on LinkedIn or at the top of a résumé; and interview coaching. Typically, participants are nominated to attend the workshop through a Defence establishment and exhibit a degree of skepticism initially. This is assuaged through effective facilitation delivered by peer-to-peer mentors who are, themselves, veterans, and therefore have lived experience that is both communal and shared with attendees. During the first and second components of the workshop, it is often revelatory to participants that their military skills have value in the civilian world. This is partly because Defence places emphasis on teamwork, rather than individual aspiration and achievement: with the program's participants sometimes expressing the belief that individual aspiration has been removed from their sense of collective identity. As will be outlined in the data section, outside of a team context, veterans often feel they have little to contribute when separating from the military. During the skills translation session (second component), participants are given a framework to support identification and translation of skills. The framework applies a simple taxonomy, where skills are grouped as "military," "trade," "rank," or "civilian." The third component of the day addresses the structure, crafting and drafting of a personal "bio" that can be used as a LinkedIn profile or personal statement at the top of a CV or résumé. The final component of the day comprises an introduction to interview coaching, where participants are given access to templates and best practice examples to enable them to prepare.

Semistructured life narrative interviews were undertaken with ten participants of StoryRight, supplemented by ethnographic insight. The sample is dominated by former regular members of the Australian Army with one from the Royal Australian Navy. Of the total sample, nine were males and one female, a distribution broadly representative of the current gender constitution of the ADF (Hoglin 2024). Three in the sample were commissioned officers, one a noncommissioned officer, and the remaining enlisted personnel. The average age of those in the sample were 33.2 years, close to the average age of those currently serving in the Regular service being 34 years. Six of the ten veterans interviewed had been deployed, representing their service during Australia's post-2001 operations in Afghanistan and Iraq, with three officially being discharged for medical reasons, the remaining separating voluntarily.

The next section of the chapter outlines the results of subjecting the interview data to thematic and narrative analysis. First, data will be presented outlining the ways in which CE was experienced by the veterans rather than CE involving discussion of deployment or other critical moments in their service history, the participants in the study focus on the informal and everyday aspects of military life, emphasizing how these experiences were often enjoyable and positively contributed to their sense of self. It is important to note that this is expressed despite simultaneously voicing frequent expressions of disenchantment with military life and command. Data relating to discharge and what they experienced as the major hurdles for securing meaningful employment will then be outlined in relation to how it challenged their symbolic connection to their past CE experiences in the military. While direct quotes are used as evidence, the demographic details or personal circumstances of the respondents are not provided for the purposes of anonymity.

Assumed Transferability and Degradation

Our data indicates that Defence Force personnel during their years of service infrequently entertained the prospect that they would have trouble in securing and thriving within civilian employment upon discharge. As illustrated in this quote from a participant in the study, this commonly relates to military personnel conceiving of their work ethic as superior to their civilian equivalents, an important context for experiencing and making meaning of their later difficulties in finding meaningful civilian employment:

> I also left the military with the unrealistic expectation that I would have career success because I'd been moderately successful in the army, I thought I'd have career success outside the army. . . . And you know, and I had an unrealistic attitude of what I could do. . . . God it hurt, it really destroyed . . . the ego, your sense of self-worth and identity . . . and it led to me being suicidal. (Lieutenant colonel, age fifty-three)

What is most evident in the ways in which the veterans perceive their civilian employability during military service is that unlike their civilian equivalents, they see themselves as getting their jobs done without complaint or being delayed by unnecessary personal issues. Indeed, it was clear that their ability to engage and interact in teams is a key aspect of their sense of military exceptionalism and identity. Not all work experiences are related to CE, but what is notable in the data is the way in which, through common work experiences, military personnel distinguish themselves positively as superior to civilian workers.

However, as illustrated in these quotes, upon searching for civilian employment most veterans interviewed noted that they immediately realized that they didn't have the vocabulary or cultural awareness to comprehend what was being asked of them or describe themselves in ways that could demonstrate to potential employers that they had the necessary skills to be qualified for the advertised role. This theme was common in the interviews sample irrespective of the rank of the participants.

> What does an acting troop sergeant do, you know? And you say acting troop sergeant on your resume, like what does that—or in an interview, you know, what does that mean to a HR rep who's twenty-three and had no exposure to the military at all, you know? (Trooper, age thirty-one)

> I'd use common military terminology, and a lot of my speech was, and my terminology was very kind of aggressive, not aggressive as in like forceful to somebody, but it was still very tactical . . . you're used to talking to people, like talking to soldiers where you're in charge. (Sergeant, Age Thirty-Three)

> I was, I was like I've spent all these years doing all this sort of stuff, I was always ambitious like what by twenty-one got to SF [special forces]. Whatever I wanted I could achieve it and then suddenly I left the army, and I didn't believe I could achieve a thing, I'd had no idea what I'd even learnt, I didn't even know if I had any skills or any qualities that might even look dazzling to the new age employer. (Private, age thirty-two)

On the surface this would seem a simple matter of the common belief about the institutionalization of military personnel, or a consequence of themselves being diminished as a consequence of institutional traumatic experiences. However, such an explanation fails to appreciate the way in which military identity is formed through everyday CE experiences. What is notable is that when the participants frequently spoke without being prompted about the positive dimensions of military life it was not about the emotional highs or the thrill of training and combat, but rather it was more about everyday group interactions and general habitus factors. Consider these quotes, which illustrates both how even relatively mundane activities reinforced a sense of the group identity and belonging, something they contrast to civilian work:

> Really enjoyed the culture, the structure, the organization, the way that the organization sort of has a constant focus on development and improvement, so it's not an individual led thing, it's a cultural thing within Defence. (Midshipman, age thirty-two)

> But it's just being in that culture, it's somewhere that's familiar, it's somewhere there's—you know, there's that familiar structure, the familiar routine, and it's—and I suppose it's also a place where I have a sense of belonging and status within the group that you really don't have in the modern workplace. (Lieutenant colonel, age fifty-three)

> I really enjoyed the training aspects of [the] army. It's always going on, . . . always learning new skills, opportunities to travel. (Captain, age twenty-six)

This data illustrates the distinctive way in which military personnel have a sense of self and identity, with this being tied to the group and attained through their experiences of organizational everyday CE. Significantly, the previous quotes come from interview participants who had also experienced trauma and abuse in the military, but it is not these negative aspects of the military, those related to it as a total institution "cut off from the wider society" (Goffman, 1961, xiii), that they nominate when discussing the difficulties they experienced in their military to civilian work transition. What is also notable in the data is that seldom do the veterans discuss any ideological conflicts in their difficulties interviewing and attaining civilian jobs or in managing their integration into workplaces once they had secured employment. Rather the overall emphasis, as will be further illustrated later, is on the challenge of presenting themselves in certain ways and attaining deep meaning from their work.

Rather than being "docile bodies," participants interviewed for the study often greatly enhance their prospects in attaining and remaining within meaningful employment following participation in StoryRight. As we will see, these individuals had received transition training in the past, but what they nominate as special and motivating from StoryRight is that it was directly focused on facilitating attainment of civilian employment by demonstrating how their everyday military service could be translated to civilian employers. In doing so, StoryRight often helped participants retain not only the meaningfulness of military identity but a connection to the CE associated with service by providing avenues for their military habitus to be culturally recognized by representatives of the civilian sphere. The quotes that follow illustrate how attaining employment following StoryRight resulted in veterans recapturing a sense of pride in their service that had become diminished through their subsequent difficulties in securing meaningful civilian employment. As was the case previously discussed, what is notable in the quotes is that there is an emphasis on the more informal aspects of military service (King 2006).

> So I was of the opinion that the whole thing [military service] had been a bit of a pointless exercise, and doing the program really showed me that actually there was some value in a lot of the stuff I had been doing, even the stuff that I thought was extremely mundane actually had a lot of value and could have a lot of value in the civilian world. (Midshipman, age thirty-two)

> I saw the effects of that course and I saw it have a strong impact on those who I did the course with because suddenly they saw it within themselves which gave them confidence and a boost in order to believe that they—their time and service wasn't all for nothing. (Private, age thirty-two)

Those interviewed frequently contrasted StoryRight with the various transition services that they had been provided with upon their discharge from the military. This data is significant as it points to military to civilian transition difficulties not being an inherent reflection of different value spheres, as suggested by the institutionalization and trauma tradition of analysis. Rather many transition assistances involve actions by both the military and civilian agencies to sever access to the CE experiences that form the basis of the veterans' pride in service and what would be otherwise enduring symbolic connections to the esprit de corps experienced relatively informally in the military. While the exact transition programs each interview participant had undertaken prior to StoryRight differed, reflecting the heterogeneous and localized nature of ADF transition services, all in the sample described their experience in terms that equates to what Garfinkel (1956) termed "degradation ceremonies." For Garfinkel, degradation ceremonies are communicative acts that seek to lower an individual's status, attempting to evoke a sense of indignation and shame in ways that affect their complete identity. After deciding to separate from the military, veterans frequently reported being treated with a level of disdain by military personnel, acts they note were undertaken to symbolically distinguish them from those still actively serving in the ADF. In some cases, this occurred as part of the official provision of transition services, while in other instances it was part of the everyday interactions military personnel have with others in uniform in the time between officially declaring their decision to separate from the military and being formally discharged. Interview participants discussed how symbolic degradation also occurred in more subtle ways through transition support services. As illustrated in these quotes, this included the focus on mundane and technical issues or a standardization of programs across services and ranks resulting in a sense of recognition denial, and resulting in "reduced mode of being" (Taylor 1992, 25) and transition services being outsourced to civilian contractors that lack the cultural knowledge of the military to comprehend the personal and emotional challenges veterans were facing.

> I know there were like checkboxes you know, that I had to fill out when I left. So you know, it was go and see the transition person and that kind of stuff like to be honest it wasn't, I don't really think that I got much support. I just filled out the paperwork and made sure my super was organized and that was pretty much it. I know they did check to see you know, where am I going to be living and do I have a plan sort of thing. (Captain, age twenty-six)

> It was just sort of all being thrown into a group . . . there were five other guys . . . and they'd all decided to leave Duntroon [the Royal Military College] within a few weeks of arriving there. So there is a very clear difference between these guys (and me). . . . I had lost most of my faith in the process at that point and just wanted it done with. (Midshipman, age thirty-two)

Because of these factors, contemporary veterans often have a sense of being excluded from Defence but left without any clear sense of how to successfully secure and integrate into civilian work after being discharged. The extent of difficulty experienced is in some ways dependent on whether a veteran's military role has a civilian equivalent. As one interview participant notes, "My job as a tank commander, there's nothing really else that you can do in the civilian sector unless you worked for a dictator or you're like private security or something like that" (Sergeant, age thirty-three). However, in cases where clear connections might be perceived, military personnel often are not eligible for equivalent civilian positions, as military training in Australia is not systematically aligned with civilian qualifications required for such roles. Army medics and civilian paramedics is one case in point. In other cases, injuries prevent veterans from continuing the same work they undertook during their military service, with drivers of trucks and other heavy vehicles being a prominent example. Many veterans also choose to pursue different career paths, with this sometimes being part of a strategy to emotionally move on from military service, including when it has an association with traumatic experiences. However, as illustrated in the first quote here, in nearly all cases veterans struggle in finding meaningful civilian work, as it involves projecting and selling themselves in ways which runs counter to their military habitus. For example, interview participants often spoke about job descriptions and criteria that use individualistic language codes that clash with veterans' identity as it has been formed through CE experiences in the military. As illustrated in the second quote, the acknowledgment of knowing what work suits a veteran is even the case when the veteran has significant civilian educational and trade qualifications.

> Job descriptions . . . I didn't have the literacy to know that my competencies lied within that criteria, it's just that I—because I didn't have the verbal criteria, the knowledge in order—or the literacy in order to know what I was actually reading, I took it literally and I was like I don't know what they're saying, so I don't fit in that job. And so that's what StoryRight do, they offer StoryRight, they offer literacy to be able to understand where you fit within the current job landscape, which I believe is very important when it comes to confidence, finding purpose and meaning. (Private, age thirty-two)

> My psychiatrist . . . didn't even understand . . . I was having trouble getting work, and it was really destroying my sense of self-esteem, and she said, well you really, maybe you're setting your aspirations too high, because it's not as if you have any civilian qualifications, and I said, well hang on, I've got two masters, a bachelor's degree, a graduate cert in applied finance, I'm mining management competent. (Lieutenant colonel, age fifth-three)

In contrast to the ADF-sponsored transition support programs that the veterans characterize above as ineffectual, StoryRight is seen as making a significant difference for many participants. As one participant in the study noted, it "made me realize that I wasn't a—wasn't a piece of shit, and I can actually make a go of having a—a successful life outside of Defence" (Trooper, age three). Besides its other differences, being led by veterans is an important characteristic of StoryRight, as it results in most participants having a high level of trust in the program. This is not only a sense that those delivering the program have commonly experienced the bonds of solidarity associated with military experience, but that they are aware of the disenchantment that comes both during military service and after separation. As one interview participant notes of their workshop facilitator, "I trust him to tell it like it is, in that as an ex-veteran he has been through the process himself.

He knows . . . we've really been screwed over here, and he can sort of address that" (Midshipman, age thirty-two). This trust is important, as the program involves not only a translating of military service for civilian employers, and addressing potential assumptions that are made about veterans, but informing veterans about the ways in which they will need to alter their military habitus to attain and succeed within civilian employment.

Awareness of the divides between the civilian and the military spheres provided by StoryRight is seen by participants as having an ongoing significance in managing their civilian careers after securing employment. After a high degree of job security in the military and being within an institution that rewards collectivist identification with the group, the requirement to continually market oneself within a competitive and individualist workplace culture is a major challenge. However, the interviewed veterans also consistently remarked that the difficulty they experienced in fitting into the civilian workplace was not only about interactions as such, but unlike the military, their new work occurred in an environment that was not orientated to a larger selfless cause, and as such is problematic for providing life with purpose. Many veterans in the sample noted that they were continually searching for employment that was better orientated to the type of meaning and interactions they experienced in the military. In the absence of such alternatives, as evident in the participants' quotes here, various veterans sought ways to limit their identification with their employer, such as through taking up contractor roles rather than being employees subject to normal work routines and rituals.

> It's not just getting a job, it's getting the right job. . . . I was working in an organization that didn't have—didn't sort of believe in those kinds of things, or that's what you do in your own personal time, that doesn't affect your work time. They didn't believe in that sort of overall wellness; they didn't believe in values. It was all very much about making money and chasing the customer. (Captain, age thirty-seven)

> . . . and that's why being a subcontractor, working for myself is actually—it makes, it allows me to sit outside the corporate structure, and I don't expect them to give me anything—you know, there's not—I don't have to rely on false promises because none are made to me. . . . I manage myself, and I'll be damned if I'll let anyone do it again. (Lieutenant colonel, age fifty-two)

As indicated in these quotes, the habitus of veterans means that the process of military to civilian transition for contemporary veterans is commonly ongoing and something that might not ever be fully accomplished. However, StoryRight, in contrast to the traditional transition support services provided by the ADF as described in the data, does empower veterans to have a greater agency in navigating their civilian careers. In part this occurs by being more attentive to the civil/military divide, particularly in how the transition to civilian employment requires new performative techniques and different expectations. However, significantly veterans are empowered by attaining translation skills that allow them to engage in civilian work without having to discard or completely segregate their former military identity and the CE meanings they associated with it.

Discussion

The data section profiled the way in which CE in the military is closely connected to more everyday interactions and activities, something that is significant for both understanding the difficulty veterans experience in securing meaningful civilian work and how this social problem can be effectively addressed. Whereas sociology has been traditionally focused on CE in terms of it being a positive function of society, and more recent studies have been concerned with the way it is motivating for protest and holding power to account, the focus of this chapter has been the downstream consequences and problems of having been previously and deeply emersed in a social environment laden with CE, something that was lost with a move between value spheres. In the context of the military, this mobility is frequent, typically caused by high rates of injury, the difficulty of maintaining a military career and family life as well as rising disenchantment with other aspects of life in the armed forces. While attachment to this everyday CE in the military was functional for a military career, following discharge it causes a social problem. Firstly, this is due to its associated habitus not in the first instance being viewed positively by civilian employers. Specifically, we evidenced that veterans frequently encounter difficulty in marketing themselves in individualistic ways. Secondly, veteran's perceived need for this type of CE in the workplace limits their ability to find civilian employment meaningful. In both cases, veterans become marginalized, not only from the civilian work value spheres for which they are needing to transfer, but also from the military value sphere as their pride in service had in part been based on the belief that their military habitus was effective and recognized in the civilian work sphere.

StoryRight is one way to better facilitate military personnel to the transition to civilian work. It focuses on the transferability of military skills that were attained as part of the everyday CE experiences in the military. While the data reveals that civilian workplaces do not generally provide the functional equivalent of the CE veterans experienced in the military, StoryRight promotes a way for them to view civilian work in relation to their military habitus. Veterans are thus able to symbolically retain a connection to their past CE experiences. While the data did indicate that StoryRight, in contrast with other transition programs, was successful in empowering veterans to secure civilian employment, what is most significant for the well-being of these veterans was that the new skills for presenting their selves was undertaken in the context of them being able to successfully market their military service and translate it to civilian employers.

The symbolic translation and performance skills facilitated by StoryRight allowed veterans to overcome the inclination for boundary maintenance at the heart of values sphere dynamics and underpinned by an associated habitus that "bind their adherents through faith, sacrifice, and passion" (Friedland 2014, 219). Appreciating the tensions between value spheres is significant in comprehending military to civilian work transition, and for policy and program development in the area, as it allows for an understanding of how the perceived differences between the relevant value sphere are in part imagined but also something that is reinforced through acts that seek to promote cultural distinctiveness and exclusion to avoid encroachment from competing domains. The divide between the civilian and military sphere is both real and imagined. It has been highly evident in our analysis that civilian employers lack a positive recognition of military habitus. Similarly, while the military often assumes, and indeed promotes, that military service provides generalist skills recognized by civilian employers, we have shown that as part of formal and informal discharge rites, exiting personnel are subject to "degradation" rituals (Garfinkel 1956) that symbolically robs them of their military identity and CE experiences. Yet, as Weber acknowledges, engagements within values spheres, and as we have argued between value spheres, often involves social actors "strive to gain power over our lives . . ." (Weber [1919] 1946, 149). From this perspective we have shown that military habitus has a creative character, that is, being able to be translated and transformed to become somewhat transferable across value spheres.

Weber's insights into value spheres are also a more broadly useful accompaniment to Durkheim's CE theory that conceives of CE being stored within symbols, which outside of ritual engagement provide an enduring socializing effect. However, there is little sense from this Durkheimian perspective of how CE can be retained when it is produced within a specific value sphere and social actors are periodically forced to select or move between them. Collins makes a similar argument to Durkheim in his influential thesis on contemporary CE being manifested through ritual interaction chains (2004; 2014). Collins sees that collective beliefs are ultimately reliant upon "a group of people concentrating their attention to generate a common mood" (2004, 58). The associated emotional energy is orientated to a totem with the social intensity of the occasion giving it a sacred power that allows it to direct beliefs and action for periods between ritual activity. However, Collins's emphasis on languages does allow for a stronger basis to understand how CE can have a transferable dimension across value spheres. Reflecting the findings of this chapter on the significance of veterans reimagining themselves through presentations of the self in written employment applications and job interviews, Collins argues that language has a ritualistic dimension, with speech acts themselves being "the product of a pervasive natural ritual . . . involving . . . group assembly, mutual focus, common sentiment" and "as a result words are collective representations, loaded with moral significance" (1998, 47). In this way, Collins similarly to Durkheim, emphasizes the primacy of ritual, that "beliefs are often only an interpretation of the practices" (Durkheim 1975, 22) and that "individual minds can meet and communicate only if they come outside themselves, but they do this only by means of movement" (Durkheim [1912] 1995, 232).

The problem with both Durkheim's and Collins's arguments about CE, though, is that it neglects an appreciation that social actors themselves symbolically embody CE, with habitus having a totemistic quality. As Freeman argues, in Durkheim's classic study of Australian Aboriginal societies from which he formulated his theories of ritual and CE, it is not just that the totem is sacred and orientates behavior and belief, but the relationship between the symbol and the person is often sacred because "the individual feels he [*sic*] is the totem and evolves beliefs that he [*sic*] will become the totem or that his [*sic*] ancestors are the totem" (2000, 419). Watts points to this symbolic element of habitus in arguing that it "is not merely comprised of the social traditions that makeup our self, it is also *expressive of them*" (2024, 190). Habitus from this perspective works as Collins suggests as a kind of "social battery" (2004, 125), but the conceptualization of habitus as an embodied symbol of CE also allows for an appreciation of how it can contribute to both an affectual empowerment and disempowerment.

Collins largely contends that once someone has attained emotional capital through experiencing CE "they are systematically advantaged in their social encounters . . . able to accrue other economic and political benefits" (King 2019, 43). In contrast, we have outlined that habitus as a symbol of CE attained within a particular value sphere can eventually result in negative consequences. Rather than inherently being a source of empowerment, when moving between value spheres CE can contribute to marginalization, a source of stigmatization, and discrimination. Rather than being inherently positive, like any symbol, the meaning of CE and the associated habitus it affords is open to meaning-making processes, including performative factors in which individuals conceive of their sense of self in relation to how others view them. For societal symbols Durkheim acknowledges the significance of disenchantment as a consequence of social change, that "the great things of the past which filled our fathers [*sic*] with enthusiasm do not excite the same ardor in us" (Durkheim [1912] 1968, 475). However, disenchantment can also emerge from changes to the relative status of value spheres or by acquired CE and the value of one's habitus being lost through persons being required or selecting to transition between value spheres. In such circumstances, persons become increasingly reflexive on their habitus with a new audience emerging for the presentation of self around which judgment of worth are made regarding past experiences of CE, which can also prompt creative processes of reimagining.

Conclusion

Using a dual Durkheimian and Weberian lens to study the role of CE in military to civilian work transition, the chapter provides an alternative perspective to the current dominant understanding of veteran well-being that is dominated by a focus on institutionalization, instrumental power, abuse, and trauma. It was found that the military CE was aligned with more everyday interactions and involvement in organizational culture than the more intense or heightened moments of training and combat involving violence. This finding is significant as it relates to how we think about military habitus, the sources of anomie experienced by veterans and how these may contribute to the difficulties veterans experience in securing meaningful civilian employment and associated well-being challenges. From one perspective it could be suggested that it is the ongoing attachment of interview participants to military CE experiences and associated habitus that limited their employability, for example by reducing their ability to project themselves in ways that are attractive for employers and to find such employment meaningful. However, this conclusion is problematic in that it tends to assume that the civilian and military spheres exist in a zero-sum game. The chapter evidenced through the StoryRight transition program that the everyday nature of the military habitus means that veterans do not necessarily have to leave behind their military identity, and as a consequence their accumulated CE capital, but rather they can translate it for civilian employers and themselves. This finding not only challenges the dominant sociological comprehension of veterans being "docile bodies" as a consequence of institutionalization and trauma, but also illustrates the need for a more dynamic comprehension of military habitus with current applications failing to fully comprehend Weber's insights into the politics of value sphere and the ways that parties activity attempt to police symbolic boundaries. By showing how military habitus can be utilized in ways that facilitates movement between value spheres, the chapter has highlighted the need for a more multidimensional understanding of CE and the ways it can have various outcomes, both positive and negative. This differs from conceptions of CE from both Durkheim and Collins who only largely associate it with empowerment.

While the focus of the study was on military veterans, the findings indicate the potential of further Durkheimian analysis of CE and value spheres. In the last two decades, social stratification within the study of CE has been largely limited to the analysis of subcultures. For example, studies of new social movements and taste-based groups, including numerous analyses of occasions such as political demonstrations and music festivals, have been prominent within the tradition (Kearney 2018; Liebst 2019; Niekrenz 2014; Stephens et al. 2022). While such scholarship accounts for cultural diversity in society, it has a tendency for empirical concern with the esoteric and exotic. In contrast, the study of values spheres arguably better accounts for actual and potential structural change as it relates to the more established institutional dimensions of social life. However, there is also a strong case to be made for greater Durkheimian attention to the military (West and Crosbie 2021). With the world again being subject to dangerously high levels of geopolitical tensions, in part through the economic rise and rapid militarization of China, directly analyzing the changing relationship of the military and the civil sphere is of paramount importance.

REFERENCES

Alexander, Jeffrey C. 2018. "The Societalization of Social Problems: Church Pedophilia, Phone Hacking, and the Financial Crisis." *American Sociological Review* 83 (6): 1049–1078.

Alexander, Jeffrey C., and Philip Smith. 2018. "The Strong Program in Cultural Sociology: Meaning First." In *Routledge Handbook of Cultural Sociology*, edited by L. Grandstaff, M. Lo, and J. R. Hall. Routledge.

Baker, D., S. Rice., N. Sadler., J. Cooper, and D. Wade. 2022. *The Next Post: Young People Transitioning from Military Service and Their Mental Health.* Orygen, https://www.orygen.org.au/getattachment/Orygen-Institute/Policy-Areas/Population-groups/The-next-post/Orygen-Policy-paper-young-veterans-update-Jun2022.pdf.aspx?lang=en-AU&ext=.pdf.

Bourdieu, Pierre. 1994. *Practical Reason.* Polity.

Bulmer, Sarah, and Maya Eichler. 2017. "Unmaking Militarized Masculinity: Veterans and the Project of Military-to-Civilian Transition." *Critical Military Studies* 3 (2): 161–181.

Calhoun, Craig J. 2013. "For the Social History of the Present: Bourdieu as Historical Sociologist." In *Bourdieu and Historical Analysis.* edited by P. S. Gorski. Duke University Press.

Collins, Randall. 1998. *The Sociology of Philosophies: A Global Theory of Intellectual Change.* Harvard University Press.

Collins, Randall. 2004. *Interaction Ritual Chains.* Princeton University Press.

Collins, Randall. 2014. "Interaction Ritual Chains and Collective Effervescence." In *Collective Emotions: Perspectives From Psychology, Philosophy, and Sociology*, edited by C. Von Scheve and M. Salmela. Oxford University Press.

Durkheim, Émile. 1968. *The Elementary Forms of Religious Life*, translated by J. W. Swain. Allen & Unwin. Originally published in 1912.

Durkheim, Émile. 1975. "Concerning the Definition of Religious Phenomena." In *Durkheim on Religion: A Selection of Readings*, edited by W. S. F. Pickering. Routledge and Kegan Paul.

Durkheim, Émile. 1995. *The Elementary Forms of Religious Life.* Free Press. Originally published in 1912 by Allen & Unwin.

Elias, Norbert. 1939. *The Civilizing Process.* Wiley-Blackwell.

Elias, Norbert. 1950. "Studies in the Genesis of the Naval Profession." *The British Journal of Sociology* 1 (4): 291–309.

Foucault, Michel. 1975. *Discipline and Punish.* Pantheon.

Freeman, Walter J. 2000. "A Neurobiological Role of Music in Social Bonding." In *The Origins of Music*, edited by N. Wallin, B. Merkur, and S. Brown. MIT Press.

Friedland, Roger. 2009. "The Endless Fields of Pierre Bourdieu." *Organization* 16 (6): 887–917.

Friedland, Roger. 2014. "Divine Institution: Max Weber's Value Spheres and Institutional Theory." *Research in the Sociology of Organizations* 41:217–258.

Garfinkel, Harold. 1956. "Conditions of Successful Degradation Ceremonies." *American Journal of Sociology* 61:420–424.

Goffman, Erving. 1961. *Asylums: Essays on the Social Situations of Mental Patients and Other Inmates.* Doubleday.

Hoglin, Philip. 2024. "Who Do We Think We Are? Demographic Changes in the Australian Defence Force and Implications for Social Legitimacy." In *The New Australian Military Sociology*, edited by Brad West and Cate Carter. Berghahn Books.

Kearney, Matthew. 2018. "Totally Alive: The Wisconsin Uprising and the Source of Collective Effervescence." *Theory and Society* 47:233–254.

King, Anthony. 2006. "The Word of Command: Communication and Cohesion in the Military." *Armed Forces & Society* 32 (4): 493–512.

King, Anthony. 2019. "Emotion, Interaction and the Structure-Agency Problem: Building on the Sociology of Randall Collins." *Thesis Eleven* 154 (1): 38–51.

Liebst, Lasse Suonperä. 2019. "Exploring the Sources of Collective Effervescence: A Multilevel Study." *Sociological Science* 6:27–42.

Malešević, Siniša. 2022. *Why Humans Fight.* Cambridge University Press.

Mauss, M. 1934. "Les Techniques du Corps." *Journal de Psychologie* 32 (3–4): 271–293.

Mellor, Philip A., and Chris Shilling. 2010. "Body Pedagogics and the Religious Habitus: A New Direction for the Sociological Study of Religion." *Religion* 40 (1): 27–38.

Morgan, Marcus. 2022. "A Cultural Sociology of Populism." *International Journal of Politics, Culture, and Society* 35 (2): 179–199.

National Mental Health Commission. 2017. *Review into the Suicide and Self-Harm Prevention Services Available to Current and Former Serving ADF Members and their Families: Final Report,* 28 March, Sydney.

Niekrenz, Yvonne. 2014. "The Elementary Forms of Carnival: Collective Effervescence in Germany's Rhineland." *Canadian Journal of Sociology/Cahiers Canadiens de Sociologie* 39 (4): 643–666.

Shils, Edward A. 1950. "Primary Groups in the American Army." In *Studies in the Scope and Method of "The American Soldier,"* edited by Robert Merton and Paul F. Lazarsfeld Free Press.

Smith, Philip. 2008. "Meaning and Military Power: Moving on from Foucault." *Journal of Power* 1 (3): 275–293.

Stephens, Neil, Photini Vrikki, Hauke Riesch, and Olwenn Martin. 2022. "Protesting Populist Knowledge Practices: Collective Effervescence at the March for Science London." *Cultural Sociology* 16 (2): 212–230.

Taylor, Charles. 1992. "Politics of Recognition." In *Multiculturalism and the Politics of Difference*, edited by Amy Gutmann. Princeton University Press.

Wadham, Ben, and James Connor. 2024. *Warrior Soldier Brigand: Institutional Abuse within the Australian Defence Force.* Melbourne University Publishing.

Watts, Galen. 2024. "Capital and Distinction or Goods and Traditions? Toward a Post-Bourdieusian Cultural Theory." *American Journal of Cultural Sociology* 12 (2): 171–211.

Weber, Max. 1946. *From Max Weber.* Edited by H. H. Girth and C. W. Mills. Oxford University.

Weber, Max. 1978. *Economy and Society: An Outline of Interpretive Sociology.* University of California Press. Originally published in 1921 by J. C. B. Mohr.

West, Brad. 2022. *Finding Gallipoli: Battlefield Remembrance and the Movement of Australian and Turkish History.* Palgrave Macmillan.

West, Brad, and Thomas Crosbie. 2021. "Militarization and the Paramilitarization of Culture: Accounting for New Civil-Military Complexity." In *Militarization and the Global Rise of Paramilitary Culture*, edited by Brad West and Thomas Crosbie. Springer.

11

Sensorial Snags and Evaluative Effervescence

Exploring Virtual Justice Rituals

Lisa Flower

Justice Rituals

As discussed in previous chapters of this book, a ritual is a set of organized practices and ceremonies that symbolically reinforce the beliefs, values, and norms of a community or society and are crucial to community building and creating a sense of togetherness (Durkheim [1912] 1995).

Law, morality, and religion are all forms of social control for Émile Durkheim, that is, ways of regulating and integrating society. This means that both laws and rules of conduct are established and internalized and make it possible for societies to function smoothly and indeed, to exist (Vogt 1993). Durkheim writes, "Moral ideals are the soul of the law. A legal code gets its authority from the moral ideal that it incarnates and that it translates into a precise formulae" (Durkheim cited in Vogt 1993, 71).

This, in turn, means that legal proceedings, such as a trial, are an extension, enactment, and enforcement of the moral ideas important to society. A trial is thus a ritualistic forum for upholding morals and values. Moreover, Karstedt (2002) argues that justice rituals play an acutely integral role in society as they have the potential to change one emotion into another. For instance, one particular justice ritual seen in restorative justice conferences wherein those harmed by a crime and those responsible for the harm take part in a restorative meeting where they talk about what occurred. This can lead to feelings of fear and anger in the harmed individual being transformed into forgiveness or understanding, and for the offender to show remorse for their actions and work toward being reintegrated into the community (see also Rossner 2013).

Such a ritual can thus transform emotions, and even transform the self, which Schechner (1981) describes as a transformative ritual. A transformative ritual entails the performer being changed, for example the social identity of a boy is transformed into a man during the ritual of a bar mitzvah. In contrast, transportational rituals entail the performer being transported and swept up in the rush of the ritual, before returning to their everyday life, without any fundamental shift in social identity or, perhaps even, emotional state. Here, Schechner (1981) suggests that many theater actors and audience members remain—transported for a brief time before returning to their original status.

Using this interpretation, the goal of a restorative justice ritual is to function as a transformative process for the defendant, metamorphosing negative emotions into positive ones, producing reintegrative shame in the offender (Braithwaite 1989). In this way, their social identity is transformed into one who can be accepted back into, and morally align with, the wider community. Similarly, as already noted, for the victim, the ritual can serve to transform negative feelings of anger into positive feelings of forgiveness. The enactment and reenactment of such justice rituals serves not only to create and affirm group membership, they can ritual also function as the source of morality and public order (Rossner 2013).

The trial as a justice ritual thus serves a function to gather society, produce solidarity, and to perhaps even transform emotions. Given the possibility for justice rituals to entail shared intersubjectivity—with all participants focused on, and interacting with, the presentation and evaluation of evidence—they can also spark collective effervescence. This is because, as Collins (2004, 35) argues, collective effervescence can emerge, not only in the large-scale gatherings as explored by Durkheim, but also in small-scale interactions such as dinner parties, provided there is shared experience, heightened intersubjectivity, and bodily co-presence (Collins 2004, 35).

So, even in a small trial with only a handful of people present (judge, lawyer, prosecutor, defendant, plaintiff, and witnesses), the relevant ingredients are in place for a successful interaction ritual and for collective effervescence to emerge. The participants can therefore be swept up in the collective effervescence of the ritual and be transformed in different ways or merely transported for a brief time—engaged in the ritual and perhaps even excited or enriched by it, but not changed.

For legal professionals working on mundane, everyday cases, the ritual of a trial is transportive—immersing them in the ceremonial setting of a court but without changing their core self. This is not to say that a lawyer, judge, or prosecutor leave every trial in the exact same condition as when he or she entered it. Rituals tend to mark individuals—whether implicitly or explicitly—however, this transformative effect is perhaps more unusual here.

Turning to the lay participants: in the best of worlds, they will leave the courtroom feeling that justice has been served. However, a more likely outcome is that while some participants may leave with this feeling, which can be understood as a form of Collins's (2004) emotional energy, an outcome of an interaction ritual, others may leave with a feeling of not being heard or seen by the legal institution: of not being fairly treated.

Because "effervescent events play vital roles in how we make meaning because they alter the way we experience ourselves and our connections with other people" (Tutenges 2023, 5), the trial as an effervescent event is particularly fascinating to explore as it entails the intermingling of different emotions that may nevertheless lead to the emergence of collective effervescence—changing how participants experience themselves and their connections to others—yet result in differing emotions in the participants.

Criminal trials constitute a particularly interesting point of study as they are often characterized by intense, yet varied, emotions among lay participants. For instance, an angry defendant who feels they have been wrongly accused of a crime, a scared victim who is facing their attacker, and a sad witness retelling the events they have witnessed are joined together in a justice ritual. The emotional landscape of the courtroom may therefore be eclectic, yet together these emotions construct a collective effervescence—a feeling of being part of something bigger—a part of justice. Just as Durkheim describes how funeral ceremonies of the Aboriginal Kurnai people in Australia included the intermingling of anger and sadness leading to violent clashes among mourners (Durkheim [1912] 1995, 397) with the burial ritual bringing a state of effervescence, even in a trial, "the intense feelings are different, the wild intensity is the same" (Durkheim [1912] 1995, 403).

Although collective effervescence is fundamental to Durkheim's approach, he remains somewhat vague in pinpointing specific types of effervescence beyond creative (Durkheim [1912] 1995, 430) and congenial (Durkheim [1912] 1995, xiii). Other scholars have since identified a wider typology including joyful and sad (Pickering and Rosati 2008) along with compassionate, drunken, psychedelic, sexual, violent, and melodramatic (Tutenges 2023). In this chapter I add to this typology by focusing on the trial as producing evaluative effervescence as it is an event designed for presenting, examining, and weighing the evidence of a case in a factual manner.

In particular, my focus is on how the emergence of this effervescence and the success of the interactional ritual of trial—understood in terms of all participants feeling justice has been served—face an important snag given that the parameters of success demand bodily co-presence that leads to the question to be addressed in this chapter: How can collective effervescence emerge when participation is virtual, that is, when there is an absence of bodily co-presence that may disrupt the shared intersubjectivity?

This is an important question to answer because, as already noted, justice rituals gather, shape, and indeed, change people and thus form society itself, leading to feelings of solidarity and shared morality. This, in turn, leads to trust in the legal system. Failed justice rituals thus have important implications for democracy. The COVID-19 pandemic led to a boom in the use of video links in trials across the globe, which means that the "new normal" (Rossner 2021) for participating is for virtual participation, via video link, without being physically present in the courtroom leading to a shift from traditional justice rituals to *virtual* justice rituals.

In this chapter I will therefore begin by showing how a criminal trial can be understood as a justice ritual and discuss the factors that should be considered when designing virtual justice rituals. I will focus on three key aspects: 1) the physical courtroom; 2) sensorial symbolism, and 3) co-presence. By drawing on interactionist theory and my ethnographic research on Swedish courts spanning the past decade, along with international research on video links, I will identify the key role these three aspects play in virtual justice rituals and show how they impact on the construction of collective effervescence.

Video Links

Participating in a trial via video link has become routine in courts across the globe, enabling judges, prosecutors, lawyers, defendants, and witnesses to appear in proceedings from locations other than the courtroom. Also referred to as virtual trials, for remote hearings, or distributed hearings, I use the term "virtual trial" to encompass them, and "virtual participation" to signify involvement via video link. Another trial type, "virtual reality trial," unfolds entirely in a digital environment using avatars, as I will outline in more detail later.

Video links are not novel to courtrooms, originating in the United States during the 1970s, primarily for bail hearings via closed-circuit television. Over time, their use expanded to protect witnesses and enhance court access in geographically vast countries (Smith, Savage, and Emami 2021; Wallace 2008). Their practicality and cost-effectiveness led to gradual implementation and increased usage (Briggs 2016; Plotnikoff and Woolfson 2019). It was not until the COVID-19 pandemic, when courts were faced with the battle of enabling trials to be held despite lockdowns and social distancing restrictions that video links began to be used regularly and widely. Many jurisdictions were already facing enormous backlogs prior to the outbreak, for instance Brazil had a backlog of seventy-eight million lawsuits (Brehm et al. 2020), India had forty-four million cases waiting (Thakur 2021), the average backlog in state and local courts across the United States increased by one-third during the pandemic (Jurva 2021), and other countries such as England struggled to keep the courts functioning smoothly (Robins 2021; Godfrey, Richardson, and Walklate 2022). The pandemic thus forced many countries to either introduce video conferencing, for instance in Ireland, San Marino, Andorra, and Switzerland or further develop those capabilities already established, such as in Australia, Canada, China, Kenya, Norway, England, and the United States (e-Justice 2020; Sanders 2021; see also Worldwide 2023 for comprehensive information).

Video links are therefore currently an established form of participation in trials, removing the customary demand of bodily co-presence in a physical courtroom. This leads to questions regarding how the collective effervescence that emerges from the "justice ritual" (Rossner 2021) of a criminal trial is impacted when lawyers, prosecutors, witnesses, defendants, plaintiffs, and even judges, are interacting via cameras and screens—when a virtual justice ritual is at play.

The next step in virtual participation is the total removal of physical co-presence, as is the case with virtual reality trials where participation is in the form of avatars. Such trials have already taken place with tech companies poised to implement the technology in US courts (PingWest 2022; Woodford 2023; Lederer 2023) and is primed to evolve beyond evidence presentation and law student training to become a central aspect of criminal and civil trial participation within the next fifteen years (Hartung et al. 2022).

The Physical Courtroom and the Justice Symbols Within

The established significance of the physical courtroom as a venue for legal rituals, symbolizing the legitimacy, solemnity, and gravity of the law, is well-documented (Rock 1993; Carlen 1976). The implications for transitioning participation from the traditional courtroom setting to the virtual realm of video conferences and how this shift affects the justice ritual in diverse ways is less well-known. Although some inquiries into conveying legal legitimacy in a virtual setting, devoid of the contextual and symbolic weight, have been initiated (Mulcahy, Rowden, and Teeder 2021), and studies on online rituals more broadly exist (Vandenberg 2022; van Ryn et al. 2017; Henry 2023), though the ways in which the absence of the physical courtroom shapes justice rituals are still unclear.

To showcase the importance of the physical courthouse in justice rituals I will use an example that is particularly pertinent in a book on Durkheim, namely Western courts designed and built to enable inclusion of Australian

Indigenous people's culture. Many courthouses are currently designed in Australia with an awareness to engage Indigenous people with Western legal systems when these systems have traditionally been a source of threat and ruin to Indigenous people (Grant and Hook 2021). Colonial Australia, write Grant and Hook (2021), was built on English law that divided, conquered, and disrupted traditional law and cultural practices. The courthouse thus became a site and symbol for oppression and marginalization.

Architecture—and within this—the use of symbols, thus plays a key role in conveying power and sovereignty that may clash with understandings and experiences of justice. Courtrooms are currently designed in a manner that ensure the amalgamation of Western and Indigenous justice rituals. The design of Kununurra Courthouse thus interweaves the history—including historical injustices—with social context, Indigenous values, and aspirations to heed the cultural, socio-spatial, and environmental needs of users. For instance, the two systems of law: Western law and traditional law/lore practice are symbolically combined in the courtroom by placing a window above the judge's position thereby acknowledging and conveying the importance of viewing the sky in Indigenous practices (Grant and Hook 2021). In this way, the significance of the judge can be retained while still attending to traditional values, hence different justice rituals are combined. By tying in these symbols, a sense of recognition and belonging can be assuaged.

Justice rituals have, therefore, clear symbols for what is going on, symbols that have been charged with meaning over centuries and that are linked to a specific jurisdiction and type of law. For instance, atop the Old Bailey in England (the oldest Crown Court in England), the building is adorned with a statue of the blindfolded Lady Justice holding a sword in one hand and scales in the other. Lady Justice is thus a symbol for the neutrality, swiftness, finality, and impartiality of the courts. In the courtroom, the judge and barristers wear wigs and robes, although with subtle differences: the judge's so-called full-bottom wig tends to be longer and more ornate, indicating their higher status, while the robes worn by solicitors, barristers, and judges also convey status, for instance with King's Counsel, who wear "silks," or different colored tabs worn below the collar of judicial robes. The judge sits in a raised, throne-like chair, and the defendant stands apart in a dock. While some of these symbols are easy to transition to virtual justice rituals with the help of background logos, similar attire, along with the specific placing of images on screens in order to make the judge most prominent, other symbols, such as the separation of the defendant in a dock are perhaps harder to convey (see Rossner et al. 2017). The last of these—positioning of the defendant—has been shown to have important implications for how the defendant is perceived by jurors, with defendants appearing in a physical dock more likely to be evaluated as guilty, compared to those appearing sitting next to their barrister, or indeed, appearing via video link (Rossner and Tait 2021).

In contrast, other countries may have fewer clear symbols. For instance, in Sweden, the justice ritual of a trial is not characterized by the same markers. While courthouses may be decorated with Lady Justice such as in Stockholm district court, judges wear similar attire to the prosecutor and defense lawyer, namely suits, and sit in a chair much like all the other chairs in the courtroom, and the defendant is seated next to their defense lawyer, at a desk like the one behind which the prosecutor and plaintiff are seated. In short, the Swedish courtroom looks like many other bureaucratic settings. This means that the gravity of events is communicated more subtly: by adhering to strict yet implicit rules for how to interact, including how to manage and display emotions (Flower 2019; Bergman Blix and Wettergren 2018), rules that are currently unknown in the virtual context. This risks inhibiting the emergence of evaluative effervescence as the lack of clarity regarding the rules of interaction leads to uncertainty and reduced mutual focus as interactants must actively reflect on what they are doing and how, in contrast to the established and habitual practices of physical courtroom interactions.

This is also important as the performances of the legal professionals in the courtroom each symbolize a key legal principle to be upheld: neutral judges, impartial prosecutors, and loyal defense lawyers. How these legal principles should be performed, or symbolized, in the physical courtroom is well-established, but how this should be accomplished in virtual settings is currently unknown, again, this threatens the smooth interaction of a trial.

Likewise, problems in enabling entrainment and failure to enter into the collective effervescence of the virtual courtroom may help to explain why defendants risk feeling they have not received suitable representation or a fair trial (Babcock and Johansen 2010; Johnson and Wiggins 2006). The absence of physical co-presence may also explain why defendants feel less "seen" by the judge and have fewer opportunities to make a good impression (Fielding et al. 2020).

So, the transference of many already-charged symbols into virtual settings can be straightforward and serve to uphold the ritual in an online sphere and help the emergence of evaluative effervescence by ensuring mutual focus. However, more subtle symbols of justice may be harder to convey, in part due to a lack of clarity regarding the rules of interaction. Moreover, the absence of fuzzier aspects is also important, as I will now show.

Sensorial Symbolism

Returning to Collins's seminal work on interaction rituals, while the "sensory character" (2004, 62) of bodily coparticipation is discussed, his focus is on, for instance, "coffee, tea, soft drinks, the party cake, the shared dinner . . . (as) ritual substances" rather than the sensorial experience of these substances: their taste, feel, sound, smell, and sight and how the full sensorium contributes to interaction rituals' success. Similarly, research on justice rituals tends to focus on co-presence, materiality, and the related symbolism of the courtroom such as the physical building, coat of arms, and judicial dress (Rossner and Tait 2021) rather than on the sensorial experiences of justice rituals.

As we draw on our senses to understand and make sense of what is going on around us and because our sensorial experiences and encounters convey the symbolism and institutional values of the legal system (Herrity, Schmidt, and Warr 2021; Flower 2021), it is crucial that we take these factors into consideration when constructing virtual justice rituals. My position is, therefore, that sensorial experiences can function as symbols of justice and thereby contribute to the emergence of evaluative effervescence. By attending to these sensorial experiences, we take yet another step closer to understanding how evaluative effervescence and successful interaction rituals can be constructed.

Visual impressions tend to spring to mind first when we think about gathering our sensorial experiences and making sense of them—to try and interpret what they convey to us. The sounds of a courtroom: the scraping of the witness chair, the sobbing of a plaintiff, the tapping noise of the legal clerk annotating, the silence of the courtroom, are noticed and captured more readily than the scent of the waiting room, the smell of energy drinks and bad coffee, or the whiff of perfume. Yet all these sensorial experiences play into creating and recreating justice rituals. They contribute to the sense of a certain type of something going on. For some they denote a break from the normal, a deviation from the day-to-day sensory experiences usually encountered. For others, these sensorial impressions indicate mundanity. Whatever the case, when a trial moves online, so, too, do our sensorial impressions and the absence thereof shape the ritual and the experience.

Focusing on the sensorial experiences, there are several aspects that make attunement to courtroom proceedings tricky even in physical courtrooms. These sensorial snags—a disruption of a sensory experience—prevent or at least hinder the mutual focus and shared mood of attunement.

I begin by taking an unexpected focus and turn my attention to the spectators: those family members, reporters, school classes, and colleagues who are sitting in the public gallery to support parties, report on proceedings, or to merely observe. In particular, I want to discuss the symbolism and role of light. As already noted, access to daylight can be integral to the design of some courtrooms, however lighting also plays other symbolic roles. For instance, before participants are allowed to enter a Swedish courtroom, the light on the screen outside detailing which proceedings are taking place within, should switch from red to green. In Sweden these colors signal "stop" and "go" just as in many other countries. Their simplicity belies the intricacy taking place behind the doors, yet they act as a beacon of normalcy. Something that the lay participant can easily understand in a landscape filled with the unfamiliar. It indicates a switch from mundanity to something else.

During ethnographic fieldwork for a study I conducted in 2019, I attended a trial at a newly built courthouse and wrote the following fieldnote:

> The courtroom has a bizarre design for those of us here watching the trial. The glass is slanted between the court and gallery which reflects the overhead lights from the ceiling in the gallery. This means that when I'm trying to observe what's going on in the courtroom, I'm faced with the visually distracting fluorescent lights which obscure my view of the trial taking place. I can observe the reflection of the lights, but not much else.

It becomes apparent to me that the focus of the courtroom design has been on ensuring the interactions within the courtroom run smoothly with clear lines of sight running between all participants. The judge can clearly see the defendant, plaintiff, witness, prosecutor, defense lawyer, and counsel for the plaintiff. These clear lines of sight can contribute to ensuing interactional engagement—individuals are able to see and interpret each other's body language and nonverbal gestures—that can contribute to attunement by enabling shared focus and mutual emotions.

In contrast, for those sitting in the gallery, it is far harder to follow proceedings, to follow the subtle nuances of exchanges, to interpret what is going on when we cannot clearly see. For me, this led to feelings of frustration and irritation. It made me feel like an outsider—not a part of the proceedings, in a way that I had not experienced in any of the other fifty-plus trials that I had previously observed. I began to focus on other things, on the people sitting in the gallery, and then I began to lose interest in the trial. It is perhaps ironic that Sweden's transparent justice system became harder to observe due to the glass window and lighting. My point here is that by attention to the small details, such as lighting, it is possible to understand which factors can impact on the success of a ritual and which factors should be considered when designing rituals.

This, in turn, indicates that lines of sight and clearly being able to see what is going on constitute vital aspects in justice rituals and the emergence of evaluative effervescence, again, vital aspects that are lost when direct eye contact is not possible via cameras and screens as in virtual justice rituals (Flower, Klosterkamp, and Rowden 2023).

My field notes from trials in Swedish district courts also reveal that there tends to be discrete artwork hung on the walls of courthouses. Neutral colors with neutral motifs. The walls themselves are painted in Scandinavian shades of white or muted tones of beige. Curtains may add a splash of color but nothing too jovial. The flooring is often wooden, reflecting the Scandinavian aversion to carpet. There are coffee and other vending machines selling drinks and snacks—the solid staples of Sweden—foam sweets and chocolate wafer bars, instantly recognizable and comforting in a space created for neutrality. The seating areas have sofas and tables that, in some courthouses, display dog-eared magazines aimed at the middle-aged range reader. Nothing more offensive than adverts for a well-known brand of caviar with banana flavoring (to be eaten with a boiled egg). Nothing to incite passion (with perhaps the exception of Kalles Kaviar adverts that can incite strong waves of disgust) again, in line with the neutrality of law and the justice ritual. All of it becomes striking in its mundaneness. We have already seen how culturally important rituals can be integrated into legal rituals as in the newly built Kununurra courtroom and here we see that other symbols can awaken other rituals such as of bureaucracy and of waiting.

For instance, sitting on the hard benches and leafing through a dog-eared magazine that you would otherwise never read triggers other occasions of sitting and waiting: at the dentist's office, or the reception area of a doctor's clinic, for a job interview or a vet appointment. A dog-eared magazine symbolizes waiting. It symbolizes that this is a public space where many others have passed through before. It symbolizes that the wait may be long enough to become boring. Perhaps also that the occasion that awaits is one that we prefer not to think about, the magazine serving as a distraction. It may also symbolize that this is a space where your well-being has been considered, where it is important enough for someone to place out a magazine available for your perusal. It is an emotion management tool, distracting and perhaps even calming.

The dog-eared magazine is thus part of the emotional landscape of the courthouse, a landscape that not only consists of the emotions of legal professionals and lay participants, but a landscape that evokes emotions through the senses. It is a subtle sensory experience, reflecting and reproducing the impartiality of law, all contributing to the justice ritual of a trial. It prepares participants for the interactions ahead, setting the mood for the evaluative effervescence to come.

The absence of sensorial experiences can thus serve as a snag to the construction of evaluative effervescence and thus to the smooth flow of a trial.

Co-Presence and Virtual Justice Rituals

As already noted, successful interaction rituals and the emergence of collective effervescence have traditionally demanded physical co-presence but, in today's digital age where interactions are increasingly taking place via cameras and screens, a contemporary spin on traditional interactionist theory is necessary.

The important of bodily co-presence in interaction rituals, as introduced by Goffman (1963) and later developed by Collins (2004) is, as already made clear, a potentially problematic obstacle for virtual justice rituals. Bodily co-presence is understood as a key ingredient in successful interactions as it enables two or more people assembled in the same place to "affect each other by their bodily presence" (Collins 2004, 48). Within this, eye contact is a central facilitator of mutual focus, shared emotion, and rhythmic entrainment as "by seeing another person's eyes and face, and the orientation of their body, you know what they are paying attention to. An exchange of glances communicates, I-see-you-seeing-me, and also, I-recognize-what-we-are-both-looking-at" (Collins 2020, 482).

This means that not only is physical co-presence important for affecting each other, more specifically, it is the possibility of seeing and interpreting the facial expressions of the person one is interacting with that ignites successful interactions. Virtual justice rituals by this rationale are trickier to be successfully fulfilled due to technological issues in enabling eye contact and other interactional disruptions due to lagging as well as poor picture and sound quality.

Focusing on the sociological issues at hand, and moving technological issues to one side, questions regarding the continued veracity of Goffman's and Collins's prerequisite of physical co-presence in order for micro-sociological analyses of interactions to be conducted have blossomed in recent years in conjunction with the development of new digital technologies enabling direct and immediate audiovisual communication via cameras and screens. Rather than attempting to understand these online interactions as requiring separate and isolated theories from those regarding physically colocated people, I suggest we refine existing theories and frameworks. As Campos-Castillo and Hitlin (2013) note, the unification of traditional theory with contemporary nuances enables us to understand the range of different forms of encounter that may take place within a single setting—including face-to-face and mediated—as is the case with a trial.

Hence, rather than assuming that physical co-presence, where interactants are "close enough to be perceived in whatever they are doing, including their experiencing of others, and close enough to be perceived in this sensing of being perceived" (Goffman 1963, 17), is necessary for ensuring that interactants are able to share a social reality as to "what is going on here" (Goffman 1974, 8)—including understanding one's own role and the expectation for oneself and others, I propose an alternative approach. This approach moves beyond physical co-presence while still upholding shared understandings and a shared definition of the situation (Goffman 1974, 302). By questioning the fundamentality of physical co-presence in providing present "unique informational conditions" (Goffman 1969), which make it possible for us to send out and receive social cues about ourselves, we can instead move forward to a framework for understanding virtual face-to-face interactions.

For instance, Rettie (2009, 425) argues that video links enable synchronous mutual monitoring, because even though interactants are not colocated, "they share a time-frame and a mediated copresence: as the interactants converse they collaborate on what we can call a mediated encounter." Consequently, although interactants are not physically copresent in a mediated encounter, their mutual focus, shared temporality, and social reality means that they are able to accomplish Goffman's (1983, 3) "sustained, intimate, coordination of action" as is central to social situations and hence justice rituals (see also Walsh and Clark 2019; Walsh and Baker 2017; Humphreys 2005; Pinch 2010).

Similarly, by drawing on Goffman's (1963) two principal dimensions of co-presence whereby we are entrained toward others, and we believe them to be reciprocally entrained toward us, Campos-Castillo and Hitlin (2013) present co-presence as a continuum of mutual entrainment. People can thus be mutually involved in conversation to varying extents with co-presence per se by not necessarily precipitating shared entrainment but by not automatically preventing it either.

This means that the success of a virtual justice ritual is not a question of co-presence, rather of mutual focus of attention and of shared temporality. Hence, video links and other virtual interactions can be successful as they constitute a continuous and synchronous form of communication (Rettie 2009, 435). Indeed, some scholars take for granted that communicating via webcams entails "digitised face-to-face work in real time" (Jenkins 2010, 262) and that a "digitized interaction order" (Jenkins 2010, 263) is at play, which as Rettie (2009) writes, requires co-presence in *time*—temporal co-presence—not physical co-presence. However, Campos-Castillo and Hitlin (2013, 182) find that "all else being equal, mediated forms of interaction decrease copresence." If mutual attention and shared emotion are constrained, mutual entrainment will be decreased. So, online interactions can be successful, just to a lesser extent.

Despite the bodily co-presence problem, Collins's theory has been applied to online interactions. For instance, DiMaggio and colleagues (2019) expand its scope to show that it applies to online communication in the context of an organizational intranet for employees. They find that mutual entrainment and synchronized flow between parties emerges in these online settings indicating a degree of flexibility to the theory. Hence, while they show that the rhythm of an interaction is important, they conclude that successful online interactions must be a bounded event with a clear beginning and end; occur in real time; entail participants who have previously engaged in face-to-face interaction with each other (or how have a biographical knowledge of each other); center on a topic that all participants are interested; and include both visual information as well as offline communications (DiMaggio et al. 2019, 109).

Other studies have explored online interactions as rituals. For instance, an analysis of online raves by Vandenberg et al. (2021) finds that new symbols can emerge, using emojis to express emotions, with replications of others' emoji usage indicating that participants are closely monitoring each other and have a level of collective awareness. However, they find that although online raves can establish ritual activities and transform collective focus into collective emotions, these rituals were based on preestablished face-to-face rituals that had been translated into the online environment (as in DiMaggio et al.'s 2019 study). Indeed, the online ravers studied lamented the loss of the physical crowd and the absence of this physical proximity led to a lesser level of collective effervescence. The ritual thus became a type of "dead ceremonialism" (Vandenberg et al. 2021, 149) wherein preexisting group memberships were upheld rather than a collective consciousness emerging, which is required in order to feel social solidarity and resistance. They conclude that these online interactions should be understood as "a surrogate for social interactions, but not a substitute" (Vandenberg et al. 2021; see also Vandenberg 2022). This is in line with Collins's skepticism.

Conclusion

In this chapter I have introduced evaluative effervescence as a key aspect of successful virtual justice rituals and discussed the physical, technological, and sensorial factors that may disrupt entrainment in trials. To sum up, the jury is still out as to whether interaction rituals can be successful and lead to the emergency of evaluative effervescence in digital screen-to-screen interactions. While a contemporary understanding of virtual co-presence may alleviate some of the issues, the fact remains that interactional obstacles remain.

By continuing to focus on physicality, sensorial experiences, and co-presence, we can continue to explore the established notion of "legal place" (Mulcahy 2010, 11) and unpack the traditional interlinkage of time, place, and process associated with legal proceedings. Moving forward we will therefore be able to show if court can be understood as a space, rather than a place (DeNicola 2012; Jeffrey 2019; Hine 2000) and identify whether claims that justice is "conceptually impossible" without a courtroom (see Resnik and Curtis 2011) are valid, or whether virtual justice rituals can be successful in terms of feelings of fairness and justice. By questioning previous claims that physical presence is vital for an interaction to be successful (Collins 2004), in particular an interaction with the gravity integral to a trial (cf. Vandenberg et al. 2021; Vandenberg 2022), we will be able to show whether appropriate service and advice is possible via video link (Legg and Song 2020). In short, there is much to discover when it comes to virtual justice rituals.

These are vital issues I will address in my imminent research project on video links in courts. If it is correct that "the more human social activities are carried out by distance media, at low levels of IR intensity, the less solidarity people will feel; the less respect they will have for shared symbolic objects; and the less enthusiastic personal motivation they will have in the form of EE" (Collins 2004, 64), there is a risk that the legitimacy of the legal system becomes weakened by video links (Tyler 2003).

However, while video links may comprise a threat to successful interaction rituals by inhibiting the emergence of evaluative effervescence and feelings of being fairly treated, they may also contribute to more legally secure trials. This is because a trial is characterized by organic solidarity, with legal professionals working interdependently in their specialized roles to accomplish an interaction grounded in rationality and cooler sentiments, functioning as counterweight to the passionate emotions that can emerge when collective norms and values are broken (Durkheim 1884 [1893]). Video links could thus be seen as an extra tool for further increasing the distancing of social bonds and the intrinsic emotions within a trial. In other words, video links can function as a way of further calming passions and constructing a setting whereby less affective and more effective evaluative effervescence can be achieved.

REFERENCES

Babcock, Emily, and Kate Johansen. 2010. "Remote Justice—Expanding the Use of Interactive Video Teleconference in Minnesota Criminal Proceedings." *William Mitchell Law Review* 37 (2): 652–682.

Bergman Blix, Stina, and Åsa Wettergren. 2018. *Professional Emotions in Court*. Abingdon: Routledge.

Braithwaite, J. 1989. *Crime, Shame and Reintegration*. Cambridge University Press.

Brehm, Katie, Momori Hirabayashi, Clara Langevin, Bernardo Rivera Muñozcano, Katsuma Sekizawa, and Jiayi Zhu. 2020. The Future of AI in the Brazilian Judicial System. The National Council of Justice: Institute for Technology and Society of Rio de Janeiro.

Briggs, Lord Justice. 2016. *Civil Court Structure Reivew: Final Report*. Judiciary of England and Wales.

Campos-Castillo, Celeste, and Steven Hitlin. 2013. "Copresence: Revisiting a Building Block for Social Interaction Theories." *Sociological Theory* 31 (2): 168–192. https://doi.org/10.1177/0735275113489811.

Carlen, P. 1976. "Magistrates' Justice." In *Law in Society*, edited by C. M. Campbell and P. N. P. Wiles. Martin Robertson & Company Ltd.

Collins, Randall. 2004. *Interaction Ritual Chains.* Princeton University Press.

Collins, Randall. 2020. "Social Distancing as a Critical Test of the Micro-Sociology of Solidarity." *American Journal of Cultural Sociology* 8 (3): 477–497. https://doi.org/10.1057/s41290-020-00120-z.

DeNicola, Lane. 2012. "Geomedia: The Reassertion of Space within Digital Culture." In *Digital Anthropology*, edited by Heather A. Horst and Daniel Miller. Berg.

DiMaggio, Paul, Clark Bernier, Charles Heckscher, and David Mimno. 2019. "Interaction Ritual Threads: Does IRC Theory Apply Online?" In *Ritual, Emotion, Violence*, edited by B. Elliot Weininger, Annette Lareau, and Omar Lizardo. Routledge.

Durkheim, Émile. 1884. *The Division of Labor in Society.* 3rd ed. Macmillan. Originally published by Mamillan in 1893.

Durkheim, Émile. 1995. *The Elementary Forms of Religious Life.* The Free Press. Originally published by F. Alcan in 1912.

e-Justice, European. 2020. "Impact of COVID-19 on the Justice Field." European Justice, accessed October 1, 2023. https://e-justice.europa.eu/content_impact_of_the_covid19_virus_on_the_justice_field-37147-en.do#tocHeader2.

Fielding, Nigel, Sabine Braun, Graham Hieke, and Chelsea Mainwaring. 2020. *Video Enabled Justice Evaluation.* Sussex Police and Crime Commisioner and University of Surrey.

Flower, Lisa. 2019. *Interactional Justice: The Role of Emotions in the Performance of Loyalty.* Routledge.

Flower, Lisa. 2021. "Rumbling Stomachs and Silent Crying: Mapping and Reflecting Emotion in the Sensory Landscape of the Courthouse." In *Sensorial Penalities*, edited by Kate Herrity, E. Bethany Schmidt, and Jason Warr. Emerald Publishing.

Flower, Lisa, Sarah Klosterkamp, and Emma Rowden. 2023. "Video links and Eyework." In *Courtroom Ethnography*, edited by Lisa Flower and Sarah Klosterkamp. Palgrave.

Godfrey, Barry, Jane C. Richardson, and Sandra Walklate. 2022. "The Crisis in the Courts: Before and Beyond Covid." *The British Journal of Criminology* 62 (4): 1036–1053. https://doi.org/10.1093/bjc/azab110.

Goffman, Erving. 1963. *Behavior in Public Places: Notes on the Social Organization of Gatherings.* The Free Press.

Goffman, Erving. 1969. *Strategic Interaction.* University of Pennsylvania Press.

Goffman, Erving. 1974. *Frame Analysis: An Essay on the Organization of Experience.* Harvard University Press.

Goffman, Erving. 1983. "The Interaction Order: American Sociological Association, 1982 Presidential Address." *American Sociological Review* 48 (1): 1–17.

Grant, Elizabeth, and Martyn Hook. 2021. "Reimagining Spaces for Indigenous Justice: The Architecture and Design of the Kununurra Courthouse." In *Courthouse Architecture, Design and Social Justice*, edited by Kirsty Duncanson and Emma Henderson. Routledge.

Hartung, Dirk, Florian Brunnader, Christian Veith, Philipp Plog, and Tim Wolters. 2022. *The Future of Digital Justice.* Bucerius Law School, Boston Consulting Group and Legal Tech Association.

Henry, Alistair. 2023. "Digital Ritual: Police–Public Social Media Encounters and 'Authentic' Interaction." *The British Journal of Criminology* azad036. https://doi.org/10.1093/bjc/azad036.

Herrity, Kate, Bethany Schmidt, E., and Jason Warr. 2021. "Introduction: Welcome to the Sensorium." In *Sensory Penalities: Exploring the Senses in Spaces of Punishment and Social Control*, edited by Kate Herrity, E. Bethany Schmidt, and Jason Warr. Emerald Publishing.

Hine, Christine. 2000. *Virtual Ethnography.* Sage Publications.

Humphreys, Lee. 2005. "Cellphones in Public: Social Interactions in a Wireless Era." *New Media & Society* 7 (6): 810–833. https://doi.org/10.1177/1461444805058164.

Jeffrey, Alex. 2019. "Legal Geography 1: Court Materiality." *Progress in Human Geography* 43 (3): 565–573.

Jenkins, Richard. 2010. "The 21st-Century Interaction Order." In *The Contemporary Goffman*, edited by M. H. Jacobsen. Routledge.

Johnson, Molly Treadway, and Elizabeth C. Wiggins. 2006. "Videoconferencing in Criminal Proceedings: Legal and Empirical Issues and Directions for Research." *Law & Policy* 28 (2): 211–227.

Jurva, Gina. 2021. *The Impacts of the COVID-19 Pandemi on State & Local Courts Study 2021: A Look at Remote Hearings, Legal Technology, Case Backlogs, and Access to Justie.* Thomson Reuters.

Karstedt, Susanne. 2002. "Emotions and Criminal Justice." *Theoretical Criminology* 6 (3): 299–317.

Lederer, Fredric I. 2023. "Courtroom Technology from the Judge's Perspective—a 2022–23 Update." *Court Review: The Journal of the American Judges Association* 59:52–57.

Legg, Michael, and Anthony Song. 2021. "The Courts, the Remote Hearing and the Pandemic: From Action to Reflection." *University of New South Wales Law School* 44 (1): 126–166.

Mulcahy, Linda. 2010. *Legal Architecture: Justice, Due Process and the Place of Law.* Routledge.

Mulcahy, Linda, Emma Rowden, and Wend Teeder. 2021. Exploring the Case for Virtual Jury Trials during the COVID-19 Crisis: An Evaluation of a Pilot Study Conducted by JUSTICE.

Pickering, William S. F., and Massimo Rosati. 2008. *Suffering and Evil: The Durkheimian Legacy.* Berghahn Books.

Pinch, Trevor. 2010. "The Invisible Technologies of Goffman's Sociology: From the Merry-Go-Round to the Internet." *Technology and Culture* 51 (2): 409–424.

PingWest. 2022. "A Chinese Local Court Recently Opened a Hearing in Metaverse, Saying it Helps Drive the Digitization of the Judicial System." Last Modified September 30, 2022, accessed 6 October. https://en.pingwest.com/w/10840.

Plotnikoff, Joyce, and Richard Woolfson. 2019. Falling sShort? A Snapshot of Young Witness Policy and Practice. NSPCC.

Resnik, Judith, and Dennis Curtis. 2011. *Representing Justice: Invention, Controversy, and Rights in City-States and Demoratic Courtrooms.* Yale University Press.

Rettie, Ruth. 2009. "Mobile Phone Communication: Extending Goffman to Mediated Interaction." *Sociology* 43 (3): 421–438.

Robins, Jon. 2021. "Courts Backlog Increasing before Pandemic and Will be a Problem 'For Years to Come.'" *The Justice Gap.*

Rock, Paul. 1993. *The Social World of an English Crown Court.* Oxford University Press.

Rossner, Meredith. 2013. *Just Emotions: Rituals of Restorative Justice, Clarendon Studies in Criminology.* Oxford University Press.

Rossner, Meredith. 2021. "Remote Rituals in Virtual Courts." *Journal of Law and Society* 48 (3): 334–361.

Rossner, Meredith, and David Tait. 2021. "Presence and Participation in a Virtual Court." *Criminology & Criminal Justice* 23:135–157.

Rossner, Meredith, David Tait, B. McKimmie, and R. Sarre. 2017. "The Dock on Trial: Courtroom Design and the Presumption of Innocence." *Journal of Law and Society* 44 (3): 317–344.

Sanders, Anne. 2021. "Video-Hearings in Europe before, during and after the COVID-19 Pandemic The COVID-19 Crisis—Lessons for the Courts: Academic Article." *International Journal for Court Administration* 12 (2): 1–21.
Schechner, Richard. 1981. "Performers and Spectators Transported and Transformed." *The Kenyon Review* 3 (4): 83–113.
Smith, Russell, G., Rebecca Savage, and Catherine Emami. 2021. "Audiovisual Link Technologies in Australian Criminal Courts: Practical and Legal Considerations." In *AIC Research Reports*, edited by Australian Government. Australian Institute of Criminology.
Thakur, Pradeep. 2021. "Pending Cases in India Cross 4.4 Crore, Up 19% Since Last Year." *The Times of India*, April 15 2021. https://timesofindia.indiatimes.com/india/pending-cases-in-india-cross-4-4-crore-up-19-since-last-year/articleshow/82088407.cms.
Tutenges, Sebastien. 2023. *Intoxication: An Ethnography of Effervescent Revelry.* Rutgers University Press.
Tyler, T. R. 2003. "Procedural Justice, Legitimacy, and the Effective Rule of Law." *Crime and Justice* 30 (1): 283–357.
Vandenberg, Femke. 2022. "Put Your 'Hand Emotes in the Air': Twitch Concerts as Unsuccessful Large-Scale Interaction Rituals." *Symbolic Interaction* 45 (3): 425–448.
Vandenberg, Femke, Michaël Berghman, and Julian Schaap. 2021. "The 'Lonely Raver': Music Livestreams During COVID-19 as a Hotline to Collective Consciousness?" *European Societies* 23 (sup1): S141–S152. https://doi.org/10.1080/14616696.2020.1818271.
van Ryn, Luke, Tamara Kohn, Björn Nansen, Michael Arnold, and Martin GIbbs. 2017. "Researching Death Online." In *The Routledge Companion to Digital Ethnography*, edited by Larissa Hjorth, Heather A. Horst, Anne Galloway, and Genevieve Bell. Routledge. https://doi.org/10.1002/symb.605.
Vogt, W. Paul. 1993. "Chapter 3: Durkheim's Sociology Of Law: Morality and the Cult of the Individual." Taylor & Francis Ltd.
Wallace, Anne. 2008. "Virtual Justice in the Bush: The Use of Court Technology in Remote and Regional Australia." *Journal of Law, Information and Science* 2 (1).
Walsh, Michael James, and Stephanie Alice Baker. 2017. "The Selfie and the Transformation of the Public–Private Distinction." *Information, Communication & Society* 20 (8): 1185–1203. https://doi.org/10.1080/1369118X.2016.1220969.
Walsh, Michael James, and Shannon Jay Clark. 2019. "Co-Present Conversation as 'Socialized Trance': Talk, Involvement Obligations, and Smart-Phone Disruption." *Symbolic Interaction* 42 (1): 6–26.
Woodford, Isabel. 2023. "Colombia Court Moves to Metaverse to Host Hearing." Reuters, February 24, 2023. Accessed August 13, 2023. https://www.reuters.com/world/americas/colombia-court-moves-metaverse-host-hearing-2023-02-24/.
Worldwide, Remote Courts. 2023. Accessed January, 25, 2023. https://remotecourts.org.

12

Digital Dance Floors

Distinguishing the Ineffectiveness of Collective Effervescence Online

Femke Vandenberg

Why do we go to concerts? Listening to music at home, through speakers or headphones, often provides better quality sound, and viewing a performance on YouTube guarantees an unhindered view of the artist, both without having to leave the comfort of our couch. An important distinction between recorded and live music—and one that helps account for the allure of the "live" aspect—lies in the social nature of musical events. Taking place in public space, they allow for interaction between the participants, that is, between performing artist and audience, but also among the members of the audience (Kjus and Danielsen 2014). Concerts accommodate both *small-scale* and *large-scale interaction.* While small-scale interpersonal interaction—between new or old acquaintances—is no doubt an important part of any music event, it is the large-scale collective engagement that makes concerts so attractive (Hesmondhalgh 2013). It is in this group-based interaction that the audience can reach a heightened emotional state, what Émile Durkheim calls *collective effervescence* (1995). Since the early 2000s, scholarship on interaction has argued that communication in smaller groups can generate similar emotional outcomes (Collins 2004). Large-scale interaction, however, remains a relatively rare occurrence (Ling 2008, 88),[1] giving it in the traditional Durkheimian sense a more "sacred" quality.

For the most part, our daily lives are made up of a multitude of small-scale interactions: talking to a cashier at a local shop, catching up with a friend over a beer, meeting someone at the coffeemaker at work. And when we do find ourselves in a crowd, for example on a busy street or in a classroom, these situations are not necessarily large-scale interactions per se. For a crowd to convert from individuals merely occupying the same space to an "interaction ritual," with the outcome of collective effervescence, participants must enter a state of "rhythmic entrainment"—cognitively and emotionally synchronizing (Collins 2004). In sociophysiological terms, rhythmic entrainment is the process by which the nervous system of interacting participants becomes mutually attuned (Heinskou and Liebst 2016). For small-scale interaction, this occurs through actively participating in conversation, where entrainment forms through a shared discourse and effective turn-taking (although body language is important to assess the sincerity and emotional state of the speaker). When the group gets too large and it becomes no longer possible to synchronize with each participant individually, the manner under which rhythmic entrainment is established must take another form (Ling 2008). For large-scale interaction, rhythmic entrainment is then based on visual cues (moving bodies and emotional expressions) and the overall noise of an excited crowd, who—for instance through the music—largely act in unison.

But what happens when this type of interaction occurs online? Is it possible to establish large-scale interaction rituals in the virtual sphere? As a society we are moving more of our interactions online, and with technological developments, spurred on by COVID-19 lockdowns, cultural events are finding a permanent place in this virtual space. Randall Collins, a prominent scholar in post-Durkheimian studies, has extensively criticized the success of online interaction rituals (2004, 2014, 2020). His critique lies in the ability to establish rhythmic entrainment, he states, "Interaction mediated by telephone, internet, or other distant media, are weak in producing emotional amplification and micro-rhythmic entrainment, and thus generate less solidarity and emotional energy" (2014, 309). For example, he gives the concrete example of emailing, and the lack of flow that accommodates the slow turn-taking process of email exchange (Collins 2004, 63). However, in the time since he wrote this a lot has changed; emailing is now only one of many ways to communicate online, with social media platforms and messenger apps increasingly gaining popularity. The telephone calls that Collins also refers to seems less relevant today, with millennials swapping calling for messaging, choosing text-based interaction over picking up the phone (Buchanan 2016).

More recently, a growing number of studies are challenging Collins's strict definitions, using his interaction rituals model to analyze online gameplay (Burroughs 2014; Simpson et al. 2018), dating (Nexø and Strandell 2020), social media (Bartholomew and Mason 2020; Boyns and Loprieno 2013; Maloney 2013), and forums (Burcar Alm et al. 2023; DiMaggio et al. 2018). These studies are generally favorable toward the virtual sphere's capacity to accommodate successful interaction rituals, though they tend to focus on small-scale, text-based exchanges. Elsewhere I have argued (Vandenberg 2022) that it is far more difficult for large-scale interaction to unfold successfully online, making collective effervescence generated through such interaction highly unlikely.

In the rest of this chapter, I dive into the issues that virtual text-based interaction presents for the establishment of collective effervescence. I use empirical data from three previous studies (Vandenberg et al. 2021; Vandenberg 2022; Vandenberg and Berghman 2023), all presented elsewhere but in this chapter are compared for the first time. These studies all focus on audience interaction during livestreamed concerts. These concerts were chosen based on their genre, with the aim of reaching audiences from classical music, Dutch folk music, and techno. They span across two platforms (Facebook and Twitch) and use a range of methodologies: discourse analysis of chat sections, interviews with participants, and observations of screen and webcam recordings (depicting viewers on- and offline engagement during the livestream). This triangulation of data allows for a rich analysis of large-scale, text-based interaction and the possibility of establishing collective effervescence.[2]

Chat Sections as Dance Floors

One of the issues with online interaction, according to Collins, is the lack of bodily co-presence. Since Durkheim's original account, the importance of *social morphology* (the ratio of people per spatial area) has been widely noted as an important ingredient for the establishment of collective effervescence (Liebst 2016, 2019; Swartjes and Vandenberg 2022). Collins writes, "Human bodies moving into the same place starts off the ritual process. There is a buzz, an excitement, or at least a wariness when human bodies are near each other" (2004, 53). Online, in many cases, bodily co-presence is swapped for a profile picture and a username, meaning that interaction is no longer between two actors but between an actor and an abstract representation of another actor (Hogan 2010).

The livestream audiences researched here seem to be aware of the loss of physical co-presence, with copious comments seen reflecting the importance of listening to live music physically together:

> "This is super-hot, but I can't dance . . . not alone in a room."
>
> "It is just painful to watch this from the couch, when all I want to do is be there with you guys dancing 😭😭😭."

These posts can almost be read as outcries of frustration with the inability of the livestreamed event to follow traditional conventions and provide the usual experiences. Here viewers of the techno livestream recognize that they would normally dance to this music, but without the rest of the physical audience, a key feature of the event cannot be accomplished as usual. The virtual audience seems to provide a poor substitute for a physical one. A similar lament for physical concerts was also seen among the folk audience:

> "I miss concerts, hope we can go again very soon."
>
> "Go away corona, then we can have music parties again."
>
> "This provides so much comfort in troubled times. Hope we can do this in real life soon."
>
> "I look forward to the real thing, sick of doing nothing."
>
> "Corona party anywhere?"

In their longing for physical concerts, they disclose that the livestreamed event does not live up to their expectations, dismissing the virtual event as a concert. It is important to mention here, however, that these livestreams took place during the first months of the COVID-19 lockdowns, where physical concerts and their audiences had no other option but to move online. After the initial lockdown passed, these livestreamed concerts also ceased, demonstrating that they served more as a temporary substitution, and not a supplement or permanent replacement.

However, is this longing for physicality something limited to livestreams during COVID-19, where prior concerts and thus the scene were based purely *in real life* (IRL)? In the most recent of the three studies presented here, this was a primary question. The research was not only conducted a year later (when venues were once again opening) but focused on Twitch, a platform where artists perform predominantly online for a "virtual community," and thus have no physical IRL counterpart.

To understand the importance for physicality in this context, during the interviews with Twitch audiences the respondents were asked about how they experienced the presence of the other viewers. One respondent explained:

> "They are just these random user names that I see popping up and I don't put any value in that."

The fact that the other viewers are, for a large part, invisible—meaning there is less perception of the other viewers or what they are really doing or feeling—makes the experience more superficial for this respondent. Another respondent stated when asked the same question:

> "With my friends on Twitch, I feel very alone, like physically alone. I'm like 'Okay, I'm in my room I'm enjoying this,' but then I wish I had

> someone next to me to say 'this is a good song are you feeling this as well?' like, I really want to see the reaction of the people"

Although a large number of people are watching together, the virtual representation of the audience does not seem to provide the same experience as a physical encounter. Interacting with people on the virtual dance floor, that is, the chat column, provides a space to verbally express one's enjoyment, but the honest reaction that accompanies the statement is missing, hidden behind two screens. In a Goffmanian sense, these interactions provide "impression given," but not those "given off" (Goffman 1959, 2), meaning the sincerity in the messages are difficult to read.

Interaction can be more meaningful, however, if between acquaintances who know one another also in the physical realm. This was expressed by the same interviewee in the previous quote, when commenting on the meaning of interacting on the chat column during the livestream:

> "Most of the time [interaction] stays online, and you just turn off your computer and just move on with your day so um the fact that I could have my best friend there after the stream ends, we can reminisce about it, . . . just like turn off your computer but still take it to your daily life."
>
> "I have to say, in regard to the chat, I found this one a lot more fun. Being with my friends in real life is more fun, but it does give something extra that they were in the chat. You can talk about things a little easier or say things that they already know about. You don't have to explain yourself; they know exactly what you mean."

While her "Twitch friends" provided little feeling of presence—with these interactions and their outcomes remaining online—having a friend in the chat gives the experience more weight. Due to the preestablished relationship, the comments, which are often short, are imbued with more meaning. The topics of comments are based on past experiences rather than the generic topics usual to the Twitch chat. These messages are endowed with respect for mutually defined symbols of the physical relationship, preserving already established feelings of solidarity, and confirming group membership. Mutual attention and emotion are then based on these past feelings, creating a synchronicity among the friends. In these interactions, bodily co-presence seems to be less of a drawback than when between strangers, reflecting DiMaggio et al.'s (2018) hypothesis that a history of face-to-face interaction leads to a more intense interaction.

Sharing a similar sentiment, Boyns and Loprieno (2013) construct a theoretical account suggesting that parasocial interaction can serve as a replacement for direct physical presence. Originally coined by Horton and Wohl (1956), parasocial interaction characterizes the bond formed with media figures, wherein frequent exposure and increased knowledge of the persona creates a sense of intimacy and friendship. Boyns and Loprieno argue that these experiences can cultivate a "parasocial presence," mimicking face-to-face encounters and leading to increased emotional involvement. Online conversation between old friends from the physical realm would seem to work a similar way, where (in this case reciprocal) knowledge of the other helps to provide a shared emotion through common memories and experiences built prior IRL.

This is also clearly seen in the interaction with the artist. One of the positive affordances to livestreaming (particularly on Twitch) is that artists can read out and address comments seen on the chat, in this, interacting directly with their audience. Despite the infrequency and brief nature of this type of communication, many of the respondents came to see the artists as a "sort of friend," as one respondent stated. While communication, and thus information, predominantly flows in one direction (from artist to viewer), a perceived bond is forged through frequent exposure. This parasocial connection is often perceived as more important and meaningful than many interactions among fellow audience members. Consequently, the emotional energy derived from these exchanges is greater, enhanced further by the sense of privilege they feel when their name and comment are singled out from a multitude of others.

When looking at the data of the webcam recordings—where we can see the screens and home environment of the respondents while they interact with the livestream—it is clear that the interaction with the artist indeed resulted in the greatest emotional response. In these moments, respondents were more inclined to let out an uncontrolled grin or laugh, seen also physically moving toward or away from their screens. In comparison, leaving a reply on the chat section, in any other situation, led to little to no bodily reaction or emotional change. Without the physical bodies of the audience the intensity of the emotional experience is considerably lower, where even if text-based interaction does result in an emotional response, it is concealed behind a screen and thus very difficult to share, subsequently complicating synchronization and rhythmic entrainment. It is important to mention here that these interactions are small-scale in nature. In the following section I move on to examining large-scale interaction.

Virtual "Crowdspeak"

Let's turn our focus now to the ability of the virtual sphere to produce rhythmic entrainment among a crowd of (online) audience members. During the research it became apparent that livestream audiences were very receptive to one another's comments, with the chat on specific moments flooding with the same word or image:

> VIEWER 1: Nice man 🔥 🔥 🔥
> VIEWER 2: Greetings from Germany 🥴
> VIEWER 3: He is going nicely! 🔥 🔥 🔥
> VIEWER 4: <3 🔥 🔥 🔥 🔥 🔥 I miss you
> VIEWER 5: 🔥

Here the audience of a techno livestream uses the "flame" emoji to communicate the phrase "lit" or "hot." This was predominately seen during the "drop"—a climactic change in the bassline of electronic music. Use of this symbolism not only marks participation and displays an understanding of the group's discourse, but in replicating it in a series of replies it signals close observation of what others are doing and a collective awareness of one another. The emojis here perform a social role to "maintain and enhance social relationships" (Riordan 2017, 555) while simultaneously indicating a form of collective action.

Something similar was seen with the audience of the Dutch folk music livestream. In this stream the viewers did not so much acknowledge the beginning, end, or "drop" in a track, but kept a continuous stream of reciprocal comments going for the entire virtual show:

> VIEWER 1: Yes yes yes, everyone take their shirt off
> VIEWER 2: Party team back together!!!
> VIEWER 1: Hahaha
> VIEWER 3: Hoppa
> VIEWER 4: Take your shirt off and wave it
> VIEWER 5: Party
> VIEWER 1: We should come together some time [*sic*], for a beer
> VIEWER 2: This is a good plan
> VIEWER 1: Which bus should I take?

Though brief and seemingly spontaneous, these comments display reciprocity and coordination of behavior. Through addressing another viewer by (user) name, directly asking a question, or echoing discourse and previously discussed topics, they display a conversational tone and highly engaged manner of interaction.

This matching of discourse and emojis is an important part to online text-based communication (Al Rashdi 2018; Nexø and Strandell 2020). Like face-to-face interactions, mimicry functions as a demonstration of comprehension, suggesting that the interaction, and the situation as a whole, are being perceived similarly (Campos-Castillo and Hitlin 2013). Due to the constraints of textual communication and the higher chance for misunderstanding this form of interaction affords, mimicry is particularly important online. Using similar emojis and phrases signals a shared cultural capital while simultaneously signifying a common focus and emotional state (Nexø and Strandell 2020).

On Twitch this type of reciprocal interaction is such a common occurrence it has been dubbed "crowdspeak" (Ford et al. 2017). Studies like that of Ford et al. (2017), Taylor (2018), Jodén and Strandell (2021), and Hamilton et al. (2014) emphasize the collective experience that this form of interaction affords, comparing the attained intersubjectivity to that seen at IRL events. It would seem then, that this is the large-scale interaction of text-based interaction, and if group-based collective effervescence should occur, it would be through engaging in these streams of messages.

When asking the respondents interviewed how they experienced this type of interaction they stated that they use them to show their appreciation for the track. One of the respondents explains:

> The chat was just, like, hand emotes[3] in the air, and just kind of vibing emotes, where it showed that they're kind of enjoying the music, basically. That maybe it wasn't even a conversation, but it was more even, like, to show that they're there and they love what's going on. . . . Very, like, I would say that, like, digital yelling that you are enjoying it, you know.

In the digital realm, the audience's enthusiastic screams are replaced with a form of "digital yelling," while limited to text this echoes the conventions and collective engagement observed at concerts. When explaining his experience of joining in one of these streams, a respondent stated:

> It is fun. Even if it is as lame as putting the letter "F" in the chat, you are still active. And if a lot of people do it, and you get a waterfall of "Fs," it looks cool. And then you feel like you actually took part in something. . . . Yes, I'm not sure, maybe it creates that feeling of belonging. That you are all doing something together. . . . Yes, a little, how do you say that? Active. And that you fit in.

Similar to the flame emojis, through regular participation, the letter "F" materializes from random letters with little meaning into a shared symbol. By employing it accurately the viewer marks their membership in the group while cultivating positive emotions through being able to accurately predict the actions of other viewers. These symbols carry emotional weight, securing a position in the collective memory of the participants (Collins 2014).

The appreciation of this type of interaction is clear from the positive feelings expressed by the respondents during the interviews. Yet, when looking at the analyzed webcam recordings, there was no emotional or bodily response. When leaving a comment as part of crowdspeak, the facial expression of the respondents remained, to a large extent, neutral, with little change in bodily position. When asked about this, a respondent relates it again to the anonymity of the platform, stating it is because "I don't really see the people." Similarly, in comparing the experience of interacting as part of an online audience to that of an offline one, another says,

> So, when you're, for example, in a live concert you laugh with the people. You embrace each other randomly, with also people you don't know, because you can give a face to them. Like, you can, you can see them, you can feel them, you can feel the presence. In this case it's more like, okay, you have, like, people that want to show their support, but it's a different way. I don't know. It's more, like, distant.

The anonymity on Twitch seems to present a barrier to experiencing collective interaction of high intensity. Thus, although the "digital yelling" in unison on these streams can equate to feelings of group membership and an individual positive emotional experience, sharing these emotions is again difficult. Without being able to see or hear the excited expressions of the audience, synchronizing these emotions to foster collective effervescence is (arguably) not possible.

Digital Rituals

What the previous two sections demonstrate is that there is no shortage of shared symbols being produced on these livestreamed concerts as seen in the flame emoji and the letter "F" collectively used in the chat. But (and perhaps even more common) was the reproduction of old symbols. A clear example of this was seen in the use of emojis on the Facebook livestreams where, for example, the viewers of classical music livestreams would leave in their comments bouquets, roses, and clapping hands; the viewers of Dutch folk music would comment with dancing figures and mugs of beer; and the viewers of techno would comment emojis of pills. Interestingly, these emojis visually represent the central aspects of each of these concerts, in their use marking the conventions of each genre. As with the new symbols, commenting with one of these emojis in the chat works to mark group membership, but also an understanding of the usual IRL event proceedings.

Highlighting the genre conventions was a common occurrence also in textual exchange. For example, the techno audience would leave comments such as

> "see you at the left of the stage"
> "do you have a cigarette?"
> "where is the toilet?"
> "does someone have a popper for me?"
> "where is the bag at?"
> "someone for a line?"

Similarly, the Dutch folk audience left phrases such as

> "Cheers everyone"
> "Everyone jump!"
> "SOON, the whole room will go from left to right"
> "I'm singing along already. Can you hear me?"
> "I'll grab your shoulders"

These comments are very much a verbal representation of the ritual activities of the IRL counterpart of these events. However, while at IRL events, ritual activities (whether types of customary dance, dress, or applause) work to foster rhythmic entrainment, online without physical co-presence, these ritual activities become totemic. According to Durkheim (1995), the totem represents the group in symbolic form, reflecting the *collective consciousness* established through the strong emotions conjured up during ritual interactions. Through consecutive participation in rituals, the collective meaning of the symbols is continuously charged with emotion. In the livestream chat, the activities most common to the concert take on symbolic significance, acting as new totems, with much of the interaction focused on recognizing them. In this context, these interactions work less in providing collective engagement needed for collective effervescence and more as what we have coined *totem-defining interaction* (Vandenberg and Berghman 2023), meaning that while they work as a reminder of past effervescent experiences, establish a common ground and signify membership, they do little to recharge the collective consciousness.

This presents a fundamental distinction from online, small-scale interaction rituals. In two-way interaction active turn-taking (Meredith 2019) and mutual focus remain largely feasible through direct messaging, resulting in higher levels of emotional energy. This explains previous findings regarding the effectiveness of online interaction rituals in interpersonal conversations (see, for example, DiMaggio et al. 2018; Nexø and Strandell 2020). However, the necessary conditions for fostering collective effervescence in the Durkheimian sense—as intense group-based emotions—are simply not met. Although the experience of the music may potentially evoke similar emotions among the viewers, as a group they lack the means to collectively express this.

When considering the concert as not only made up of ritual activities but as a ritual in and of itself, another problem arises. For example, a large number of the respondents interviewed alluded to the issue of participating from within their domestic space:

> For me, the one thing that makes the difference is that the [concert] is not in your own house. It's something you go out for. You enjoy it because you go there. You go to the venue, you have people around, you have things going on around you. Because, [with livestreams] I'm alone at home watching it.

Another respondent stated, "[After a livestream] I don't feel that excitement. . . . Like, after a concert I would be more excited, and it would last longer." She credits the underwhelming experience of livestreams to the solitary nature of watching them from her "kitchen table." The livestreams were not only seen as unmemorable but even evoked a sense of guilt in consumption:

> "I feel a little guilty if I'm just sitting here, I don't know, on a Wednesday afternoon. . . . 'I haven't done anything with my life,' that's sometimes how I feel. I don't want to waste my day."

To combat the feeling of wasting time behind their computers, many of the livestreams were watched as a secondary activity in combination with other practices, such as work, study, and cooking. The feeling of guilt is also very telling regarding the experience itself, where the "special" or sacred nature of a IRL concert is swapped for a mundane and almost routine chore. According to Collins (2004), successful interaction rituals result in high levels of emotional energy, moments that will stand out as positive in one's memory and remain prominent also after the experience has ended. By contrast, the stated insignificance of livestream events situates the experience as a mediocre or perhaps even failed interaction ritual—at least in terms of the large-scale interaction.

The anonymity and public nature of the online sphere creates what boyd (2007) has named "context collapse," where "people, information, and norms from one context seep into the bounds of another" (Davis and Jurgenson

2014, 477). It becomes more difficult to act in accordance with the context as the situation is less defined (a physical venue swapped for a two-dimensional generic interface) and your audience less clear. This presents a challenge to the maintenance of genre conventions and the overall success of large-scale interaction rituals. Genre conventions, seen as ritual activities at concerts, turn into totem-defining interaction, great for redefining the context of the (virtual) situation and celebrating the community, but not so capable in establishing rhythmic entrainment. Furthermore, viewing a livestream alone at home creates "social convergence" (boyd 2008), where the profane (domestic space) collides with that of the sacred (concert space), meaning that the effect of participation in a ritual itself is also significantly diminished.

Concluding Remarks

Interactions during virtual concerts are thus considerably different than IRL concerts. Where in physical concerts collective effervescence acts as a primary ingredient to the concert experience, the virtual sphere seems to lack the affordances for this. The issue mainly arises from the inability of the chat column to establish rhythmic entrainment. While the inadequate speed of message exchanging (or turn-taking) no doubt affects entrainment, messages can also only convey *impressions given* and not those *given off*, meaning that honest emotions (seen in uncontrolled excited body language and noises) remain inaccessible. While messages may present an emotional tone (excitement, joy, sadness), the genuine feeling of the writer is difficult to affirm, making the attunement of emotions problematic and the interaction ritual less intense. This is specifically challenging for large-scale interaction where interaction is primarily based on the sights and sounds of an excited audience and not verbal discourse.

Due to context collapse where social space is diminished to a two-dimensional screen, interaction is often "totem defining." Defining the situation and signaling knowledge of the community's conventions becomes a central part of the event. And while the symbols used can directly relate to ritual interactions IRL, stating a ritual (and being in on the joke) provides a very different experience to partaking in one. IRL ritual activities are precisely the moments where participants can find rhythmic entrainment. Through collectively dancing a traditional dance, shouting a conventional call, or collectively drinking the same drink, the interacting members attune, resulting in a collective effervescence not possible from merely writing a symbol in the chat. As rhythmic entrainment is not only a key feature for the success of large-scale interaction rituals, but a necessary ingredient for the formation of large-scale interaction in general, the virtual sphere (as it is today) would seem to not be able to accommodate this type of communication.

However, this is not to say that the online sphere cannot accommodate meaningful interaction. Small-scale interaction—between two respondents or with the artist—is far more successful. Intense emotional outbursts are seen when the participants interact with, specifically, people they know (either from the physical realm or through a parasocial relationship with the artist) (see also DiMaggio et al. 2018). This implies that although rhythmic entrainment is hindered online, these conversations can have significant intensity and accommodate an influx of emotional energy. The difference is that small-scale interaction online has a capacity for direct and prolonged turn-taking, which means that there is more of a chance of conveying and thus sharing an emotional state. Furthermore, the capability of a reciprocal exchange of messages means that there is more of a likelihood for a re/charge of collective symbols marking solidarity. We may be tempted to see this as rhythmic entrainment; however, I would argue (as does Collins 2004) that the pace of online messages cannot match the flow of face-to-face conversation, meaning the buildup of rhythm needed for collective effervescence is out of reach.

To end on a slightly more positive interpretation of digital cultural consumption, livestreamed concerts are still popular, particularly on Twitch. Users of these platforms are active and find creative ways to overcome the drawbacks of these spaces, not only maintaining coherent and meaningful interaction (see also Meredith 2019; Paulus et al. 2016) but also finding ways to establish community sentiments. For example, emojis present an online tool used as collective symbols, fostering group membership. Similarly, the opportunity to converse in real time with people in the chat and directly with the artist allows for the forming of new relationships and positive social experiences—although one lacking collective effervescence.

NOTES

1. Only found in events such as concerts, sports competitions, protests, rallies, and marches.

2. For a more detailed account of the methodologies used see Vandenberg, Berghman, and Schaap 2021; Vandenberg 2022; Vandenberg and Berghman 2023.

3. On Twitch, emotes work similar to emojis, representing objects, symbols, or facial expressions in a small visual format.

BIBLIOGRAPHY

Al Rashdi, F. "Functions of Emojis in WhatsApp Interaction Among Omanis." *Discourse, Context & Media* 26 (2018): 117–126.

Bartholomew, D. E., and M. J. Mason. "Facebook Rituals: Identifying Rituals of Social Networking Sites Using Structural Ritualization Theory." *Journal of Consumer Behaviour* 19, no. 2 (2020): 142–150.

boyd, danah. "Facebook's Privacy Trainwreck." *Convergence: The International Journal of Research into New Media Technologies* 14, no. 1 (2008): 13–20.

boyd, danah. "Why Youth (Heart) Social Network Sites: The Role of Networked Publics in Teenage Social Life." In *Youth, Identity, and Digital Media,* edited by D. Buckingham. MIT Press, 2007.

Boyns, D., and D. Loprieno. "Feeling Through Presence: Toward a Theory of Interaction Rituals and Parasociality in Online Social Worlds." In *Internet and Emotions,* edited by T. Benski and E. Fisher. Routledge, 2013.

Buchanan, D. "Wondering Why That Millennial Won't Take Your Phone Call? Here's Why." *The Guardian*, August 26, 2016, https://www.theguardian.com/commentisfree/2016/aug/26/whatsapp-phone-calls-smartphone-messaging-millennials.

Burcar Alm, V., E. Hannerz, and D. Wästerfors. "Hard Work and Fun: Collective Online Interaction in a Case of Photo Fraud." *Symbolic Interaction.* 2023. [Advanced online publication], https://onlinelibrary.wiley.com/doi/10.1002/symb.677.

Burroughs, B. "Facebook and FarmVille: A Digital Ritual Analysis of Social Gaming." *Games and Culture* 9, no. 3 (2014): 151–166.

Campos-Castillo, C., and S. Hitlin. "Copresence: Revisiting a Building Block for Social Interaction Theories." *Sociological Theory* 31, no. 2 (2013): 168–192.

Collins, R. *Interaction Ritual Chains.* Princeton University Press, 2004.

Collins, R. "Interaction Ritual Chains and Collective Effervescence." In *Collective Emotions*, edited by C. Von Scheve and M. Salmela. Oxford University Press, 2014.

Collins, R. "Social Distancing as a Critical Test of the Micro-Sociology of Solidarity." *American Journal of Cultural Sociology* 8, no. 3 (2020): 477–497.

Davis, J. L., and N. Jurgenson. "Context Collapse: Theorizing Context Collusions and Collisions." *Information Communication and Society* 17, no. 4 (2014): 476–485.

Dimaggio, P., C. Bernier, C. Heckscher, and D. Mimno. "Interaction Ritual Threads: Does IRC Theory Apply Online?" In *Ritual, Emotion, Violence: Studies on the Micro-Sociology of Randall Collins*, edited by E. B. Weininger, A. Lareau, and O. Lizardo. Routledge, 2018.

Durkheim, E. 1995. *The Elementary Forms of Religious Life*. Free Press.

Ford, C., D. Gardner, L. E. Horgan, C. Liu, A. M. Tsaasan, B. Nardi, and J. Rickman. "Chat Speed OP: Practices of Coherence in Massive Twitch Chat." *Conference on Human Factors in Computing Systems—Proceedings*, Part F1276(2017).

Goffman, E. *The Presentation of Self in Everyday Life.* Doubleday, 1959.

Hamilton, W. A., O. Garretson, and A. Kerne. "Streaming on Twitch: Fostering Participatory Communities of Play within Live Mixed Media." *Conference on Human Factors in Computing Systems—Proceedings,* 2014.

Heinskou, M. B., and L. S. Liebst. "On the Elementary Neural Forms of Micro- Interactional Rituals: Integrating Autonomic Nervous System Functioning into Interaction Ritual Theory." *Sociological Forum* 31, no. 2 (2016): 354–376.

Hesmondhalgh, D. *Why Music Matters.* Wiley Blackwell, 2013.

Hogan, B. "The Presentation of Self in the Age of Social Media: Distinguishing Performances and Exhibitions Online." *Bulletin of Science, Technology & Society* 30, no. 6 (2010): 377–386.

Horton, D., and R. Wohl. "Mass Communication and Para-Social Interaction." *Psychiatry* 19, no. 3 (1956): 215–229.

Jodén, H., and J. Strandell. "Building Viewer Engagement Through Interaction Rituals on Twitch.tv." *Information, Communication and Society* 25, no. 13 (2021): 1969–1986.

Kjus, Y., and A. Danielsen. "Live Islands in the Seas of Recordings: The Music Experience of Visitors at the Øya Festival." *Popular Music and Society* 37, no. 5 (2014): 660–679.

Liebst, L. S. "Exploring the Sources of Collective Effervescence: A Multilevel Study." *Sociological Science* 6 (2019): 27–42.

Liebst, L. S. "Reassembling Durkheimian Sociology of Space." In *Spatial Cultures: Towards a New Social Morphology of Cities Past and Present*, edited by S. Griffiths and A. von Lünen. Design and the Built Environment, 2016.

Ling, R. *New Tech, New Ties: How Mobile Communication Is Reshaping Social Cohesion.* MIT Press, 2008.

Maloney, P. "Online Networks and Emotional Energy." *Information, Communication & Society* 16, no. 1 (2013): 105–124.

Meredith, J. "Conversation Analysis and Online Interaction." *Research on Language and Social Interaction* 52, no. 3 (2019): 241–256.

Nexø, L. A., and J. Strandell. "Testing, Filtering, and Insinuating: Matching and Attunement of Emoji Use Patterns as Non-Verbal Flirting in Online Dating." *Poetics* 83 (2020): 101477.

Paulus, T., A. Warren, and J. N. Lester. "Applying Conversation Analysis Methods to Online Talk: A Literature Review." *Discourse, Context and Media* 12 (2016): 1–10.

Riordan, M. A. "Emojis as Tools for Emotion Work: Communicating Affect in Text Messages." *Journal of Language and Social Psychology* 36, no. 5 (2017): 549–567.

Simpson, J. M., J. D. Knottnerus, and M. J. Stern. "Virtual Rituals: Community, Emotion, and Ritual in Massive Multiplayer Online Role-Playing Games—A Quantitative Test and Extension of Structural Ritualization Theory." *Socius: Sociological Research for a Dynamic World* 4 (2018): 1–13.

Swartjes, B., and F. Vandenberg. "Festival Atmospheres: Social, Spatial, and Material Explorations of Physically Distanced Festivals." In *Remaking Culture and Music Spaces: Affects, Infrastructures, Futures*, edited by I. Woodward et al. Routledge, 2022.

Taylor, T. L. *Watch Me Play: Twitch and the Rise of Game Live Streaming.* Princeton University Press, 2018.

Vandenberg, F. "Put Your 'Hand Emotes in the Air': Twitch Concerts as Unsuccessful Large-Scale Interaction Rituals." *Symbolic Interaction* 45, no. 3 (2022): 425–448.

Vandenberg, F., M. Berghman, and J. Schaap. "The 'Lonely Raver:' Music Livestreams During COVID-19 as a Hotline to Collective Consciousness?" *European Societies* 23, suppl. 1 (2021): S141–S152.

Vandenberg, F., and M. J. Berghman. "The Show Must Go On(line): Large-Scale Interaction Rituals at Livestreamed Concerts?" *Poetics* 101782, no. 103 (2023): 1–13.

13

A Taylor Swift Concert Is Watching My Face Right Now

Viral Publics and Platform-Afforded Collective Effervescence

Ashley Mears

Can collective effervescence take place online? Collective effervescence, that intense group energy and sense of unity, is experienced by a group of people at a shared activity or event (Durkheim, 1912 [1965]). Émile Durkheim reasoned that it occurred in physical gatherings, such as at religious rituals and festivals. Scholars have since used the concept to describe the energy found at nightclubs, churches, and social movements (Tutenges, 2013). In the digital era, internet technologies have given rise to "networked publics" in virtual public spaces where people interact, share information, and construct identities (boyd, 2014). What happens to collective effervescence, that critical element found at social movements, concerts, dance parties, and rituals, when our social gatherings transpire on a screen?

This chapter develops the idea of *platform-afforded collective effervescence*, rooted in science and technology studies and micro-sociology, to show how social media platforms construct and compel strong feelings of co-presence among digitally mediated crowds.

I consider this question through a study of "viral publics," when massive online audiences come together and disperse very quickly. Virality is often approached as an issue of circulation; when something "goes viral" on the internet, it spreads to many users in a short amount of time (Nahon and Hemsley, 2013). Scholars have studied how and why we consume memes (Shifman, 2014), but my approach is different. I think of virality as labor, and I examine what kinds of work it takes to go viral, and what kinds of emotional energy people harness as they experience it.

Based on an ethnography of high-performing content creators on social media, I document their experiences of "going viral." In this chapter, I document the platform architecture that affords emotional energy to users and creators, and the creators' interactions with the platform, their audiences, and each other, as they make sense of these experiences. Platforms give creators tools to access data metrics in real time, like counts of live viewers, likes, shares, comments, and emojis. Creators describe interacting with these metrics in terms of awe, rush, and addiction. In other words, the platform provides the sensorium of an energized crowd for creators to experience and manipulate; we can say collective effervescence is a platform affordance (Bucher and Helmond, 2017).

People who go viral have a number of techniques to make sense of their experience. They often compare the size of their audience to in-person events, like Taylor Swift concerts. This technique, which I call *upward comparison*, allows them to make sense of online attention with reference to celebrities in live performances. Their accounts of online attention echo Durkheim's writings on collective effervescence, also described as a feeling of "getting high" in microstudies of cultural experiences from religion to opera (Benzecry and Collins, 2014). Yet instead of feeling the physical co-presence of the crowd, creators often sit alone, and watch counts of live viewers on their screens. Viral creators develop collective strategies for dealing with both the high and the lows of the viral rush; it is a collective sense-making experience.

Ultimately, the experience of going viral can forge a powerful sense of commitment to keep making content. It binds content creators to the platform in ways that parallel the role of rituals in the formation of groupness. The high of collective effervescence, in other words, keeps creators coming back to make more content, and this labor dynamic is important in platform capitalism—it compels workers to work more.

In what follows, I sketch this emerging field of research, then I outline my research setting and methods. My argument unfolds with my data in four steps: First, I describe the platform architectures that afford a sense of collective effervescence in virality. Second, I show how creators make sense of their experience with upward comparisons to celebrities. Third, I show how creators cope with the loss of a viral high, even physically separating the technology from their bodies. Finally, in the discussion, I argue that online collective effervescence is an important mechanism to compel workers to enjoy overworking, a key dynamic that drives platform capitalism.

Previous Research

Platform Affordances and Viral Publics

In communication and media studies a great deal of research on social media focuses on user experiences, and this research has fruitfully advanced an understanding of how collective effervescence can take place online. Virtual events like online concerts, livestreamed trials, news and sports events, and webinars can create a sense of shared experience on platforms like Facebook and TikTok. In these online spaces, users construct their "imagined audiences," those people they have in mind when posting (boyd, 2014). Sometimes imagined audiences are quite powerful, such as influencers who refer to their audiences as "my community" (Christin and Lewis, 2021) and dieters who refer to their "fitfam," or fitness family, those unknown strangers who engage in similar diets (Baker and Walsh, 2018). Gaming and virtual worlds like Second Life allow people to engage deeply with each other, without even knowing their "real" identities (Boellstorf, 2008 [2015]). Platform design features help people feel connected via the likes, chats, live comments, emoji reactions, and viral hashtags, which build and communicate shared enthusiasm.

Across these platforms, scholars note how design architectures afford certain kinds of experiences; we could say the experience of online emotional energy is an *affordance*. The term "affordance" has origins in perceptual psychology to refer to what an actor's environment enables her to do (Gibson, 1979). In social studies of technology and science, affordances describe those capabilities that are created and constrained by technology design. For instance, a standard intersection affords a pedestrian four easy options of which way to walk, but not five (McClain and Mears, 2012).

In media studies, affordances are the material artifacts like technologies that *afford* users certain capabilities when they interact with the platforms (Bucher and Helmond, 2017). On social media, platforms enable content creators to "see" their audiences via metrics like follower counts. This marks a powerful "scopic regime" that constructs fields of attention and connection among actors, as Knorr and Brügger (2002) observed in financial markets when real-time trading platforms allowed traders to "see" markets through their screens, enabling them to act instantly based on live data. Performance metrics like views and followers are further powerful because research suggests that most people feel a dopamine rush when they receive likes on their social media posts (Bail, 2021, p. 52).

Fandom is one example of how affordances change communities. People now come together online in mutual admiration (or hate) of a cultural object on platforms such as TikTok or Weibo to express themselves, and their sentiments are mediated by platform algorithms, making a "computed sociality" (Alaimo and Kallinikos, 2017). Fans who shout louder, or say more outrageous things, often find their voices amplified by engagement-based ranking algorithms (Yin, 2020). Thus, contemporary cultural practices of fandom have become enmeshed in technological affordances.

Often infused with emotions, and aimed at steering emotions too, online communities like fandoms can be called affective publics (Papacharissi, 2015). In this chapter, I use the term "viral public" to refer to a transient, emotionally driven group of people who come together around content that spreads rapidly through digital networks. These publics are marked by intense but short-lived engagement, driven by the viral nature of social media's algorithmic amplification. Even as "the action," as Goffman (1969) calls it, happens on a screen, users share high emotional stakes with each other.

What kinds of social connections come out of these emotional experiences? Durkheim had theorized that rituals and their attendant collective effervescence had the power to mold individuals into groups, to produce collective consciousness. Can this similarly happen to participants in viral publics? To answer this question, we can take lessons from research on social movements as they play out on social media. As Tufecki (2017) documents in the Arab Spring protests, #BlackLivesMatter, and other online-mediated social movements, digital technologies enable unprecedented speed and scale of connections among disparate populations. But how strong are the bonds produced in this kind of "clicktivism," as opposed to traditional grassroots forms of organizing? Liking a hashtag or clicking on a cause does not entail the same intensity of engagement as did earlier generations of activists. Civil rights movement activists, for example, put in countless hours of physical and emotional work—the proverbial sweat, blood, and tears of any movement—that cemented durable bonds among their fellow activists and to their causes. Networked publics, those that are connected online (boyd, 2014), come together quickly but they can disperse with just as much speed, without cementing the kinds of social bonds that Durkheim theorized were enabled by experiencing physical co-presence.

Hence, we can say that the internet can indeed facilitate forms of collective effervescence, but the online experience lacks some of the physical and sensory elements of in-person gatherings (see Vandenberg's chapter in this book). Regardless of their power to cohere individuals to groups, there is no doubt that group energy flows through "networked publics" online (boyd, 2014). We now turn to how platforms construct and channel that energy to create shared experiences of the viral high.

The Creator Economy

My analysis focuses on viral content *creators*, not the users (or consumers) of content, because creators' labor shows us concretely how people "see" and "work" digital crowds. My study develops the growing body of research on the creator economy, also called the "attention economy," in which one goal of creators is to use platforms to harness attention for profits. As a job, "content creator" is only two decades old, ranging from bloggers to influencers to content farms like the one I studied. Studies of creators have taught us about how they are attuned closely to metrics (Christin and Lewis, 2021), how they form collective "pods" to work together to increase their visibility (Cotter, 2019), how they are attuned to "gossip" about what the platforms and algorithms want (Bishop, 2020), and how they try to embody lifestyles that they can rarely afford (Duffy, 2017) or find personally satisfying (Foster, 2021). The picture we have from such existing research is that content creators are employed precariously, subject to whimsical spikes in their popularity and success, and highly attuned and adaptable to platform metrics.

Platforms afford creators new ways of interacting with and even "seeing" their audiences. Platformed cultural production differs from radio and television in past eras of media: on platforms like YouTube, audiences and artists interact more frequently, and intermediaries like talent managers, agents, and producers play a lesser role in gatekeeping than other platforms, which convert audience interactions into metrics. Content creators have direct access to these metrics to understand what their viewers want, which alters the performer-performance relationship—artists can connect to massive audiences in real time, simultaneously bringing them closer and farther away.

Metrics also *feel* emotionally powerful, and their power is dependent on social processes of constructing affect (Kennedy and Hill, 2017). Affect is the capacity of bodies to sense and feel one another. Affect theory proposes that the collective circulation of emotions across bodies and spaces creates social effects, and that this is a central part of work in late capitalism (Ahmed, 2004). When programmers code algorithms to promote certain types of content, they are producing emotional states that transmit across bodies, with the goal of producing capital in the form of money for advertisers (Underman, 2020, p. 16). Hence, we can say that digital spaces afford affective highs, aided by technological design (for an elaboration, see Mears and Beauvais 2025). In this chapter, I consider the following question: How does collective effervescence translate from physical co-presence to being together on a screen?

Research Setting and Methods

From December 2020 to July 2022, I conducted an ethnography of a social media content publishing company that I call "Magic Media Productions" (a pseudonym). At the time, Magic Media managed over 120 monetized Facebook pages and Snapchat channels with roughly 150 independent contractors creating content for their individual pages. The company shares skills and resources in exchange for a share of each page's earnings, akin to a talent agency or multichannel network. Based on the West Coast of the United States, Magic Media also offers data analytics, props, and workspaces including a "collab" (collaboration) house. Companies like this are sometimes called content farms or mills because they produce a lot of content quickly. Magic Media's mainstay are short, scripted videos, ranging in length from three to twenty minutes, like pranks, cooking and crafting hacks, magic tricks, and scripted dramas.

The company aims to go viral primarily on Facebook. Its goal is to make "banger" videos, with tens of millions of views. Facebook is the world's largest platform with 3.07 billion monthly active users as of 2025. Facebook launched its Watch feature in 2018 to promote video content, and its algorithms boost the visibility of popular videos in users' feeds. Two features of Facebook are important regarding virality: number of views and profits.

First, its videos can reach hundreds of millions of views. Facebook's Feed (previously known as its News Feed) was redesigned in 2009 to model the contagion properties of Twitter, about which Facebook's own data scientists used epidemiological terms like "viral contagion" to describe how fast content could reach mass audiences (Sun et al., 2009). Unlike YouTube, which is search-based—users search specific terms to plug into niche communities—Facebook content can more easily go viral by design to keep users engaged.

Second, viral videos generate high profits. Facebook makes money as ads roll over content, yielding over $100 billion in revenue in 2023. Facebook gives creators 55 percent of the money it makes per thousand views of an ad, known as CPM. The rate might be as high as $40 per one thousand viewers, if the video's audience is "high value" (i.e., North American). The CPM drops the further a video travels from wealthy countries: advertisers pay as little as one dollar per thousand views in Pakistan, a pricing system used across the global advertising market.

Viral creators focus their efforts to post on Facebook, over and above TikTok and other platforms, because of its high pay. As such, their experiences are shaped by the specific affordances of Facebook, in particular its speed and high rates of pay. As an AdShare program, both Facebook and its creators have an interest in the fast accumulation of massive views; the leaked papers in October 2021 revealed that the company *could* slow down the speed of viral content, for example, to stem the flow of misinformation, but it has not done so out of financial interests (Hagey and Horwitz, 2021).

The 120 pages at Magic Media collectively earned about $5 million a month and five to seven billion views monthly. Creators' median monthly earnings were $30,000 per page in mid-2021; 6 percent of its pages earned more than $200,000 a month; 94 percent of its pages earned over $5,000 a month. Clearly outliers, this sample captures the "winners" in the winner-take-all creator economy that has few highly paid creators at the top of a steep pyramid (Jin, 2020). This study provides rare insights into elite creators for whom virality is a regular occurrence, which allows me to examine the experience of being at the center of online crowds.

Ethnography

I conducted digital and in-person ethnography with Magic Media for over eighteen months and interviewed sixty content creators, almost all of whom regularly experience virality. Upon agreeing to the terms of the study, Magic Media added me to their private Facebook group for digital observations, which included over a dozen hours of training videos on how to make viral videos. I logged in at least twice daily and kept systematic notes on their online discussions.

Magic Media also set up a monetized Facebook page for me to begin to make and upload my own content, so that I could learn from immersion. I filmed, acted in, edited, and uploaded over a dozen videos to my own page, and studied the performance metrics. I also observed Magic Media's work on the West Coast on six field trips that lasted between five and ten days between March 2021 and August 2024, including during "meetup" events with sixty-plus creators filming together in small teams. I stayed in their collab house, and spent days filming videos with them, acting in their videos, driving to Wal-Mart for prop runs, and sitting beside them as they studied their laptops.

Of the sixty viral creators I interviewed, fifty-three of them work with Magic Media and the other seven worked for competitors. Most interviews were conducted on Zoom and lasted one to two hours, though several were conducted in-person during my fieldwork. There were thirty-seven men and twenty-three women, predominantly white ($n = 50$), and their median age was thirty. Of the sixty, forty-eight of them did this job full-time as their main source of income at the time of the interview.

All interviews were recorded and, like my field notes, transcribed using AI software, then edited for accuracy. All names of viral creators and companies have been changed to protect their privacy.

Findings Part I: Platform-Afforded Collective Effervescence

Platforms afford a high level of collective emotion, most obviously with how they convey visibility in real time. Viral creators kept the Facebook Creator Studio open constantly; this was the platform's portal to a dashboard suite of performance metrics, since replaced with Meta Business Suite, and some similar tools, in October 2023. Creator Studio simplified how creators understood their success with clear and commensurate indicators, bright colors, and emotionally evocative numbers that track how frequently users click, view, and engage with their content. Creator Studio offered line and pie charts as well as tables to convey numbers of views, likes, emojis, followers, average time watched, and comments. Rendered into concrete data points, audience tastes become visible like never before (Mejias and Couldry, 2019). They look like scores on a game and exemplify the gamification of labor, turning work into an addictive game of chance (Van Doorn and Chen, 2021).

Further, when a video goes viral, Facebook shows the number of live viewers in the upper left-hand corner of the screen: it is like a ticker tape counting the number of people currently watching—a scoreboard tracking popularity. Every creator described following this view count closely, tracking its movement up or down. They reported their state of amazement, akin to hitting the jackpot in lottery play, when it peaks. For instance, Alex, a twenty-seven-year-old former magician's assistant, had a video that reached 160,000 live viewers:

> I'm bad at numbers anyway, but I just can't fathom 160,000 people, and they all leave and a new set comes in. . . . I just can't fathom it. You can't comprehend what that means. . . . It all seems like a dream for me, like I'm about to wake up.

These metrics can be overwhelming, presented on the screen with minutia that are constantly changing, what Gregg (2015) calls the spectacle of data. Typically, most of the views and money made take place in a video's first thirty days of posting. The speed with which videos "pop off," as they say, leaves many in shock. Olga said,

> Yeah. It was, mind-blowingly like, you would check the numbers daily and you're like, I cannot, I can't even describe it. Like you can't. I just can't believe it. Like, I literally, I'm in shock. I was in shock daily by the numbers. Um, yeah, but it feels really, really good.

Those thrills are certainly amplified by money, in particular, by the specific ways that platforms distribute monetary rewards. Like view counts, money is tallied on electronic screens that creators constantly refresh. Most creators I interviewed had experienced watching a single video yield sums ranging from $10,000 to $100,000. Financial success of this scale was new for almost every creator interviewed. Several viral creators reported making more in one month than they typically earned in a year. "This doesn't happen to many people, to make more money than neurosurgeons," said Alex, herself a community college dropout.

Creators showed strong emotional and even physical reactions during Zoom interviews when describing their high view counts and earnings. Some laughed uncontrollably, some shouted. Kim, twenty-eight, previously earned $25,000 a year as a public school teacher in Minnesota, a job she loved but quit after one month into making Facebook videos full-time with her best friend. Now her monthly income is between five and ten times what she used to make in a year—details she disclosed in a fit of laughter, as if she herself couldn't believe it.

Several creators cried talking about the rush of views and money. Avery got emotional on Zoom as she recalled her first several paychecks. She had previously toured the country playing stadium shows and she even appeared on the popular American TV show *The Voice*. But money didn't always follow these successes. After she focused full-time on Facebook videos, her income jumped dramatically:

> Okay, so $6,000 [in that first month], to next month $80,000, next month $150,000 and I'm losing my damn mind! I'm a sobbing wreck every other day like, this isn't *real*. And it just, I tear it up even thinking about it still [tearing up]. It was the most—it was just absolutely life changing.

Like Avery, creators frequently spoke quickly about the rush of metrics. The cadence of their voices would speed up, and they narrated numbers moving upward, as if reliving the feeling. This was the case talking to Josh, a twenty-seven-year-old magician who heads a content team in Mexico (and held number one spots on Tubularlabs leaderboard for five out of the past twelve months). Prior to 2018, Josh was "famous," he said dryly with air quotes, from his magic tricks on YouTube and Instagram. He had some money in his bank account, he explained, but he wasn't making what he would call "crazy money." One week after getting monetized on Facebook, he had two videos go viral. He described that moment:

> I mean, Jesus, I mean—[pauses] I remember the Creator Studio was going up, and it was like alright, $1,000 [*snaps* his fingers] $2,000 [*snap*] $30,000 [*snap*] $31,000, $32,000. And it was going up by ten thousand an hour. It was going up [he laughs]. It was *going up!* And we was like "*OHMYGOD, we're rich!* [he shouts]. *We're rich! We're rich! This is it! We've done it!*" . . . I couldn't believe it. I just could not *believe* that I was being paid for these videos. It was amazing.

By the time I interviewed him, Josh expected a majority of his roughly five videos posted weekly to be "bangers," which to him means at least fifty million views; for that, he could expect the video to earn between $50,000 and $100,000. The rush from the influx of money and views was like winning the lottery. Avery compared her work as such: "You're sitting on a lottery ticket."

Creators' accounts have parallels with the biophysical markers of gambling, with distinct embodied sensations of spiked endorphins, sleeplessness, and feelings of euphoria. Emotional excitement runs so high that some people report not being able to sleep when they go viral. Said Lynn and Coby, who make content together with their family:

> We were just watching the numbers come in with our jaws dropped. I mean we couldn't sleep, I mean it is *amazing.*

Trish, formerly a musician, captured her first time going viral on camera: "So I actually have a picture of myself on the plane crying, like happy tears, like freaking out."

Collins (2004) argues that emotional energy is contagious and can spread among individuals in a social setting. Such contagion is observable even for people interacting online. We can clearly see the movement, or affective circulation, from the digital crowd—rendered in metrics—to the creator. The creator "feels" an excitement from the group, even physically, even as she sits alone processing it all on her phone. Similarly to how Yin (2020) describes fandom as an "algorithmic infrastructure," these platform affordances spike affect and build excitement.

Because virality brings immediate financial rewards, it is difficult to disentangle the effects of money and views because the platform conveys both pieces of information via metrics that can scale up high and fast. As Josh put it, "It was *going up!*" Only two creators in my interviews were explicit that their excitement stemmed *only* from money, and *rather than* views, like Chris:

> When our video was going viral [130 million views], I thought, "Oh, cool, this might make us a lot of money." . . . I think they did a study where, like neurologically, money and cocaine had the same effects in your brain, you know? I've seen that in a lot of the people in this company, they get addicted to the money. 'Cause it's a *high*. It's a really big high. So for me, it was awesome, because this might make a lot of money, but it wasn't like, "Oh, great, I'm an influencer and hundreds of millions of people have seen my face." Nah, I don't care about that.

Chris is rather exceptional because most creators talked about views and money as intertwined. On the other hand, five content creators explicitly stated that they experienced excitement from view counts alone, even if the videos did not yield high payouts. For instance, Henry, twenty-seven, who had been posting on YouTube since he was a teenager, described his first hit video as affirming his self-image:

> It got thirty-six thousand views overnight. And my little brain was wondering, "How I can make that happen again?" Now I didn't get any money, at that time. But I was like, "Oh my God, like, if I can get this many views, then the world would know I am funny." Like, that's all I wanted people to know, that I was funny.

While money is surely a pleasurable reward, as Henry suggests, the attention itself is the high. The rush of visibility metrics alone could feel like winning the jackpot on a slot machine. Visibility matters, as many creators jarringly explained to me how peculiar it felt that millions, even hundreds of millions, of people were looking at them.

Findings Part II: Upward Comparisons and Labor Commitment

How do creators make sense of the experience of such a massive amount of attention? View counts, seconds watched, emoji reactions, comments: platforms give creators an abundance of tools to "see" and understand their audiences. Of course, none of this is absolutely meaningful as information; metrics are all inferences about who audiences are, what they want, how they engage. To make sense of metrics, creators collectively arrive at meaning. As I show in the following text, I identify the interactional processes that allow creators to experience virality as a pleasurable high that I call "upward comparisons."

Upward comparison is when a person compares herself to status superiors favorably. In this case, creators drew comparisons between their reach to that of celebrities who command big audiences. When describing live viewers, they compare their audience to in-person shows: a Rolling Stones concert, a live show at Madison Gardens, and Hollywood awards ceremonies. For example, two creators—Kim, a former public school teacher, and Jane, an events photographer—described what it feels like to see live viewers:

> KIM: I remember laying in my bed and seeing that we had like forty thousand live viewers on our video and being like, "Oh my gosh,

thousands of people are watching our faces right now." . . . There's a Rolling Stones concert watching your video. When you put it in terms like that, it's *literally* insane.

JANE: It does help to use concert perspectives. Like, "Oh my gosh, a Taylor Swift concert is watching my face right now." It's like really hard to comprehend that so many humans are staring at you.

KIM: When you do quantify it though, it's crazy. . . . Like just this one video, more people have watched that than saw The Rolling Stones play in the *entire* decade of the eighties. *Which is insane!*

What Kim and Jane describe is a new, unfamiliar form of collective effervescence, but it seems even to them that the screen—the online rendering of the audience—cannot make sense, so they compare it to the terrain in real life that we already know: The Rolling Stones and Taylor Swift. They are "anchoring" virality to IRL events, that is, they integrate this strange new experience into an existing framework to better comprehend it (Moscovici, 1984). Instead of feeling that energy from physical co-presence with a crowd, creators feel it as they sit alone, watching counts of live viewers on their laptop and smartphone screens.

Performers in particular drew parallels to the thrills of being on stage to explain the rush of virality, like Quentin:

> It's incredibly rewarding and it's, it's instant gratification. . . . I think this is more rewarding than doing a live show a lot of the time. And you *are* doing a live show in a sense. I mean, there is a little number in that upper left-hand corner of the screen when a video is taking off and they tell you how many people are watching it live, *right now.* And when you've got a good video and you see that you've got fifty thousand to seventy thousand people watching it, *right now.* I mean, *that's crazy!* That's selling out Madison Square Garden, what, *three times?*

To make sense of these numbers, creators rely on upward comparisons, thus situating themself on par with celebrities. Said Jude, who had one of the world's most watched YouTube pages from repackaging his Facebook videos, "I'm the most viewed artist in the world, even more than Banksy." Six months later, he said, "I'm one hundred million views behind Mr. Beast," a top celebrity influencer.

Interestingly, these are all positive ways of imagining the online community. They are not, for instance, imagining themselves as maligned figures who get booed on the stage. Rather they draw comparisons between themselves and beloved culture icons like Taylor Swift. As creators mobilize these "imagined communities" of adoring fans, they construct their collective identities as adored entertainers, thus constructing a positive vision of themselves.

They further build collective positive identities by celebrating "bangers." They call to congratulate each other on their live view counts. The head of Magic Media gives trophies to creators for bangers that get over one hundred million views. Creators proudly display these trophies in their homes.

They also compared their audience size to other well-known events like the Super Bowl, the Oscars, and to nights at Madison Square Garden, and the Oscars. Jenni situated the scale of her audience relative to the size of the U.S. population:

> I even received an award from Facebook for one, for being in the top ten most viewed videos. And I believe that video has, like, 360 million views right now, probably even more. . . . That's, that's more than the population of the United States.

Upward comparisons to celebrities, famous events, and geographies may sound like boasting, but I understood them to be collective strategies of sense-making of the experience of hypervisibility, and a way of elevating the meaning of their metrics. In fact, creators frequently came together to talk about their experiences; they had well-worn narratives of their first time going viral and being in unity with each other about feeling the high.

Creators also constantly compare themselves with each other as well as with their own past performances. Creator Studio tools consistently display their performance metrics alongside competitors and their recent performances. This pushes creators to compare themselves against the very top performers, since they tend to imagine competing against the highest achievers—including their own past record highs. This, too, is a platform affordance. Upon opening Creator Studio, at the top appeared a set of numbers and arrows, a scored percentage indicating how the creator was doing compared to how she was doing over the average of the prior week. If she were performing better than last week, her scores appeared in green accompanied by a green arrow pointing upward; if she were performing worse, they appeared in red with red arrows pointing downward. Other colorful figures tracked how she is doing compared to other content creators like her. By comparing to her past performances, the creator must be constantly improving, or she risks being "in the red." Said Hana,

> With so many high-level performers around us we are stuck in a bubble of successful people. Okay we have half a billion views in total, that's good. But Avery pulls in one hundred million [dollars] a week!

Through communicating, comparing, and celebrating their experiences, they arrived at shared discourses about the physical thrill of virality, using terms like "high," "addiction," "dopamine," and "cocaine" to describe its sensation. For example, Fabian folds social media into several addictions:

> You know what I consider a social media? Like a casino. People go into the casino because they want to gamble. Yeah. Okay. And that's the addiction that they have, and social media is addictive. So social media, drugs, like alcohol and gambling, is the same.

Likewise, Margo said,

> It really becomes an addiction, a little bit. Like, you're just on the back end looking at all the numbers, looking at the live viewers, looking at the money coming in and you're like "*Oh my gosh* this is crazy, I have to do this again!"

As Margo suggests, and Fabian explicitly says, platform metrics gamify success that's akin to a game of casino gambling. The platform affords them ways of imagining an audience and sensing an effervescent excitement of unseen others watching them.

In fact, physically, the viral high can cause behaviors that creators see as problematic, like not being able to put their phones down when their numbers are rising. When Alex first went viral, her boyfriend and fellow creator physically closed her laptop and told her, "Don't look at it." Jake, whose first viral hit occurred earlier in the day we met, was reaching for his phone in his jacket pocket incessantly while we chatted. Almost all creators try to set limits, even if they don't enact them in practice, on checking their view counts after uploading a video. Said Freddie,

> I found myself not having to check it that often because it can be addictive. . . . Yeah, it's an addiction and I already can feel the—the expectations start to change. So now that this video is at ninety-seven million in four days, I now want every video to go super viral. Whereas if I have a video that gets three million, that's still a good money maker. . . . But to me, it's going to be like, "Oh, well, what did I do wrong?" So it's an addiction for sure. I can see that.

Elsa, similarly, had been "chasing" the viral success she had found months ago, with a video that went on to get one billion views, at the time, the highest banger in the company. Success on that level was unlikely to replicate, but she talked passionately about what it felt like to reach that high, and to feel it fade:

> Oh, I need it. Like not even thinking about the money, you just want to see those numbers of users go up. Like it's crazy. It just feels like such a success when you do hit that. And then whenever you don't, it just feels like you're constantly disappointing yourself. Like your creativity isn't good enough.

All metrics are comparative and hence competitive; they reduce qualitative questions like "Is this good or bad content?" into quantitative ones such as "Am I scoring more or less than someone else?" (Espeland and Sauder, 2016). The result is a structure of anxiety where creators are constantly at risk of losing a game predicated on forever growth, even when they have achieved a celebrity-sized following.

Conclusion: Pushing the Boundaries of Collective Effervescence

In the classical thought of Durkheim, collective effervescence emerges through co-presence and mutual focus of people close to each other. This is a powerful feeling, so powerful as to make a person feel one with the crowd: she could lose a sense of herself momentarily with such a profound sense of connection and belonging to the collective.

As crowds have moved online, so, too, do these powerful sensations. But how powerful are they? As this book is an invitation to push forward the concept of collective effervescence, I see my chapter as advancing Durkheim's concept into the online world of virtual crowds. This chapter has shown how "going viral" illustrates a type of collective effervescence, akin to Durkheim's original concept. Lacking the co-presence of in-person crowds, social media platforms mimic elements of co-presence via live view counts, in real-time metrics, and streamed comments, all of which can circulate and increase at great speeds, amplified by engagement-based ranking algorithms.

Perhaps going viral falls short of the lived experience of deep interhuman connection that Durkheim theorized: that which involves rhythmically synchronized bodies and emotions, all being overtaken by a collective force, one that could have its own agenda independent of the individuals that constitute it. Indeed, online crowds lack this mutual bodily awareness. Yet still we see a surprisingly embodied and emotional account of online crowds that can mobilize strong feelings, like the overwhelming sense of being looked at by millions of strangers. Viral creators make sense of this with appeals to in-person events like a Taylor Swift concert, arguably this decade's most iconic scene of groupness (e.g., "Swifties"). Online, even sitting alone in their bedrooms, strong emotions arise, like the "high" of being seen and seeing the metrics tick upward. This high is much more than mere appreciation for big paychecks. As I demonstrate, meaning-making processes, like upward comparison and group celebrations, generate a sense of togetherness and sociality. Creators derive visceral pleasure from the numbers, and they collectively make sense of them. After all, numbers only make sense in webs of interactions, in this case, in a company of creators who are steered by the platform and who steer each other to feel the excitement of high reach. In experiencing the high of their online imagined communities, creators also create connection with each other.

Thus, interaction ritual chains and collective effervescence can translate from physical presence to the screen. They can be thought of as platform affordances because the carefully designed digital architecture delivers the right metrics to "see" one's virtual community. In the end, I found creators highly committed both to each other, and to the platform, to keep making more content.

Future research should consider how emotional energy varies across platforms. My case centered on Facebook creators who were drawn to its high CPMs and financial rewards. Because different platforms offer different kinds of experiences, further studies should explore what kind of emotional states are produced and how they circulate on other platforms. On TikTok, for example, rates of pay are far lower, and it encourages the production of memes with tools to make imitation videos. Reddit, meanwhile, allows users to give "awards" to content, often paid for with real money. In the popular press, we frequently hear about people experiencing the destabilizing impacts of virality, paradoxically, alongside its pursuit. This suggests that a phenomenology of virality as pleasurable exists across platforms, but we expect it to be mediated by different design architectures.

Finally, this analysis of online collective effervescence is applicable to other superstar markets, where affect surely plays a role in spiking labor commitment and market participation. In venture capitalism, where financiers "chase unicorns," and in crypto markets where investors push coins "to the moon," market actors harness affect and tech affordances to propel growth (Sheehan, 2024). The emotional states of Wall Street drives markets around the world. As more and more fields become platform based, more people will be able to visualize and pursue extreme success in parallel winner-take-all economies. A central part of that experience, as I have shown here, is platform-afforded collective effervescence.

REFERENCES

Ahmed, Sara. 2004. "Collective Feelings: Or, the Impressions Left by Others." *Theory, Culture & Society* 21 (2): 25–42.

Alaimo, C., and J. Kallinikos. 2017. "Computing the Everyday: Social Media as Data Platforms." *The Information Society* 33 (4): 175–191.

Bail, Christopher. 2021. *Breaking the Social Media Prism: How to Make Our Platforms Less Polarizing.* Princeton University Press.

Baker, Stephanie Alice, and Michael James Walsh. 2018. "'Good Morning Fitfam': Top Posts, Hashtags, and Gender Display on Instagram." *New Media & Society* 20 (12): 4553–4570.

Baym, Nancy K. 2018. *Playing to the Crowd: Musicians, Audiences, and the Intimate Work of Connection.* New York University Press.

Benzecry, Claudio, and Randall Collins. 2014. "The High of Cultural Experience: Toward a Microsociology of Cultural Consumption." *Sociological Theory* 32 (4): 307–326.

Bishop, Sophie. 2020. "Algorithmic Experts: Selling Algorithmic Lore on YouTube." *Social Media + Society* (January–March): 1–11.

Boellstorff, Tom. 2015. *Coming of Age in Second Life: An Anthropologist Explores the Virtually Human.* Princeton University Press.

boyd, d. 2014. *It's Complicated: The Social Lives of Networked Teens.* Yale University Press.

Bucher, Taina, and Anne Helmond. 2017. "The Affordances of Social Media Platforms." In *The SAGE Handbook of Social Media*, edited by J. Burgess, A. Marwick, and T. Poell. SAGE.

Christin, Angèle, and Rebecca Lewis. 2021. "The Drama of Metrics: Status, Spectacle, and Resistance among YouTube Drama Creators." *Social Media + Society* 7 (1): 2056305121999660.

Collins, Randall. 2004. *Interaction Ritual Chains.* STU-Student edition. Princeton University Press.

Cotter, K. 2019. "Playing the Visibility Game: How Digital Influencers and Algorithms Negotiate Influence on Instagram." *New Media & Society* 21 (4): 895–913. https://doi.org/10.1177/1461444818815684.

Duffy, B. E. 2017. *(Not) Getting Paid to Do What You Love: Gender, Social Media, and Aspirational Work.* Yale University Press.

Durkheim, Émile. 1965. *The Elementary Forms of the Religious Life.* New York: Free Press. Originally published by Paris: Félix Alcan in 1912.

Espeland, Wendy Nelson, and Michael Sauder. 2016. *Engines of Anxiety.* Russell Sage Foundation.

Fine, Gary Alan, and Ugo Corte. 2017. "Group Pleasures: Collaborative Commitments, Shared Narrative, and the Sociology of Fun." *Sociological Theory* 35 (1): 64–86.

Foster, Jordan. 2021. "'My Money and My Heart:' Buying a Birkin and Boundary Work Online." *Communication, Culture and Critique* 14:639–656.

Gibson, James J. 1979. *The Ecological Approach to Visual Perception.* Houghton Mifflin.

Goffman, Erving. 1969. *Where the Action Is: Three Essays.* Allen Lane.

Gregg, M. 2015. Inside the Data Spectacle. Television & New Media 16 (1): 37–51.

Jin, Li. 2020. "The Creator Economy Needs a Middle Class." *Harvard Business Review*, December 17.

Kennedy, Helen and Rosemary Lucy Hill. 2018. "The Feeling of Numbers: Emotions in Everyday Engagements with Data and Their Visualisation." *Sociology* 52 (4): 830–848.

McClain, Noah, and Ashley Mears. 2012. "Free to Those Who Can Afford It: The Everyday Affordance of Privilege." *Poetics: Journal of Empirical Research in Culture, the Media, and the Arts* 40 (2): 133–149.

Mears, Ashley, and Taylor Beauvais. 2005. "Learning to Like the Likes and the Hate: The Labor of Internet Fame in the New Attention Economy" *Social Problems.* https://doi.org/10.1093/socpro/spaf028.

Mejias, U. A., and Nick Couldry. 2019. "Datafication." *Internet Policy Review* 8 (4). https://doi.org/10.14763/2019.4.1428.

Moscovici, S. 1984. "The Phenomenon of Social Representation." In *Social Representations*, edited by Robert M. Farr and Serge Moscovici. Cambridge University Press.

Nahon, Karine, and Jeff Hemsley. 2013. *Going Viral.* Polity.

Papacharissi, Z. 2015. *Affective Publics: Sentiment, Technology, and Politics.* Oxford University Press.

Sheehan, P. 2024. "To the Moon: Hype and Start-Up Work." *Contexts* 23 (4): 26–31.

Shifman, Limor. 2014. "The Cultural Logic of Photo-Based Meme Genres." *Journal of Visual Culture* 13 (3): 340–358.

Sun, Eric, Itamar Rosenn, Cameron Marlow, and Thomas Lento. 2009. "Gesundheit! Modeling Contagion through Facebook News Feed." In *Proceedings of the International AAAI Conference on Web and Social Media*, vol. 3. https://doi.org/10.1609/icwsm.v3i1.13947.

Tufekci, Z. 2017. *Twitter and Tear Gas: The Power and Fragility of Networked Protest.* Yale University Press.

Tutenges, Sébastien. 2013. "Stirring up Effervescence: An Ethnographic Study of Youth at a Nightlife Resort." *Leisure Studies* 32 (3): 233–248.

Underman, Kelly. 2020. *Feeling Medicine: How the Pelvic Exam Shapes Medical Training.* New York University Press.

Van Doorn, Niels, and Julie Yujie Chen. 2021. "Odds Stacked against Workers: Datafied Gamification on Chinese and American Food Delivery Platforms." *Socio-Economic Review* 19 (4): 1345–1367.

Yin, Y. 2020. "An Emergent Algorithmic Culture: The Data-ization of Online Fandom in China." *International Journal of Cultural Studies* 23 (4): 475–492.

Contributors

Sarah H. Awad is associate professor of sociocultural psychology at Aalborg University, Denmark. She received her Ph.D. in cultural psychology from Aalborg University and her M.Sc. in social and cultural psychology from the London School of Economics and Political Science. Her research interests are in visual culture and the analysis of public images and their influence on identity, collective memory, and politics within a society. Her recent books include *Remembering as a Cultural Process*, with Brady Wagoner and Ignacio Brescó de Luna (Springer, 2019), *Street Art of Resistance* with Brady Wagoner (Palgrave, 2017), and *The Psychology of Imagination: History, Theory and New Research Horizons*, with Brady Wagoner and Ignacio Brescó de Luna (Info Age, 2017).

Pierre Bouchat is an associate professor (MCF HDR) of social psychology at the Université de Lorraine. He earned his Ph.D. in psychology at the Université libre de Bruxelles in 2017 and worked as a postdoctoral researcher at the Université catholique de Louvain. His current research focuses on the role of collective emotions at the individual, intra-, and inter-group levels.

Randall Collins is professor of sociology emeritus at the University of Pennsylvania. His books include *The Sociology of Philosophies: A Global Theory of Intellectual Change* (1998), *Interaction Ritual Chains* (2004), *Violence: A Micro-sociological Theory* (2008); a sociological novel, *Civil War Two* (2018); and *Charisma: Micro-sociology of Power and Influence* (2020). Most recent is *Explosive Conflict: Time-Dynamics of Violence* (2022).

Silvia da Costa was born in Uruguay. She has a Ph.D. in psychology from UPV/EHU in Spain and is a permanent lecturer at the University of Zaragoza on the Teruel campus. She researches in the area of social psychology with one focus being group processes, collective behavior, and emotions.

Scott Draper is a professor of sociology at The College of Idaho. His research in the sociology of religion examines topics such as religious diversity, social boundaries, belief in angels and the paranormal, art/media, and God concepts. His main interest is the microsociology of religious rituals, as seen in his book, *Religious Interaction Ritual: The Microsociology of the Spirit* (Lexington Press, 2019).

Lisa Flower is an associate professor at the Department of Sociology at Lund University. Her research interests include the hidden emotion and interaction rules in courtrooms and the legal profession. She is the author of several articles and books, including *Interactional Justice: The Role of Emotions in the Performance of Loyalty* (Routledge, 2020).

Romulo Lelis is a postdoctoral associate at the Brazilian Center of Analysis and Planning, funded by the Sao Paulo Research Foundation. Working in the intersection of intellectual history, social theory, and religion, he is currently writing a book on the making of the Durkheimian sociology of religion through the collaboration of Durkheim and the Année Sociologique team. He earned a Ph.D. in sociology and a dual BA in philosophy and social sciences at the University of Sao Paulo.

Heather Margrison is a business (management) student at the University of South Australia, and currently undertaking a vacation research scholarship focused on workforce planning. She holds a degree in psychology and recently completed arts honours (Psych). Heather is passionate about veterans' mental health and plans to pursue a Ph.D. concentrating on their postservice transition to civilian employment.

Sharon Mascall-Dare is an adjunct associate professor at the University of South Australia (UniSA) and a member of Australia's Military Organisation and Cultural Studies research group. An internationally recognized journalist, broadcaster, and author, she was awarded a medal in the Order of Australia in 2023 for her service to media as a journalist. Her academic research interests are focused on military identity and veterans' transition to civilian life. Since her Ph.D. was awarded by UniSA in 2013, she has published widely on the lived experiences of military veterans. Mascall-Dare has served on the government of South Australia's Veterans' Advisory Council and is a serving member of the Australian Army Reserve with operational experience in Iraq. She is also the founder of StoryRight, a not-for-profit program that supports veterans' transition to civilian life.

Ashley Mears is professor of sociology and women's, gender, and sexuality studies at the University of Amsterdam. She works on cultural, gender, and economic sociology, studying processes of valuation and the circulation of nonfinancial forms of value. Her publications have focused on ethnographies of fashion, elites, and viral social media. She received her Ph.D. from New York University.

Darío Páez was born in Chile. He earned his doctorate degree in 1983 at the University of Louvain, Belgium, with a dissertation on the social psychology of social movements. He was professor of social psychology at the University of Basque Country from1983 to 2023. Currently, he is invited professor faculty of education and social sciences at the Universidad Andres Bello, Stgo., Chile and honorary professor faculty of psychology at Pontificia Universidad Católica del Peru, Lima, Peru. He has been honorary professor faculty of psychology University of Buenos as of 2023. His research interests include collective emotions and memory, social representations, and coping and effect regulation. His work addresses the issue of Truth Commissions as rituals of transitional justice and effects on personal and social well-being in Argentina, Chile, Peru, Paraguay, Uruguay, Equator, Brazil, and Colombia.

Margit Anne Petersen is an anthropologist and associate professor at the Centre for Alcohol and Drug Research at Aarhus University. She is currently running two collaborative research projects: one on alcohol, intoxication, and sexual relations among Danish youth, and the other on the psychedelic renaissance and the role of the internet. Altogether, her work focuses on the notion of the "The Intoxicated Self" and how individuals and groups use different intoxicants to develop or understand themselves and everyday life.

José J. Pizarro is a professor in the Department of Social Psychology at the University of the Basque Country UPV/EHU, Donostia, Spain, and visiting professor at the Escuela de Psicología of the Universidad Católica del Norte, Antofagasta, Chile. His research is mainly focused on the psychosocial effects of participation in collective events such as rituals, demonstrations, or religious gatherings. These include the study of the functionality of emotions (e.g., collective, self-transcendence) and emotional processes (e.g., collective effervescence), the creation of new social identities, or the dynamics related to intergroup conflict.

Bernard Rimé holds a doctoral degree in psychology. His research addresses the social psychology of emotion with a particular interest on the strong links existing between emotional experience and social communication. His studies document the fact that emotions powerfully stimulate social communication, that emotional information propagates across social networks, and that the social sharing of emotions impacts social ties. His current studies examine individual and collective effects of collective emotional expression in mass gatherings such as civil or religious ceremonies, commemorations, collective festivities, and sporting, musical, folk, or sociopolitical events.

David Sausdal is an associate professor at the Department of Sociology, Lund University as well as affiliated with the University of Copenhagen's Centre for Global Criminology. As a criminological ethnographer, his work focuses on issues of crime and policing within a cross-border and global perspective. Sausdal recently published an ethnography of Danish transnational detective work entitled *Globalizing Local Policing* (Palgrave, 2023) and is part of the editorial boards of *Theoretical Criminology* as well as *Qualitative Criminology*.

Daniel Smith is a senior lecturer in sociology in the School of Social Sciences, Cardiff University. He is a cultural sociologist who attempts to use classical sociological theory to understand contemporary culture's anxieties and desires, social processes, and forms, ranging from social class's relationship to the "hopes and losses" of English society, through comedy's relationship to a fraught political landscape, or the state of our mental health. He is the author of *Elites, Race and Nationhood* (Palgrave, 2016), *Comedy & Critique* (Bristol University Press, 2018), and most recently *The Fall & Rise of the English Upper Class* (Manchester University Press, 2023).

Philip Smith is professor of sociology and codirector of the Center for Cultural Sociology at Yale University. A globally known figure he is responsible for a dozen books and over seventy articles and chapters at last count. Smith authored the first comprehensive guide to the entire Durkheimian tradition. His book *Durkheim and After* (Polity Press, 2020) tracks 130 years of theoretical innovation. He is also coeditor of the *Cambridge Companion to Durkheim* (Cambridge, 2005) as well as various other writings making use of Durkheim's theoretical resources to explain social outcomes.

Sébastien Tutenges is professor at the Danish School of Education, Aarhus University, Denmark. He earned his Ph.D. in sociology at Copenhagen University in 2010 and has a master's degree in anthropology also from Copenhagen University. He is the editor in chief of the *Nordic Journal of Criminology.* Tutenges is the author of numerous publications, including the widely acclaimed book on collective effervescence among youth, *Intoxication: An Ethnography of Effervescent Revelry* (Rutgers University Press, 2023).

Femke Vandenberg is an assistant professor in audience research at the University of Groningen. She is part of the executive board of the Benelux branch of the International Association for the Study of Popular Music. She has published widely in international tier 1 journals, with a particular focus on the social and cultural significance of live music as an interaction ritual and the digitalization of cultural consumption.

Brady Wagoner received his Ph.D. from the University of Cambridge on a Gates Cambridge Scholarship and is now professor of psychology at the University of Copenhagen, Aalborg University, and Oslo New University College. At a general level his work focuses on developing a culturally sensitive psychology that explores people's meaning making as process in context. More specifically, he has applied this framework to such topics as memory, visual culture, social change, the history of psychology, and the public's engagement with science. His books include *The Constructive Mind: Bartlett's Psychology in Reconstruction* (Cambridge University Press, 2017), *Handbook of Culture and Memory* (Oxford University Press, 2018), and *Remembering as a Cultural Process* with I. Bresco and S. H. Awad (Springer, 2019). He has received a number of prestigious international awards and fellowships, including the Humboldt Prize from the Alexander von Humboldt Foundation in 2021.

David Wästerfors is a professor of sociology at the Department of Sociology, Lund University. His publications include *Violence—Situation, Specialty, Politics and Storytelling* (Routledge, 2022), *Analyze!* (Studentlitteratur, 2018) coauthored with Jens Rennstam, and *Accessibility Denied* (Routledge, 2022), co-edited with Hanna Egard and Kristofer Hansson. His research often focuses on interactions, institutions, emotions, and social control at the intersections of social psychology, cultural sociology, and criminology. His additional and related interests include ethnography and qualitative methodology.

Brad West is an associate professor of sociology at the University of South Australia. He is the immediate past copresident of the International Sociological Association's Research Committee on Sociological Theory (2018–2023), a faculty fellow at the Center for Cultural Sociology at Yale University and cofounder of the Military Organisation and Culture Studies Group. His recent publications include *Finding Gallipoli: Battlefield Remembrance and the Movement of Australian and Turkish History* and *Re-enchanting Nationalisms* as well as journal articles on the Invictus Games (*American Journal of Cultural Sociology*) and tourism of the American war in Vietnam (*Thesis Eleven*). He is also the coeditor of *Militarization and the Global Rise of Paramilitary Culture* (with Thomas Crosbie) and *The New Australian Military Sociology* (forthcoming).

Index

www.ingramcontent.com/pod-product-compliance
Lightning Source LLC
LaVergne TN
LVHW090558110826
845146LV00001B/177